The Defence Industry in East–Central Europe

Restructuring and Conversion

The Defence Industry in East–Central Europe

Restructuring and Conversion

Yudit Kiss

sipri

OXFORD UNIVERSITY PRESS

1997

Oxford University Press, Great Clarendon Street, Oxford OX2 6DP
Oxford New York
Athens Auckland Bangkok Bogotá Bombay
Buenos Aires Calcutta Cape Town Dar es Salaam
Delhi Florence Hong Kong Istanbul Karachi
Kuala Lumpur Madras Madrid Melbourne
Mexico City Nairobi Paris Singapore
Taipei Tokyo Toronto Warsaw
and associated companies in
Berlin Ibadan

Oxford is a trade mark of Oxford University Press

Published in the United States
by Oxford University Press Inc., New York

British Library Cataloguing in Publication Data
Data available

Library of Congress Cataloging in Publication Data
Kiss, Yudit.
The defence industry in East–Central Europe: restructuring and conversion / Yudit Kiss.
— (SIPRI monographs)
Includes bibliographical references and index.
1. Defence industries—Europe, Central. 2. Economic conversion—Europe, Central.
I. Stockholm International Peace Research Institute. II. Title. III. Series.
HD9743.C362K57 1997 338.4'76233'0943—dc21 96–54807
ISBN 0–19–829280–5

Typeset and originated by Stockholm International Peace Research Institute
Printed in Great Britain on acid-free paper by
Biddles Ltd., Guildford and King's Lynn

Contents

Preface   ix
Acknowledgements   x
Acronyms   xi

Part I. Introduction

**1. The end of the cold war and the collapse of the traditional defence   3
industry in East–Central Europe**
    I. Introduction   3
    II. East–Central Europe in the aftermath of the cold war   6
    III. The collapse of the defence industry   8
    IV. Consolidation and partial resurrection   9

Part II. Case studies of defence industry restructuring in East–Central Europe: the Visegrad countries

2. The Czechoslovak Federation   13
    I. The main characteristics of the defence industry   13
    II. Crisis and conversion   18
    III. Conversion   20
    IV. The road to separation   30

3. The Czech Republic   34
    I. The heritage of the breakup of the Czechoslovak Federation   34
    II. Restructuring the defence industry   41

4. Slovakia   56
    I. The heritage of the breakup of the Czechoslovak Federation   56
    II. The policy on military production and export   60
    III. Crisis and survival   64

5. Hungary   77
    I. Introduction   77
    II. The main structural features of the defence industry   79
    III. Crisis   84
    IV. The new policy on defence industry and arms exports   88
    V. Defence enterprises: the history of disintegration   94
    VI. Consolidation   102

6. Poland   105

    I. Introduction: a pioneer country with problems   105
    II. The new Polish policy on defence industry and exports   113
    III. Examples of defence industry development   123

Part III. Defence enterprises in post-cold war East–Central Europe

7. The special features of defence enterprises   133

    I. Introduction   133
    II. State protection and special social status   134
    III. Organizational features of defence enterprises   138
    IV. Special safety features of defence enterprises   140
    V. The international dimension of defence industry organization   141

8. The nature of the crisis in the traditional defence industry   143

    I. Introduction   143
    II. The identity crisis   148
    III. Financial collapse   150
    IV. The loss of markets   153
    V. The structural and technological crisis   155

9. Strategies for crisis management and survival   157

    I. Approaches to crisis management   157
    II. Survival strategies   166
    III. Results   170
    IV. Conversion experiences   174

10. New features of the defence industry in East–Central Europe   191

    I. Introduction   191
    II. Internal changes at the enterprises   191
    III. New social and economic status   194
    IV. The new role of the state   196
    V. New external links   200

Part IV. Conclusions

11. Conclusions   207

    I. Introduction   207
    II. Defence industry restructuring: alternative approaches   208
    III. Defence industry transformation as a mirror of socio-economic   214
       change
    IV. The revamped defence industry   215
    V. Renewed defence industry as a vehicle of international economic   217
       integration
    VI. The challenge of genuine conversion   219
    VII. Future prospects   221

Index   223

Tables

Table 2.1. Czechoslovak military production and sales, 1987–90   14
Table 2.2. The major Czechoslovak arms producers, 1991   17
Table 2.3. Czechoslovak Federal Government support for conversion,   21
            1989–91
Table 5.1. Hungarian military expenditure, 1990–94   85
Table 5.2. The main indicators of Hungarian military production, 1988   87
            and 1991
Table 5.3. Military production as a share of total production in the main 96
            Hungarian defence enterprises, 1988–89
Table 5.4. Military production as a share of total production in the main 97
            Hungarian defence enterprises, 1988
Table 6.1. Major arms producers in Poland, 1991 and 1993   108
Table 6.2. The trend in production and employment in 31 core Polish   116
            defence enterprises, 1991–93

Figures

Figure 3.1. Location of defence enterprises in the Czech Republic   36
Figure 4.1. Location of defence enterprises in Slovakia   58
Figure 5.1. Location of defence enterprises in Hungary   78
Figure 6.1. Location of defence enterprises in Poland   106

Preface

In 1994 SIPRI published a research report entitled *The Future of the Defence Industries in Central and Eastern Europe*. That report reached two conclusions which led directly to the decision to publish this book. First, it was clear that the paths of the countries of the former Warsaw Treaty Organization (WTO)—in spite of the common features of their recent historical experience—were diverging. New governments were now making independent evaluations of their national interests and developing individual policies to pursue those interests. Moreover, each government had specific assets and liabilities in undertaking this task. Second, defence industries could not carry on with 'business as usual' on a smaller scale. More fundamental changes would be required. It was therefore necessary to examine the specific subregional characteristics of East–Central Europe. It was also increasingly important to examine not only decisions made by governments but also the perspectives of industry—now able to have a greater voice in shaping decisions.

The subregion examined in this book is the eastern part of Central Europe, defined to include the Czech Republic, Hungary, Poland and Slovakia. This grouping has advantages from the research perspective. While the defence sector in these countries is by no means transparent, there are nevertheless significant primary sources available to researchers. It was possible to conduct 70 interviews with managers, employees and government officials responsible for different aspects of defence industrial policy in preparing the book. After the cold war these countries appeared to face a genuine choice whether to retain or relinquish defence industrial capacities. During the cold war each of them had a significant defence industry without having the extreme level of dependence that existed in some parts of the former Soviet Union. Moreover, the geographical location and the existing political dynamics of Europe seemed to make integration into the wider regional economy a more promising option for these four countries than for any other former members of the WTO.

At the end of 1996 not all the outcomes are yet clear. All four countries have sought full integration into the predominant economic, political and military structures where West European countries discuss many of their most important policies: the European Union and NATO. However, neither of these organizations has taken the final and irrevocable step into the post-cold war era by admitting former adversaries as members. If and when this decision is taken it will have some implications for the future development of the defence industries in East–Central Europe. Although further changes can be anticipated, this book charts the basic alternatives that faced the industries of the subregion and describes the approaches adopted in each country.

Adam Daniel Rotfeld
Director of SIPRI
December 1996

Acknowledgements

I would first like to thank SIPRI, under whose auspices this book was published. My special thanks go to Ian Anthony, whose support and comments were vital during this process, and to Connie Wall, who edited the manuscript.

I am indebted to all my interviewees for devoting their time and energy to answering my questions and to Karol Droppa, of the Slovak Ministry of the Economy, and Jerzy Kade, of the Polish Ministry of Industry and Trade, who authorized my enterprise visits. I am particularly grateful to Medgyesy Janos, of the Hungarian Military Industrial Office; Buda Gyorgy, of the Hungarian Ministry of Foreign Trade; Ladislav Nemec, of the Czech Ministry of Industry; and Edward Gorczynski, of the Polish Ministry of Industry and Trade, for their cooperation in organizing my visits to defence enterprises. Their helpfulness went much beyond sheer authorization, which I appreciated even more being aware of the fact that they did not necessarily share my perspective on the military–industrial sector.

I would like to thank my assistants, Yahia Said in the former Czechoslovakia, Lydia Kulikova in Slovakia and Jacek Wojcik in Poland, who took part in organizing my interviews, for collecting documentation in the local press and for translations. Very special thanks are due to Aleksandr Krestovsky in Prague, for his able assistance. I would like to thank all my friends and colleagues who helped me to contact people, gather material and manage my trips: Anna Zabkowicz, Aleksandr Sulejewicz, Konstanty Gebert and Krystina Lindenberg in Warsaw; Otfried Nassauer and Ulrich Albrecht in Berlin; and Iveta Radicova in Bratislava.

I am grateful to Andras Brody, of the Institute of Economic Research of the Hungarian Academy of Sciences, whose insight and terse comments helped me to understand better what is behind the official statistics. In a longer retrospective I thank Tamas Szentes, of the University of Economic Sciences of Budapest, who first taught me to use economics to understand wider socio-economic realities, and my colleagues at the Institute of Development Studies of the University of Sussex, particularly Robin Murray and Gordon White, who restored my confidence in economic research in a period when I had doubts. I also thank Mary Kaldor, of the Sussex European Institute, University of Sussex, for being the first to draw my attention to defence economy questions and making it possible for me to work on them.

Last, but not least, I am very grateful to the MacArthur Foundation, for providing me the Research and Writing Grant that made it possible to carry out my research and write this book.

Finally, I would like to extend my personal thanks to my family in both Budapest and Geneva for their encouragement and support.

The maps were prepared by Billie Bielckus, SIPRI, and the index by Peter Rea, UK.

Yudit Kiss
December 1996

Acronyms

For acronyms that are the names of defence enterprises, see the first mention in each chapter.

ACDA	United States Arms Control and Disarmament Agency
APC	Armoured personnel carrier
CFE	Conventional Armed Forces in Europe (Treaty)
CGE	Central government expenditure
CMEA	Council for Mutual Economic Assistance
COCOM	Coordinating Committee (on Multilateral Export Controls)
CSFR	Czech and Slovak Federal Republic
EBRD	European Bank for Reconstruction and Development
ECE	East–Central Europe
EU	European Union
GDP	Gross domestic product
GDR	German Democratic Republic
GNP	Gross national product
IFF	Identification Friend or Foe
ISO	International Standards Organization
NATO	North Atlantic Treaty Organization
NBC	Nuclear, biological and chemical (weapons)
OECD	Organisation for Economic Cooperation and Development
PFP	Partnership for Peace
PHARE	Pologne–Hongrie: action pour la reconversion économique (Assistance for economic restructuring in the countries of Central and Eastern Europe) (EU)
R&D	Research and development
WTO	Warsaw Treaty Organization

Conventions in tables

–	Nil or a negligible figure
$	US dollars
m.	million
b.	billion (thousand million)

Part I

Introduction

1. The end of the cold war and the collapse of the traditional defence industry in East–Central Europe

I. Introduction

In the classic joke about military production in the former Soviet bloc, Ivan Ivanovich's wife is expecting a baby but the couple are unable to find a pram in the empty shops of their little town. Ivan Ivanovich works in a machinery factory where, among other things, prams are produced. Seeing his growing frustration, his colleagues decide to help him out. Each of them steals a part so that Ivan Ivanovich can assemble his own pram at home. The morning after all the parts have been collected and delivered, Ivan Ivanovich's friends ask him: 'So, how does it work?' He answers laconically: 'It won't roll but it shoots great'.

In March 1993 participants in a seminar on financing conversion held in the town of Martin, Slovakia, a stronghold of the Slovak defence industry, visited the ZTS Martin enterprise. The group of economists, political scientists, engineers and conversion experts listened with enthusiasm as the representative of the enterprise described the civilian items that had replaced military production. As the participants, among them the present author, admired the tractors and the construction machinery, one of the party exclaimed: 'There's a tank flying above us!' From a parallel production line, located in a section of the plant where access was restricted, a brand new tank floated elegantly towards the workshop exit.

These two anecdotes encapsulate the subject of this book: the hidden but ubiquitous presence of military production in the cold war command economies; the half-hearted efforts to convert this capacity to civilian production after the dramatic political and economic changes in East–Central Europe in 1989–90; and the partial resurrection and modernization of sections of this industrial capacity. The transformation of military-related production is a crucial dimension of the wider transformation process launched by the countries of the region. In the past, the military sector and military security considerations occupied a crucial role in the overall political, economic and social system. The way in which the position and role of this sector have changed provides revealing insights into the overall transformation process.

This book focuses on the four countries of the Visegrad Group—the Czech Republic, Hungary, Poland and Slovakia—as well as on the Czechoslovak Federation before the breakup in 1993. For the purposes of this study, they are referred to as the East–Central European (ECE) countries,[1] using a socio-geographical category that expresses both their former membership in the Eastern bloc and their historical location close to the centre of European affairs.

The background research on which this study is based was conducted primarily in the first, decisive years of the political, economic and social transformation, which took place in the region between the late 1980s and the mid-1990s. In this crucial period many of the main issues of transformation were determined and the principal trends of future development were established. The principal questions addressed are: What happened in the military-related sector during this period? How did its representatives react to the changes? What kind of future prospects does the defence industry in the ECE region have as a result of the changes (both spontaneous changes and those introduced by decision makers) at the national and at the enterprise level?

The research was based on interviews carried out with defence industry managers, employees, government officials and academicians in five countries in 1991–94—the Czechoslovak Federation, the Czech Republic, Hungary, Poland and Slovakia. Altogether, 70 interviews were conducted and 43 military-related enterprises visited by the author. This material was complemented with other public information, some of it published in official sources and some in the international and local media. This method had both advantages and shortcomings. The principal advantage was that it provided first-hand information about the state of the sector, its individual enterprises and the prevailing managerial attitudes. When requesting an interview at an enterprise, approval was in each case needed from the respective ministry in charge. With this legitimation, in most cases the interviewees appeared to try their best to answer the questions. An average interview lasted two or three hours, which was usually enough time to get an impression of the condition of the enterprise and, most importantly, the approach of the management to the changed situation. Since the defence industry had been a closed and secretive segment of the economy, for many of those interviewed this was the first time they had spoken to an 'outsider'.

The main disadvantage was that the method rarely provided 'hard', comparable data and the sample of enterprises was not always fully representative. Despite the advocated new spirit of openness and sincerity, there was still a great deal of fear and suspicion. In several cases it was later discovered that in the interviews the author had simply been misled. It also became apparent that enterprise managers were much more prepared to discuss their companies' problems when they were asked 'how' they were proceeding rather than 'what' they were doing and 'how much'.

Another problem was the construction of the sample of enterprises. At the beginning it was intended to visit a representative list of military-related companies that included all the most important enterprises along with those that seemed interesting because of their special production profile, history, conver-

---

[1] In this book the term 'Eastern Europe' is used to refer to the countries of East–Central Europe and the other former member countries of the Warsaw Treaty Organization, the 'Eastern bloc'.

sion experience, outstanding success or total failure. However, the final sample reflected the prevailing circumstances—it was subject to the decisions of enterprise managements and government officials who still had the right to authorize or refuse factory visits, even after enterprises were formally privatized.

In spite of the new openness throughout the ECE region, it remains very difficult to find systematic, consistent data that measure the volume and value of strictly military production; the number of employees involved in different forms of production; and the costs, investments, exports and other indicators of this type. Figures for the same enterprise for the same period are inconsistent and depend on the source. This can partly be attributed to the reflex of secrecy inherited from the past. However, it also reflects the fact that issues such as what and who should be classified as engaged in military-related production, which inputs were directly channelled there and at what costs, how domestic and export prices were set, for example, were never clearly established. Often even the concept of a 'defence enterprise' was unclear. Sometimes the term has been used to describe actual facilities involved in military-related production, which could mean a workshop employing a handful of people or a large factory. However, the term has also sometimes referred to a whole network of facilities at different locations, only some of which were engaged in military activities.

Official documents usually appear to have the same tendency to use vague and inconsistent terms and definitions. Statistics reserved for confidential use in military–industrial and government circles in the ECE countries during the cold war period apparently operated with indicators denominated in physical units. Output or sales figures were calculated by multiplying the number of units by a price that did not reflect the exchange value of the item. It became even more confusing when exports or imports were dealt with. Export data were published in figures based on local currency converted into a standard unit, expressed in either convertible roubles or US dollars. However, the exchange rates were in general highly tendentious, as indicated by the devaluation of ECE currencies against the US dollar once market rates of conversion were introduced. Within the former Council for Mutual Economic Assistance (CMEA) the convertible rouble was used to describe exchanges that principally took place in kind. However, although called convertible, it could not be exchanged for currency. Transactions with the West assumed a hypothetical local currency/dollar exchange rate which did not reflect any market transaction. As long as the scope of military-related exchanges were rather limited, this was not an important issue. After the end of the cold war, when economic ties with the West became more extensive, prices and exchange rates became more realistic. However, there is no way to use recent data along with historical data or to recalculate historical data 'retrospectively'.

In addition to the traditions of secretiveness and politically motivated distortions of economic data, many of the problems with East–Central European statistics concerning the immediate past stem from the fact that even basic economic notions were used in a different way. In a market economy most statistics are collected from companies. This requires both a common under-

standing of terms and concepts used and functioning mechanisms for cooperation between industry and national statistical services.

In the former ECE command economies there was no unit of industrial
organization that was the exact equivalent of a company or corporation in a
market economy. A company is established to provide a legal agent who can be
held liable for breaches of the law and which can take advantage of the rights
and privileges established by law. A company must be registered with a
responsible national authority as well as registered with the tax authorities.

In the command economies the system of industrial organization was different. The enterprises were state-owned and the whole economic activity was
meticulously planned and organized by central state agencies (ministries and
state committees). Formal and informal lines of liability, responsibility and
authority were established between industrial entities and administrative
centres. There was a high degree of division of labour. (As a result, the names
of industrial entities were often derived from their location rather than being a
company name.) In general, design bureaus and scientific research organizations were specialized in developing products but not in producing them.
Science and production associations had the capacity to perform a wide variety
of operations within the production cycle. These could be very large and significant industrial assets with tens of thousands of workers located in several
different places. There were examples of such organizations in East–Central
Europe. Production associations were specialized in manufacturing products
developed elsewhere based on technical documentation provided to them.
Single plants and factories were engaged in more limited production tasks, perhaps a single component which would be incorporated into a more complex
product.

Moving away from this command system, changing the pattern of both the
ownership structure and industrial organization is one of the central elements in
the transformation that has occurred in East–Central Europe. However, the
creation of a new system has not been uniform or smooth and industrial
reorganization has been subject to a variety of special regulations and conditions. As a result, in each of the Visegrad countries there is a mix of industrial
entities, some private, others retaining elements of state ownership. Among
those entities that have been subject to privatization, the different approaches
adopted in different Visegrad countries have created a mix of holding companies and joint stock companies (some open to outside investors, some
closed).

II. East–Central Europe in the aftermath of the cold war

The transformation of the defence industry is presented against the background
of the spectacular, unexpected changes that reshaped the political landscape of
Europe. Countries that had been in the Soviet bloc, separated from the rest of
the continent by the cold war division and united by ideological, political, eco-

nomic and military cooperation, became independent. The breakup of the system was the result of long years of erosion that loosened cohesion both within and between the respective countries. A slow but undeniable economic transformation occurred in countries such as Hungary, Poland and the former Yugoslavia that questioned and gradually undermined the command economy—based on a rigid, hierarchical, bureaucratic method of central planning and plan fulfilment. Cyclical outbursts of popular dissent and inevitable contact with the outside world eroded the ideological–political system based on the dominance of a single political party, a vulgarized Marxist–Leninist world view and the alliance with the Soviet Union—at the same time the purest incarnation and the policeman of the values which the system advocated.

By the end of the 1980s, demands for economic and political freedom had become louder and louder in the region. The final landslide began in 1989 with a negotiated transfer of power in Poland. For the first time in East–Central Europe, the Communist Party handed over political leadership to an elected coalition. Soon afterwards other countries, through democratic elections or popular uprisings, replaced their leaderships. The spectacular changes aimed to introduce a whole new political system based on a constitutional democracy and a multi-party system. In economic terms, the objective was the quickest possible introduction of a fully fledged market economy, with the dominance of private property and the withdrawal of the state from direct economic intervention. Free competition and exchange were to be the basis of action in the domestic and international market. In foreign policy, the new objective was to put a definitive end to the policy of isolation from the rest of the world and pursue rapid integration with the economic and political structures of Western Europe. The Warsaw Treaty Organization (WTO) and the CMEA were dissolved and the Visegrad countries began to make efforts to become members of NATO, the Organisation for Economic Cooperation and Development (OECD) and the European Union (EU).

The Visegrad countries were in a relatively advantageous position to carry out this major socio-economic transformation compared with the new states of the former Soviet Union or even other East European countries such as Albania, Bulgaria and Romania. However, decades of state socialism had imposed severe deformations on their social and psychological structures. In Hungary, after the trauma of 1956, the slow, uneasy progress of economic reform and cautious political reform made the country 'the most cheerful barrack of the socialist camp'. In Poland, the mass union movement of Solidarity and the simultaneous emergence of an 'alternative society' effectively eroded the system. In Czechoslovakia, after the tragic end of the 1968 Prague Spring, the party bureaucracy reasserted its all-embracing control over society. However, a small opposition movement offered at least a theoretical alternative to the existing system. In 1989–90, when mass protests led to the abrupt, total collapse of an exhausted system in Czechoslovakia and Poland, the former opposition could take over power with an intention to realize ideals they had fought for

for decades. In Hungary the former opposition remained outside the government, which was formed by a new, conservative–nationalist coalition.

The collapse of state socialism and the end of the cold war also brought dramatic changes for the defence industry. Along with democratization and the introduction of a market economy, demilitarization was a declared aim of the transformation. A new security policy based on such elements as peaceful cooperation, military doctrines based on sufficient defence, substantial cuts in military expenditure, conversion of the defence industry and the elimination of the military's privileged place in society were put on the agenda of the newly elected governments. Conversion was advocated throughout the region both as a desirable political objective and as an indispensable dimension of economic restructuring. The enormous resources spent on the cold war military machine would be made available for the progress of the whole of society.

Conversion of the defence industry and large-scale demilitarization also appeared to be relatively easy to accomplish in the ECE countries compared with the situation in the former Soviet Union, where the military sector had overwhelming significance. According to official data, in 1987–88 (which were the peak years of output) military-related production represented 11 per cent of total industrial output in Czechoslovakia and 3 per cent in Hungary and Poland and employed between 2 and 5 per cent of the economically active population. Even taking into account distortions in the data, this was a relatively small segment of the economy.

The structure of production seemed rather favourable for conversion to civilian production. With the exception of Slovakia—where heavy weapon production dominated—the region hosted comparatively advanced sectors such as aircraft, electronics, telecommunications, optronics and light engineering. The defence industry had access to research facilities that were very well financed. However, instead of conversion, a costly and massive collapse took place in East–Central Europe in the period immediately after the old political and economic system was transformed. This has been followed by the partial reconstruction of military production.

III. The collapse of the defence industry

Four blows pushed the defence enterprises into a sudden, deep crisis. First, the collapse of the WTO military–industrial cooperation system eliminated, from one year to the next, a large and stable demand for equipment. Second, the state withdrew much of its support to the sector. Third, non-WTO markets (in particular those in Arab countries such as Iraq and Libya) were lost. Finally, the defence industry had features which placed it at a particular disadvantage in adapting to the new socio-economic conditions in the region. As these developments—each of which would have created serious adjustment difficulties—occurred more or less simultaneously, the impact was dramatic.

The unexpected and rapid collapse of the WTO and the increasing liquidity and political problems of the developing countries, which were important customers for arms, led to a 50 per cent reduction in the volume of production in 1990–91. Further cuts in military expenditure, the sudden withdrawal of state subsidies and the general economic crisis deepened the decay. By 1993 overall production had fallen to an average 70–80 per cent of the levels recorded in the late 1980s.

The characteristics of this collapse were massive lay-offs, a production standstill at many plants, and the sale of assets and machinery at rock-bottom prices. However, there was rarely any restructuring of enterprises or creative or innovative re-employment of productive assets. Instead, the defence industry went into a form of 'hibernation'. Few enterprises were declared bankrupt or liquidated their military-related production equipment. Behaviour was often motivated by a combination of inertia, scepticism about the commitment of the government to reform and a fear of risks. Most enterprises preferred to maintain military production at minimum levels (even if output was simply kept in stock) and retain a core workforce wherever possible.

The economic and political climate also underwent significant change during the first five years after the end of the cold war. In particular, the ECE region saw political insecurity increase when suppressed political, ethnic and social tensions (exacerbated by economic crises) came to the surface in the former Soviet Union and the former Yugoslavia. Meanwhile, Czechoslovakia broke up into two countries; Poland went through multiple changes of government; and in Hungary major political and personnel changes took place within the same government. In the development of a new ideology, the Visegrad states have combined the values of pluralism, a market economy and assimilation into the Western world with a reinvented national identity. The deterioration of the political landscape, reconstructed nationalism and the desire to join the major Western institutions—including NATO—have quickly rehabilitated a demand for strong national armies supported by national military industries.

IV. Consolidation and partial resurrection

Despite the difficulties created by the political and economic changes, by 1993–94 the first signs of economic and political consolidation in the region had appeared. First in Poland and then in the other countries, economic growth resumed. Even though gross domestic product (GDP) per capita and other quantitative indicators still had not reached 1989 levels by 1995 and, in addition, some major economic stabilization targets had not been met, there were signs that the economy was emerging from the crisis with a more efficient, healthier structure. In Poland and Hungary reform-led communist parties resumed power, while in Slovakia the system became increasingly authoritarian and nationalistic. In the Czech Republic the previously unquestioned dominance of the leading liberal–conservative party was seriously challenged.

Nevertheless, in spite of these very important changes on the political scene, the main dimensions of the large-scale transformation have continued to unfold. In the immediate international environment, the post-Yugoslav and post-Soviet spaces have remained unstable. However, fears that these were the first stages of a more generalized pattern of armed conflict across East–Central Europe have significantly diminished.

By 1993 both enterprises and governments had openly declared the need for a defence industry (albeit one with a new structure) in East–Central Europe. The democratically elected national governments concluded bilateral agreements on military cooperation with Eastern and Western partners and backed the commercial activities of the new arms trading companies. Those military-related enterprises that were not forced to close or change their profile completely recovered slowly from the shock caused by the collapse of the WTO production and distribution system and the 'threat' of conversion. They reorganized their production lines, introducing some inevitable changes, established new political alliances and reasserted themselves throughout the region. The crisis of the traditional defence industry brought very important changes in the sector, even if it did not lead to a genuine conversion or a thorough transformation of the majority of the military-related enterprises.

This book describes the road travelled from the promise of conversion to the reality of restructuring in the defence industries in Czechoslovakia before the disintegration of the Federation, the Czech Republic, Slovakia, Hungary and Poland. Part II presents the main features and the collapse of the traditional defence industry in each of these countries and describes the different patterns they followed in reorganization. Part III describes how military-related enterprises faced the crisis and learned to cope under the new conditions. It also describes the new features of the military sector. Part IV draws some conclusions about defence industry restructuring in East–Central Europe.

Part II
Case studies of defence industry restructuring in East–Central Europe: the Visegrad countries

2. The Czechoslovak Federation

I. The main characteristics of the defence industry

The foundations of the arms industry of the Czechoslovak Federation were laid in the last century as part of the industrialization of the Czech and Moravian lands. In a further modernization, three major arms production facilities— Skoda (located in the town of Plzen), specialized in artillery weapons, tanks and ammunition; Ceskoslovenska Zbrojovka (in Brno), producing infantry weapons and ammunition; and Ceskoslovenska Kolben Danek (CKD) Praha (in Prague), a tank and armoured vehicle producer—were established between 1920 and 1926. Production of combat aircraft was based in the Avia and Aero concerns (in Prague).

After the German occupation of the Czech lands in 1939, the Czech defence industry served as a major military supplier of the German Army during World War II. Existing enterprises were expanded and a number of new military firms were built in Moravia (in the towns of Vsetin, Uhersky Brod, Slavicin and Bojkovice) and in Slovakia (in Dubnica and Povazska Bystrica). Some of these factories had been destroyed by the end of the war, but most of them survived and the defence industry as a whole was 'larger and more efficient . . . than ever before'.[1]

After 1945 some of the Czechoslovak military enterprises shifted to civilian production. For example, artillery production at Skoda-Plzen was replaced by production of turbine engines. When Czechoslovakia joined the Warsaw Treaty Organization (WTO) in 1955, new military enterprises were established which produced, among other items, aircraft technology (including trainer aircraft), radio-electronics, radars, optical instruments and anti-tank mines. The bulk of heavy weapon production was shifted from the area near the western borders to Slovakia. While some of the Czech production capacities were transferred to Slovakia, some new large factories were also built there.

Czechoslovakia became the second largest military producer of the WTO, after the Soviet Union. In 1987, when Czechoslovak military production reached record levels, output was 29.298 billion Czechoslovak korunas ($1 billion).[2] This represented roughly 3 per cent of the Czechoslovak gross domestic product (GDP) and 10.5 per cent of total industrial production.[3] A year later, when production had dropped slightly, armaments still represented

---

[1] Cechak, O., Selesovsky, J. and Stembera, M., 'Czechoslovakia: reductions in arms production in a time of economic and political transformation', ed. H. Wulf, SIPRI, *Arms Industry Limited* (Oxford University Press: Oxford, 1993), p. 239.

[2] The average annual exchange rate in 1989–92 was: 1989, $1 = 15.05 korunas; 1990, $1 = 17.95 korunas; 1991, $1 = 29 korunas; and 1992, $1 = 30 korunas.

[3] Sauerwein, B., 'Focus on the Czechoslovak defense industry', *International Defense Review*, vol. 24, no. 8 (Aug. 1991), p. 862.

Table 2.1. Czechoslovak military production and sales, 1987–90

Figures for volume are in m. korunas, current prices. Figures in italics are percentages.

	1987		1988		1989		1990	
	Volume	Share	Volume	Share	Volume	Share	Volume	Share
Production								
Czech Republic	11 557	*39.5*	12 331	*46.1*	10 587	*55.7*	7 515	*49 7*
Slovak Republic	17 741	*60.5*	14 406	*53 .9*	8 409	*44.3*	7 592	*50.3*
Czechoslovakia	29 298	*100.0*	26 737	*100.0*	18 996	*100.0*	15 107	*100.0*
Index of production		*100.0*		*91.3*		*64.8*		*51.5*
Share in engineering industry		*11.3*		*10.0*		*6.9*		*5.7*
Sales								
Domestic	6 558	*22.4*	7 699	*28.8*	6 802	*35.8*	7 200	*47.7*
Exports	22 740	*77.6*	19 038	*71.2*	12 195	*64.2*	7 907	*52.3*
To other WTO countries	17 055	*58.2*	15 134	*56.6*	11 179	*59.8*	6 305	*41.7*
To other countries	5 685	*19.4*	3 904	*14.6*	1 016	*5.3*	1 602	*10.6*

Source: Hospodarske Noviny, no. 20 (1991).

24 per cent of total engineering and electrical engineering output in Slovakia and 7 per cent in the Czech lands.[4]

In 1987–88, 111 factories were engaged in military production: 75 in the Czech lands and 36 in Slovakia.[5] According to the Czechoslovak Federal Ministry of Defence, the sector employed 73 000 workers directly and another 50 000–60 000 indirectly.[6] On the basis of these figures, 1.5 per cent of the economically active workforce was employed by the military sector.

While the share of the defence industry in the economy was small, its weight was heavier than was first apparent. In mid-1992 the largest enterprises—each employing 6000–35 000 people—were Skoda-Plzen, Skoda Volkswagen, Tatra Koprivnice, ZTS Martin and Liaz Jablonec.[7] In addition, official figures gen-

[4] Droppa, K., 'History of armament production in Czechoslovakia', eds Z. Kominkova and B. Schmognerova, *Conversion of Military Production: Comparative Approach*, Papers presented at a conference organized by the Slovak Academy of Sciences and the Friedrich Ebert Foundation (Slovak Office of the Friedrich Ebert Foundation and the Institute of Economics of the Slovak Academy of Sciences: Bratislava, 1993), p. 7.

[5] Figures for the number of defence industry enterprises varied because of different methods of calculation. In general only end-producers and major subcontractors were taken into account.

[6] Most Czechoslovak sources used the same or similar figures until the crisis hit the sector and numbers became inflated in both the press and official publications. Western documents usually quoted different, higher numbers. The *Financial Times* mentioned 70 000 workers employed in Slovakia alone while, according to a Deutsche Bank publication, 250 000 people were employed by the defence industry, 100 000 of them directly. *Financial Times*, 22 Jan. 1991; and Deutsche Bank, *The Peace Dividend: How to Pin it Down?* (Deutsche Bank: Frankfurt, 1991), p. 34.

[7] Blaha, J., 'L'economie tchecoslovaque 1991–1992: l'an I de la grande reforme' [The Czech economy 1991–1992: the first year of the great reform], *Le courrier des pays de l'Est*, no. 369 (May 1992), p. 82.

erally excluded the vast number of subcontractors which provided services and supplied both the defence industry and the armed forces with raw materials, machines, instruments, vehicles, food and clothing.

Military expenditure represented 3.4 per cent of GDP in 1987 and reached a peak of 3.7 per cent in 1989, before falling to 3.1 per cent in 1990.[8] This share was roughly maintained in the following two years. The lower level of military expenditure absorbed 6.7 per cent of central government expenditure (CGE) in 1990, in contrast to 1.8 per cent for education and 0.4 per cent for the health sector.[9]

The Czechoslovak defence industry produced a wide range of military items. Aircraft were produced by Aero (located in Prague), Let (Kunovice), Moravan (Otkrovice) and Letov (Prague); aircraft engines at Povazska Strojarne (PS, Povazska Bystrica); armoured vehicles at ZTS Martin (Martin), ZTS Dubnica and PS Detva; rocket and tube artillery at ZTS Dubnica; ammunition and missiles at ZVS Dubnica, Vihorlat (Snina) and Adast (Adamov); ammunition at Vlarske Strojirny (Slavicin), Policske Strojirny (PS, Policka) and Zeveta (Bojkovice); small arms at Uhersky Brod; wheeled armoured vehicles at Tatra (Koprivnice); engineering and transport equipment at SSUB (Uhersky Brod), Vitkovicke Strojimy a Zelezarny (VSZ, Ostrava), Mostaren (Brezno) and Slovenske Lodenice (Komarno); optical instruments at the Meopta factories in Bratislava and Prerov; and military electronics and telecommunications equipment at the Tesla factories in Prague, Pardubice, Kolin, Liptovsky Hradok and Prelouc.

In 1987 Czechoslovakia was the seventh largest arms exporter in the world according to the US Arms Control and Disarmament Agency (ACDA).[10] In that year 77.6 per cent of military production was exported, generating 22 740 million korunas in revenue (see table 2.1). Czechoslovakia was a major supplier of tanks, armoured personnel carriers (APCs), military trucks, light weapons and trainer aircraft. The bulk of military exports went to its WTO partners— mainly to the Soviet Union—and the income was used to balance arms imports, according to WTO practice. In some sectors, for example armoured vehicles, almost all the output was exported.

Several developing countries were also recipients of Czechoslovak military hardware. They were attracted by the relatively high quality, reliability and comparatively low cost of the weapons. The main appeal for the Czechoslovak side was the hard-currency earnings although, as data on unpaid claims showed, the developing countries were not always reliable business partners. The main recipients were countries in the Middle East and a number of African countries, such as Ethiopia, Nigeria, Tanzania and Zimbabwe. In the 1980s arms exports

[8] Deger, S., Loose-Weintraub, E. and Sen, S., 'Tables of world military expenditure', *SIPRI Yearbook 1992: World Armaments and Disarmament* (Oxford University Press: Oxford, 1992), appendix 7A, table 7A.3, p. 264.

[9] World Bank, *World Development Report 1992* (Oxford University Press: New York, N.Y., 1992), p. 239.

[10] US Arms Control and Disarmament Agency, *World Military Expenditure and Arms Transfers 1988* (ACDA: Washington, DC, 1989).

to countries outside the WTO earned the country an annual average of $850 million in cash or other essential resources like oil.[11] After the collapse of the WTO, developing countries became the principal market for the Czechoslovak arms industry.

According to a report in the journal *Respekt*, in the period 1984–88 the main customers of the Czechoslovak defence industry were the Soviet Union ($1900 million aggregate value for the period, in 1989 prices), Libya ($925 million), Iraq ($675 million), Syria ($625 million), Algeria ($410 million), Cuba ($350 million), Poland ($290 million) and Hungary ($130 million).[12] However, it is not known how these data were derived, and it seems unlikely that countries like Cuba paid for arms in hard currency.

According to data from the Federal Ministry of Defence, arms exports represented 11.8 per cent of total exports in 1966, but this share had fallen to 7.2 per cent by 1989. Western sources claimed that the share was much higher: a US congressional study claimed that arms exports accounted for 25–50 per cent of Czechoslovakia's foreign exchange earnings between the mid-1970s and the end of the 1980s, although this share was decreasing.[13] ACDA claimed that in 1989, when the political transformation took place, arms sales represented more than 6 per cent of total Czechoslovak exports.[14]

Small arms, aircraft, wheeled armoured vehicles, electronic equipment and ammunition were produced from local designs, while tanks, artillery, combat aircraft, rockets and guided missiles were built under Soviet licences which normally became available some time after the equipment had been introduced into the Soviet armed forces. Czechoslovakia had to pay high licence fees, which were increased with each further technical development to the product. Moreover, it had to pay a licence fee even when its own patents were incorporated into the product if it was for use within the WTO.[15]

There was an internal division of labour in Czechoslovakia. The bulk of the Soviet-licensed heavy weaponry was produced in the Slovak Republic. Although the most important Slovak enterprises had their own research and development (R&D) institutes, and although Konstrukta—the military research institute in Trencin—was acknowledged for its projects, local innovation was relatively modest. Slovakia developed only a few successful products, including tank engines and optical instruments for tanks. In the Czech lands there was local development of more sophisticated military products, including light arms, aircraft and telecommunications equipment.

Most military enterprises produced goods for both military and civilian purposes, often using the same production facilities. This was partly to 'disguise' the function of the facility and partly to offset the significant fluctuations of

---

[11] *Defense News*, vol. 6, no. 24 (17 June 1991).

[12] *Respekt*, 27 Jan. 1992.

[13] *Defense News*, vol. 6, no. 24 (17 June 1991), p. 8.

[14] United States Arms Control and Disarmament Agency, *World Military Expenditure and Arms Transfers, 1993–94* (ACDA: Washington, DC, Feb. 1995).

[15] Fucik, J., 'The Czechoslovak armament industry', *Military Technology*, vol. 15, no. 7 (July 1991), p. 99.

Table 2.2. The major Czechoslovak arms producers, 1991

Enterprise (location)	Type of production	Total arms production (m. (1991) korunas)	Share of arms production, 1987–88 (%)
Slovak Republic			
ZTS Martin (Martin)	Heavy equipment	1 500	60
ZTS Dubnica (Dubnica)	Heavy equipment	450	70
ZVS Dubnica (Dubnica)	Ammunition	400	–
PS Detva (Detva)	Heavy equipment	400	50
PS Povazska Bystrica (Povazska Bystrica)	Aircraft engines	200	52
Tesla Liptovsky Hradok (Tesla)	Communications technology	–	57
Czech Republic			
Tesla Pardubice (Pardubice)	Communications technology	150	73
Blanicke Strojirny (Vlasim)	Ammunition	70	23
Zeveta Bojkovice (Bojkovice)	Ammunition	60	60
Tatra Koprivnice (Koprivnice)	Heavy trucks	50	–
PS Policka (Policka)	Ammunition	–	80
Meopta (Prerov)	Optical instruments	–	70
Adast (Adamov)	Rocket launchers	–	37
CZ (Uhersky Brod)	Small arms	–	32
Vitkovice (Ostrava)	Engineering technology	40	–

Sources: Derived from Cechak, O., Selesovsky, J. and Stembera, M., 'Czechoslovakia: reductions in arms production in a time of economic and political transformation', ed. H. Wulf, SIPRI, *Arms Industry Limited* (Oxford University Press: Oxford, 1993), table 12.3, p. 242, and table 12.5, p. 244.

military demand. 'Special' (i.e., military) production represented more than 20 per cent of total output in only one-third of the factories. The enterprises with the highest share of military production in 1991 are listed in table 2.2. Very often the fairly lucrative military production financed the civilian production carried out at the military enterprises.

Another characteristic of the defence industry was its regional concentration, with 32.6 per cent of the workforce employed in the central Slovak region, 23 per cent in southern Moravia and 17.4 per cent in or around Prague. Employment in cities such as Bojkovice, Dubnica, Martin, Slavicin or Uhersky Brod was mainly, if not solely, in military and military-related production. The concentration of military production was greater in Slovakia, where huge enterprises, with thousands of employees, were rather common. Over 30 000 workers were employed in the military triangle of Martin, Detva and Dubnica. In the Czech lands, Tesla Pardubice employed 6000–7000 workers at its peak capacity, and the largest concentration of factories—in Slavicin, Bojkovice and Uhersky Brod—employed around 10 000 people.

II. Crisis and conversion

According to Josef Fucik, former head of the Department of Special Production in the Federal Ministry of the Economy, the first signs of crisis appeared with the fall in WTO orders for armoured vehicles in 1986. Facing economic exhaustion, the WTO countries were considering significant reductions in overall production and trade as well as a reorganization of their trade relations. These first, vague attempts at 'economic disarmament' prompted the management of ZTS Martin, Czechoslovakia's largest military producer, to prepare emergency plans to expand civilian production to fill the gap in orders. These documents were used to prepare the law to halt tank production that was drafted in 1989 by the last communist cabinet, headed by Ladislav Adamec.[16]

The first significant cuts in defence production were made in 1988–89, as a reaction to further reductions in military orders by other WTO countries, mainly the Soviet Union and the German Democratic Republic (GDR). At the same time several customers in the developing world became insolvent or politically undesirable business partners, which contributed to a further decrease in export orders. In 1989–90, after the 'Velvet Revolution', the revised security and military concepts led to further down-sizing. One cornerstone of the new Czechoslovak policy was the radical dismantling of the political and economic heritage of the cold war to promote global, peaceful security cooperation between the nations and to convert the defence industry.

The new government of Vaclav Havel declared in January 1990 that it would halt arms sales and tank production by the end of the year.[17] Soon afterwards this position was slightly softened to a promise that the country would 'try to orient its exports away from arms . . . but existing obligations would be honoured'.[18] The cabinet's new decisions were formulated in Decisions No. 84/1989 'On the Reduction and Halt of Tank Production' and No. 42/1990 'On the Production, Export, Concept and Conversion of Special Technology, Including the Halt of the Production of Armed Personnel Carriers' of the Presidium of the Government of the Czech and Slovak Federal Republic (CSFR). Throughout the post-communist East–Central European (ECE) region, these were the only government decisions that declared and regulated a government's commitment to conversion.

New export regulations were drawn up to control and curtail the arms trade. Under Federal Government Act No. 256/1990, a licence had to be obtained from the Ministry of Trade for all military-related exports. According to a parliamentary decision of 21 March 1991, companies trading in military material required a general foreign trade licence issued by the Ministry of Trade after consultations with other state security organizations. Several other government

---

[16] Fucik, J., 'Conversion: the outline for "economic disarmament"', *Hospodarske Noviny,* no. 20 (1991).
[17] *Defense News,* vol. 6, no. 24 (17 June 1991).
[18] *International Herald Tribune,* 25 Jan. 1990.

decisions were taken to regulate the conversion of the arms industry and to maintain the necessary defence industrial capacities.

The defence budget was also radically trimmed. According to data provided by the Czechoslovak Ministry of Defence, defence expenditure was cut from 34.9 billion korunas in 1987 to 28.1 billion korunas in 1991, and development and other acquisitions fell from 12.6 billion to 3.3 billion korunas. The combined impact of these factors dramatically reduced the financial resources of the defence industry.[19] When the government's conversion programme was launched in 1990, total military output had already dropped by nearly 50 per cent. The aggregate value of military production was 15.107 billion korunas, to which the two republics each contributed roughly 50 per cent.

Czechoslovak arms exports suffered a similar decline. From their 1987 peak value of 22.740 billion korunas, foreign sales dropped to 7.907 billion korunas by 1990. Deals with non-WTO countries dropped by 77 per cent. In this period the main customers were India, Iran and Libya.[20] In 1991 arms sales dropped further, to about 12 per cent of the 1990 value.[21] Additional blows came when the United Nations imposed embargoes on Iraq and Libya, the military sector's main Arab trading partners. Another problem stemmed from the customers' insolvency or reluctance to pay. In June 1991 Czechoslovakia had accumulated claims of $1 billion for unpaid arms exports.[22] Syria alone owed Czechoslovakia over $600 million for military purchases.[23]

The effects of the unfolding crisis hit the military sector hard. Production fell to 16 billion korunas ($500 million) in 1990.[24] According to Czechoslovak sources, in 1991 output was approximately 4.5 billion korunas[25] and in 1992 it was an estimated 4 billion korunas—about 13 per cent of the level of production in 1987.[26] Most defence-related enterprises suddenly found themselves verging on bankruptcy. In contrast to the practice of previous decades, in general it was civilian activity that covered the running costs of military production.

A study prepared by a research group of the Central Institute of National Economy of the Academy of Sciences of Czechoslovakia stated that 48 fac-

---

[19] Interview by the author with Josef Fucik, Head of the Department of Defence Economy in the Federal Ministry of the Economy, Prague, 15 Apr. 1992.

[20] Deutsche Bank (note 6).

[21] *International Herald Tribune*, 3 May 1991.

[22] Sauerwein (note 3). Ivanek and Matousek quote over $7 billion worth of unpaid claims by 1990. Matousek, J. and Ivanek, L., 'Conversion of military industry in Czechoslovakia', *Peace and the Sciences*, Mar. 1992, p. 66. *The Observer*, 28 Apr. 1991, mentioned £10 billion. In 1991 Czechoslovakia had a hard currency debt of $8.085 billion.

[23] *Defense News*, vol. 6, no. 24 (17 June 1991).

[24] Sauerwein (note 3), p. 863.

[25] *Financial Times*, 11 Mar. 1992, quoted 7.6 billion korunas; the Hungarian economic weekly, *Heti Vilaggazdasag*, 28 Nov. 1992, quoted 6 billion korunas.

[26] Ivanek, L., 'Economic and social problems of conversion in the CSFR', Manuscript presented at the Seminar on Financial and Technical Assistance for Arms Conversion in the Aftermath of the Cold War, Stirin, Czechoslovakia, 2–4 Dec. 1991; Interview by the author with Jan Vrablik, Central Institute of National Economy of the Czechoslovak Academy of Sciences, Prague, 14 Apr. 1992.

tories were hit particularly hard—21 in the Czech Republic and 27 in the Slovak Republic.[27] Their estimated total loss was 9.67 billion korunas—3.53 billion korunas in the Czech lands and 6.14 billion korunas in the Slovak Republic. According to the companies, 70 per cent of the losses (86 per cent in the Czech Republic and 63 per cent in the Slovak Republic) were caused by unsold stocks and capital assets while the rest stemmed from bad debts. Another study, by Dr Ladislav Ivanek of the Czechoslovak Peace Society, estimated slightly smaller damage—4.3–6.9 billion korunas.[28] As far as the respective ministries were concerned, they acknowledged losses of 3.2 billion korunas owing to unused stocks and 1.1 billion korunas owing to non-convertible capital assets. The state created two state-owned trading companies to buy up and sell the unused capital assets of military-related companies.[29]

The crisis in the defence sector had a particularly severe impact on employment. According to official data, defence-related unemployment reached 15–18 per cent in Slovakia and 5–8 per cent in the Czech lands.[30] Moreover, for the remaining workforce the special status and advantages that made defence-related employment attractive were almost totally eliminated.[31] This created serious tensions within the traditionally well-trained, motivated workforce, which was strongly attached to military production. The fear of losing élite workers was a major concern of both the enterprises and the government agencies.

III. Conversion

The conditions for conversion to civilian production were extremely favourable in Czechoslovakia. The new leadership—specifically Vaclav Havel, Jiri Dienstbier and Jaroslav Sabata—tried to meet the ideal of a peaceful, democratic country described in the documents of Charter 77. The decision about conversion was driven by both the strong moral commitment of the new government and the need to adjust to the fall in demand that occurred in the late 1980s. Overall reduction plans envisaged a 85–89 per cent cut (from the 1987 peak level) in military production by the end of 1992. Total military output was expected to shrink to 4 billion korunas, with an 80 per cent decrease in production in the Czech Republic and 90 per cent in the Slovak Republic.

In 1990, when a wide-scale conversion competition was announced, 98 enterprises and research institutes presented 304 projects (186 from the Czech and 118 from the Slovak Republic) to a special committee appointed by the Federal

---

[27] Vrablik, J., 'The conversion of arms production', Manuscript produced for the Central Institute of National Economy with collaboration of external researchers, Prague, 1991 (in Czech).

[28] Ivanek (note 26), p. 3.

[29] Interview by the author with Zdenek Kadlec, General Director, and Ladislav Nemec, Deputy Manager, Department of Technical Policy, Federal Ministry of Industry, Czech Republic, Prague, 13 Apr. 1992.

[30] At the time general unemployment reached 12–13% in Slovakia and 3–5% in the Czech lands, *Financial Times*, 22 Mar. 1992.

[31] Dangerous workplaces such as ammunition and explosive factories did, however, retain some privileges.

Table 2.3. Czechoslovak Federal Government support for conversion, 1989–91

Figures are in b. korunas, current prices.

	1989	1990	1991
Czech Republic	–	0.35	0.3
Slovak Republic	0.4	0.85	1.2
Total	**0.4**	**1.2**	**1.5**

Source: Ministry of the Economy figures, Interview by the author with Josef Fucik, Prague, 15 Apr. 1992.

Ministry of the Economy. The committee consisted of representatives of the federal ministries of the Economy, Finance, Foreign Trade and Industry as well as local governments and banks. The committee was disbanded after the competition was completed and state subsidies were pledged.

In general, the conversion projects were elaborated by enterprise management and white-collar workers, in some cases with the help of foreign trade companies or specialized research institutes. Successful applicants could receive a state subsidy and/or apply for special loans from regional banks. Bank credits were pledged only when the plans had received official approval. A total of 125 plans were approved—60 in the Czech lands and 65 in Slovakia.

The projects were divided into those with budgets of more and those with budgets of less than 50 million korunas. Four large-scale projects were chosen by the Federal Government: the Hannomag and Lombardini projects at the Turcianske Strojarni enterprise in Martin; the mobile hydraulic cranes project at ZTS Dubnica; and the chassis production project at Podpolianske Strojarni Detva, in Detva. The first three conversion projects were for heavy weapon production and the fourth for special military engineering products. All the projects were based in Slovakia and the aggregate cost was 4.185 billion korunas, of which the state would provide 0.453 billion korunas. In the category of projects with budgets of less than 50 million korunas, the Federal Ministry of the Economy selected 121 projects and pledged 1.05 billion korunas in state participation. In a few cases—for example, Tesla (Blatna), Gumarny (Zubri), a rubber factory (Zubri), and Motorlet (Jinonice)—Czech regional banks decided to finance the projects without central participation.[32]

Between 1985 and 1990 conversion projects were financed from a Special Technology Fund; prior to 1991 state support took the form of direct transfers to the enterprises and most of this support apparently was in the form of simple state subsidies. In 1991 the government decided to finance specific projects

---

[32] Vrablik (note 27), p. 5. The aggregate cost of all projects accepted by the conversion committee was 26.3 billion korunas (8.1 billion korunas in the Czech Republic) and the state was originally asked to contribute 7.9 billion korunas (2.9 billion korunas in the Czech Republic). The state budget was obviously unable to accommodate these requests.

rather than enterprises and stated that conversion support 'will have to be spent rationally, conforming to market criteria'.[33]

After 1991 the sum allocated in the federal budget for conversion (1.5 billion korunas) was managed through the Fund for Structural Changes and was targeted towards special conversion projects. This fund financed long-term projects for structural/financial adjustment, such as environmental programmes, energy-saving projects and conversion.

In addition to subsidies to finance conversion projects, in 1991 the Federal Government provided 2.266 billion korunas to reduce the losses caused by the halt of military production and 6.5 million korunas for restructuring.[34] Plans for 1992 originally targeted 1.5 billion korunas for existing conversion projects.

State subsidies could only be used to purchase new technology and licences and to pay interest. Although the ceiling for state contributions was limited to 30 per cent of the total project cost, in exceptional cases—when the project implied complete technical restructuring—it could reach a level of 50 per cent. In theory a state contribution was granted only if the enterprise was able to cover 70 per cent of the total project cost. However, according to representatives of the Federal Ministry of Industry, there was no recorded case of a regional bank refusing to pledge credits for an enterprise that was at least nominally involved in conversion. Given the dire financial state of the enterprises, however, it was unlikely that they could meet these requirements. The fact that no application was rejected by the banks also shows that the conditions for financial support in reality were rather lenient.

The proposed new products fell into three categories. There were projects based on the extension of existing civilian production lines—for example, production of hunting guns instead of machine-guns at Uhersky Brod or consumer electronics at Tesla Pardubice in the Czech Republic. Another group of projects aimed to create new production lines to complement existing civilian production—for example, production of textile machinery and small tractors at the Vlazske engineering factory (located in Slavicin) and at Zbrojovka (Vsetin); pneumatic equipment and electromagnetic horns at PS Policka, and sliding meters and motorcycle brakes at Zeveta (Bojkovice).

The third group of projects tried to enter totally new product areas. The Zeveta Bojkovice factory, for example, proposed production of metal-cutting instruments, toys and civilian bridges instead of grenades, rockets and anti-tank weapons; the Povazska engineering factory (Povazska Bystrica) proposed production of agricultural machinery, small cars and ecological equipment as a substitute for aircraft jet engines; and the Slovak Shipyards (Komarno) suggested producing containers instead of military transport equipment.

The projects that were selected were to start production in October 1991. According to Jan Vrablik of the Research Institute of the Academy of Sciences, who took part in the work of the selection committee, of the 60 projects origi-

[33] Fucik (note 15), p. 101; and Interview with Fucik (note 19).

[34] Interview by the author with Karol Droppa, Head of the Department of Special Production, Slovak Ministry of the Economy, Bratislava, 1 Apr. 1993.

nally accepted about 30–40 had been implemented in the Czech lands by mid-1992.[35] According to Slovak Deputy Prime Minister Roman Kovac, there were 11 ongoing conversion projects in Slovakia in early 1993, whose combined value was roughly half that of total military production.[36]

Allegations have been made that financial support for conversion was often used to reduce enterprise debts or even to continue military production.[37] Many indebted defence industry enterprises treated conversion as a means to acquire further state and bank financing. In the summer of 1992 the Ministry of Control began a wide-scale investigation into how the conversion subsidies were spent. The results were not made public, but representatives of the respective ministries and some outside sources claimed that the government funds allocated for conversion were used properly.[38]

The most well-documented conversion programme was carried out in ZTS Martin, in central Slovakia. It dated from 1988, when ZTS signed a contract with Hannomag (Germany) to produce tractors and construction machinery. In 1990 another agreement was completed with Lombardini (Italy) to establish a small diesel engine plant. Although civilian production became increasingly important, the share of military output remained significant (an estimated 10–20 per cent) and was still the most profitable division of the enterprise. Conversion presented several additional problems to the enterprise managers, with whom they seemed unable to cope.[39]

The Meopta Optical Works in Slovakia and Adast in the Czech lands seemed to be potential conversion success stories.

At Meopta, by 1993 the military share of output had declined from about 50 per cent to about 10 per cent. Total output had dropped to one-third of the 1988 output, and the workforce had shrunk from 2500 to 500. The enterprise produced overhead projectors and other optical instruments—for example, a self-designed projector that projected images onto a screen directly from a computer. Meopta succeeded in entering the international market, although the management was worried about its future prospects.[40]

Adast was one of the oldest military factories, producing mechanical parts for bombs and rockets. According to the general director, by 1993 all military production had come to a halt and even the machinery and premises kept for 'cold

[35] Interview with Jan Vrablik (note 26).

[36] *Telegraf*, 19 Aug. 1992.

[37] The attitude of several enterprises during the conversion competition was revealing in this respect. Some—like Avia (Prague), Technometra (Prague), CKD (Dukla), Let (Kunovice), Bonekan (Duchov), Kras (Brno), SP Jihlava and the State Institute for Glass Research—simply applied for state subsidies without even bothering to design a conversion plan. Vrablik (note 27).

[38] Interview with Karol Droppa (note 34); Interview by the author with Ladislav Nemec, Head of the Department of Technical Policy, Federal Ministry of Industry, Prague, 8 Apr. 1993; and Mikusova, K., 'Fiscal and credit policy of the government: impact on the conversion of military production', eds Kominkova and Schmognerova (note 4). It is possible that, although the sums specifically allocated for conversion were used properly, misuse occurred in the case of additional loans provided by banks against government guarantees. Indirect support was apparently often misused or not used at all.

[39] See chapter 4 in this volume.

[40] Interview by the author with Jan Chovanec, Managing Director, and Laurenc Svitok, Commercial Director of Meopta Bratislava, Bratislava, 2 Apr. 1993.

capacities' (unused machinery, reserves and eventually labour that could be mobilized for military purposes at any time) were used for civilian purposes. The company extended its existing civilian profile—making printing machinery—and introduced a new line for production of oil pumps. Although the profitability of the years when military production was predominant was not reached, the enterprise was in a solid financial state. Most of its output was exported throughout the world, from China to the USA.[41]

There were several other successful transformations, like the Ceska Zbrojovka (Uhersky Brod) factory, which began to produce sport and hunting guns, and Blanicke Strojirny (Vlasim), which extended its rubber pipe production and introduced new lines for tools and small tractors for vineyards instead of making air bombs. Both companies started by expanding their civilian production, which meant that retooling and retraining were considerably less difficult than for a company launching an entirely new profile.[42]

The obvious pains of conversion and the relatively modest financial and technical assistance provided caused most of the military-related enterprises to be uninterested in or hostile to the whole process. In reality, fairly little conversion actually took place. The military sector responded mainly to the radical cuts in defence expenditure, the growing difficulties of customers in the developing world and the collapse of the WTO, which occurred before the launch of state-sponsored conversion projects.

Despite some positive experiences, government and industrial circles gradually adopted the view that conversion programmes took too long to develop and presented too many insoluble problems. Most of the difficulties were attributed to the lack of financial resources and markets, which the major decision makers seemed to be unable to address properly. Even though military production decreased after 1987, conversion became a scapegoat for all the defence industry's ills.

The original ideas of the 'Velvet Revolution'—stressing new forms of political engagement—were gradually replaced by more orthodox party politics and a dogmatic neo-liberal policy. In foreign policy the emphasis shifted from endorsing a European collective security system to advocating NATO membership. Conversion gradually slid down the hierarchy of economic and political priorities, which meant that there was less central state support and political commitment to it. The slow pace, lack of convincing examples of success, possible abuses and resistance from industry further decreased the enthusiasm for conversion within the cabinet. According to the original plans, the state was to contribute 1.5 billion korunas for conversion projects in 1992, but by mid-1992 the government had decided to reduce its commitment to 1 billion korunas and rethink its entire strategy with regard to conversion.

[41] Interview by the author with Jan Dosek, General Director of Adamovske Strojirny, Adamov, 7 Apr. 1993.

[42] Ceska Zbrojovka was later investigated and accused of violating the ban on exporting arms to countries under embargo—possibly including the former Yugoslavia. *Lidove Noviny*, 1 Jan. 1993.

A report on conversion by Vladimir Dlouhy, Federal Minister of the Economy, presented to the Federal Assembly in the spring of 1992 suggested that only those factories which completely stopped producing arms should receive subsidies for conversion. He stated: 'I do not want the present policy going on, which allows a tank producer to receive state subsidies for conversion only because it simultaneously started to produce Italian diesel engines as well . . . Only in the long run, when all developed countries will indeed stop arms production, will we join them'.[43]

Since even the enterprises that were most committed to conversion envisaged a gradual transformation, with a steady diversification of the product range, the government decision was undoubtedly a blow to conversion. The parallel liberalization of arms exports served as an incentive to continue producing and exporting weapons. The most unambiguous statement concerning the revised relationship of economic development and military production came from Vaclav Klaus, then Federal Minister of Finance, who said: 'Our foreign policy should first and foremost be profitable for us. I am against cheap gestures. We should not be the most peaceful country in the world, which does not sell a single bullet or gun to anyone. These ideas sound nice, but they are forced on us by countries that themselves export arms to the whole world'.[44]

Although state-assisted conversion was the most spectacular and highly publicized part of the decision, the policy on defence-related production and exports pursued by the new Czech Government after the change in the political system had other dimensions as well. Between 1990 and 1992 the official policy was to let some defence enterprises either go bankrupt or convert to civilian production. One manifest sign that the government did not intend to give special treatment to defence firms was that, after some discussion, military-related enterprises were selected to take part in the first wave of voucher privatization[45] that began in February 1992. The group of 14 companies selected to be privatized was in a way a representative sample: it included 7 Slovak and 7 Czech companies with profiles ranging from production of rocket-launcher spare parts (Adast) and ammunition (Zeveta Bojkovice, PS Policka, and Sellier & Bellot) to optical instruments (Meopta).[46]

---

[43] *Noviny*, 29 May 1992.

[44] *Rude Pravo*, 28 Apr. 1992.

[45] The word 'privatization' is used differently by different analysts and actors. Some use the word to mean a transfer of ownership from government to non-government hands. For others it connotes a wider process involving changing all aspects of production and pricing from public to private hands. Within the narrow definition of privatization, ownership can be transferred in a variety of ways. One form of privatization is the mass distribution of the means of acquisition—in the form of vouchers with a face value that can be redeemed against a share of enterprises that are put up for auction or sale. This was the pattern chosen in Czechoslovakia. Other forms were chosen in other ECE countries. For a general discussion, see Gültekin, B. and Goldstein, M., 'Privatization in post-communist economies: a theoretical analysis' and Jackson, M., 'Critical issues in privatization: a comparison of the experience in Central and Eastern Europe', Papers presented to the meeting on Privatization Experiences and Policies in NACC Countries in the Field of Defence Industry, NATO Economics Colloquium, Brussels, 1 July 1994.

[46] This later turned out to be fortunate in the case of those Slovak enterprises that were privatized before the process of large-scale privatization came to a halt in Slovakia.

The group included both fairly successful enterprises (Adast and Ceska Zbrojovka) and ailing ones (Zeveta and PS Policka). All but one were medium-sized, with a book value of up to 1 billion korunas, the exception being Povazske Strojarne in the Slovak town of Povazska Bystrica, with nearly 4 billion korunas in capital assets. Heavy weaponry and aircraft producers were missing from the list. In all the privatized companies the state preserved a 1 per cent 'golden share', and in several up to 30 per cent of the shares were allocated to the National Property Fund, the main privatization agency.[47]

Despite these spectacular signs of loosening state control over defence industry enterprises, some companies seemingly continued to receive state support in their struggle for survival on the basis of their strategic importance or potential profitability. Formally still completely committed to conversion, policy makers kept an eye on potentially profitable business enterprises, even if they were military-based. In a June 1991 interview Fucik mentioned that branches like trainer aircraft, some military electronics, and nuclear, biological and chemical (NBC) equipment would be maintained and expanded.[48]

The selection of enterprises which were to perish and those which were to be resurrected was unknown, and government policy seemed unpredictable from the perspective of enterprises. This unusual insecurity pushed many military enterprises that were already on the verge of or in bankruptcy into a state of panic. Many resorted to simple survival techniques like not paying bills, while many either sank into inertia or engaged in feverish political lobbying to secure their positions.

Reorientation

Notwithstanding their precarious economic state, between 1989 and 1992 only a handful of the defence enterprises went bankrupt and closed down. Despite spectacular drops in industrial production and productivity, the general economic crisis unfolded fairly 'smoothly' in Czechoslovakia.[49] This was principally because the new government maintained measures that helped to avoid a dramatic socio-economic collapse—even though on the surface it preached a radical free-market rhetoric. Although the Federal Parliament passed a bankruptcy law in the spring of 1991, this law was not enforced.

Forced by conversion policy, most of the defence industry enterprises did introduce or expand their civilian profiles. However limited the remaining state

---

[47] Matousek, J. and Ivanek, L., *Zbrojni vyroba, konverze, obranyschopnost* [Defence industry, conversion, defence potential], (Czechoslvak Peace Society: Prague, 1993), table 7, p. 58.

[48] Sauerwein (note 3), p. 864. Citing the need to preserve the intellectual capital of the defence industry, despite military expenditure cuts, the state already gave subsidies to some military development projects in 1991. The subsidies covered 50% of the costs of a new, dual-purpose radio sensor system (probably the Tamara) and a trainer aircraft. Interview by the author with Zdenek Kadlec, General Director, and Ladislav Nemec, Deputy Manager, Department of Technical Policy, Federal Ministry of Industry, Czech Republic, Prague, 13 Apr. 1992.

[49] By 1991 industrial production fell by 23% and productivity by 18% in the Czech Republic and by 18% and 23%, respectively, in Slovakia. Ulc, O., 'The bumpy road of Czechoslovakia's Velvet Revolution', *Problems of Communism*, May–June 1992, p. 23.

intervention was—whether in the form of conversion support, 'emergency subsidies' or just not forcing factories to close—it did help companies to stay in business. Even though government allocations were modest, especially compared to those of the past, they played an important role in maintaining the belief among company managers that the situation would improve. Most factories intended to preserve military-related production, if necessary producing only for stock. If production came to a halt they maintained the core of their military-related assets and workers. With measures such as reduced working hours, obligatory holidays, lower salaries and inter-enterprise indebtedness, they struggled to cut costs. Many enterprises were led by sheer inertia, but others sensed the political change and decided to 'wait and see'.

Minor but meaningful alterations were perceptible in Federal Government policy from early 1991. A strong 'revivalist' current emerged among representatives of the defence industry and associated ministries who began to express their views openly in the media. They claimed that the period after 1989 was a time of naïve humanism, brutally abused by other arms-producing countries. When Czechoslovakia unilaterally withdrew from the lucrative arms market, its place was immediately occupied by Western, ECE and Chinese exporters. They sold weapons not only to former clients of Czechoslovakia but also to countries under international embargo—including the former Yugoslavia. According to this view the damage caused by the conversion policy and ban on arms exports could only be repaired if the country regained its position on the international market. Their proposed new policy of 'pragmatism' envisaged arms production on a commercial basis and proposed that the best way to revamp Czechoslovak military production was to establish cooperation with Western military firms.[50]

In June 1991, in a hearing before the United States Senate, Oldrich Cerny—adviser to President Havel—claimed that the only option for the government was to retain a limited defence industry to finance conversion from export revenues and to meet army requirements.[51] However, even before this new policy was formally accepted, the Federal Ministry of the Economy and the Federal Ministry of Foreign Trade decided to act as mediators between Czechoslovak and foreign arms producers to promote cooperation.[52]

While these ideas were expressed increasingly openly in Prague, in Bratislava 'revivalist' arguments were based more on social factors. They claimed that the sudden halt of military production would cause a socio-economic catastrophe, enormous unemployment and social unrest in the most affected regions. The Slovak ideas were quickly transformed into action as well. In 1991, under pressure from Slovak politicians, the Federal Government reluctantly approved the sale of 300 T-72 tanks to Syria and negotiations for the sale of 1500 tanks to Iran. This was the first open retreat from the rejection of arms exports.

[50] Fucik (note 15), pp. 98–102; and Interview by the author with Jan Vrablik, Head of Department of the Central Institute of National Economy of the Czechoslovak Academy of Sciences, Prague, 14 Apr. 1992.
[51] *Defense News*, vol. 6, no. 24 (17 June 1991).
[52] Fucik (note 15), p. 102.

The controversies concerning conversion and arms exports surfaced in connection with the regulation of the arms trade. From 1990, KOVOM, the department in charge of the control of trade in 'special materials' of the Federal Ministry of Foreign Trade, headed by Stefan Glezgo, authorized and supervised trade in military products and materials. The department issued 'licences for general commercial activity, including arms'. By April 1992, 27 general licences were granted, mainly to military-related enterprises to sell their own products but also to state-owned and about 20 private trading firms. In addition, some 'one-off' licences were given for individual transactions. Many small and medium-scale companies involved in foreign trade managed to extend their licences to include trade in weapons as well. These developments brought the end of the monopoly of the state-owned Omnipol, which until 1989 was the only trader of arms. In 1991 Unimpex—another state-owned arms trade company and Omnipol's Slovak counterpart—was established.

Despite the apparent strict ban on arms sales, some deals were struck even in the immediate post-1990 period. According to Glezgo, in 1991 arms sales did not reach the level of 200 million korunas, which was less than 10 per cent of the total exports of that year. No finished product was sold outside the WTO, although spare parts were purchased.[53] Other sources, however, suggested that there were more Czechoslovak arms trade deals in 1990–92.

According to *Respekt*, 250 tanks were sold to Syria and 200 to Peru. The negotiations with Iran for the sale of 1518 surplus tanks (destined to be reduced under the 1990 Treaty on Conventional Armed Forces in Europe, the CFE Treaty) were completed in 1990 but the deal was cancelled in response to worries expressed by the United States. After Iran threatened to suspend its civilian trade with Czechoslovakia, worth $2 billion, a compromise was agreed with Minister of Foreign Trade Jozsef Baksay to sell three Tamara air surveillance systems instead of the tanks.

The same article claimed that, following a deal signed in April 1991, more than 600 tank-assembly experts would be sent to Libya to help to set up a tank factory near Tripoli. Another large-scale shipment of mostly hand weapons allegedly to be sent to Nigeria but probably destined for the Yugoslav Federal Army was detected in January 1992.[54] Commenting on the latter case, Stefan Glezgo, Director-General of the Department of Military Products, Federal Ministry of Foreign Trade, said: 'we certainly would not permit this deal. The problem is that the existing legislation does not allow us to prosecute people who plan such deals . . . We can refuse to give them a licence, but we cannot stop them'.[55]

The new trade law accepted by the parliament in January 1992 failed to deal with the special licences required for arms deals and was not accompanied by a

---

[53] Interview by the author with Stefan Glezgo, Prague, 14 Apr. 1992. According to *Financial Times*, 7 Nov. 1992, exports between Jan. and Aug. 1991 reached $6.54 billion, 10% of which would be higher than the sum mentioned by Glezgo.

[54] The suspicious 'Nigerian' deal was struck by the Slovak agency Unimpex.

[55] *Respekt*, 27 Jan. 1992.

detailed equipment list specifying what was to be considered 'special' military material. In March 1992 Glezgo proposed to parliament a new law, to introduce strict and legalized control over the proliferating arms market. The proposal was rejected because of the resistance from Slovak parliamentarians who considered it a 'Czech centralizing effort'. The prevailing Slovak opinion was summarized by the director of Omnipol, Stanislav Kozeny, who stated that 'the first priority of the new Slovak prime minister will be to maintain standards of living. And in Slovakia this is linked directly to allowing the arms factories, the republic's main hard currency earners, to sell'.[56]

In order to prevent illegal arms exports, however, in the spring of 1992 the government published a list of countries to which it was forbidden to sell arms. The decision significantly upset military–industrial circles. Ladislav Nemec of the Federal Ministry of Industry said in an interview: 'publishing the list of the countries where we cannot sell arms was embarrassing, because it indicated that we did not trust these countries and will most likely have a negative impact on our civilian trade with them'.[57]

The turning-point in government arms trade policy came in mid-1992 when the general ban on arms exports was waived and individual (private or state) enterprises were allowed to produce and sell arms subject to licensing but without any direct state intervention. Vladmir Dlouhy, Federal Minister of the Economy, summarized the new policy: 'Arms are goods everybody is trading with, including those who criticize us most for it. Since other countries are doing the same, we should not fear to continue selling weapons in a reasonable and regulated form. It is important however to outline clear trade conditions and certain territories where arms cannot be exported'.[58] The list of states subject to embargo remained in place.

The decision could be considered as a recognition that the government was unable to resist the pressure of military–industrial circles in the Czech Republic and the increasingly radical Slovak opposition to Federal regulations on the arms trade.[59] It seemed as if the Czech side offered this compromise to placate the Slovaks. However, following the events unfolding since mid-1990 it was clear that the Federal Government included loosening the strict ban on arms exports on its own agenda. In addition, by mid-1992 it was too late to satisfy the increasingly independent-minded Slovak politicians with more permissive arms trade regulations. The new policy on arms export was announced along with the revised policy on conversion, underlining the general shift in perspective of the Czech Government.

It is interesting to follow the arguments used to justify this shift because in each ECE country the same types of argument were used by the respective government officials. The first argument was that profits from sales of military

[56] *Financial Times*, 11 Mar. 1992.
[57] Borovicka, M., 'The renaissance of arms trade?', *Noviny*, 29 May 1992 (in Czech).
[58] *Rude Pravo*, 11 Feb. 1992.
[59] Long before the disintegration of Czechoslovakia, and in violation of the existing regulations, the Slovak regional government shipped a prototype armoured personnel carrier to Sudan and declared its intention to sell more of them. *The Economist*, 28 Nov. 1992.

equipment could be used for conversion or to import military equipment needed by the Czechoslovak armed forces but not produced locally.[60]

Then it was argued that a limited amount of arms production should be permitted in order to combat increasing unemployment.[61] General Oldrich Barak, Head of Procurement of the Czechoslovak Army, argued that maintaining some of the defence industry would help to prepare the new national army for its desired entry into NATO.[62] Finally, purely economic reasoning was used to demonstrate that substituting imports with cheaper local production and earning high profits through foreign sales would improve the macroeconomic situation and contribute to further progress in the national economy.[63]

IV. The road to separation

While there were obviously other very important factors pushing towards the disintegration of Czechoslovakia, questions of the future of the arms industry and arms trade became crucial in the escalation of economic and political tensions that led to the breakup of the Federation on 1 January 1993. Defence industrial questions acted as a catalyst and a major stage on which the ideological and political differences of the emerging new political leadership of the two republics were acted out. For those who considered separation unfortunate, conversion appeared to be a major factor to blame for it. Outgoing Czechoslovak Minister of the Interior Jan Langos claimed that the push for conversion led by Minister of Foreign Affairs Jiri Dienstbier had led to the 'loss' of Slovakia.[64]

The development of the defence industry took different directions in the two parts of the Czechoslovak Federation. The Czech and Moravian part took up production under Soviet licence mainly as a complement to historically established traditions of arms production. In Slovakia, as in the other backward economies of countries in the region after World War II, the development of a Soviet-style arms industry was seen as a means of rapid industrialization.

In a way the two parts of the Federation represented two separate industrial development patterns. Slovakia functioned as a large-scale subcontractor to the Soviet Union, while the Czech lands enjoyed slightly more independence because of their higher level of development. The Slovak arms industry later paid a double price for this heritage. Its oversized heavy military industry found it difficult to cope with the devastating effects of crisis and the challenges of conversion. At the same time it seemed much less attractive to Western

---

[60] Cerny, O., in Leopold, G., 'Czechs try to end arms exports in weak economy', *Defense News*, vol. 6, no. 24 (17 June 1991), p. 8; and Vaclav Havel, in *International Herald Tribune*, 3 May 1991.

[61] Minister of Foreign Affairs Jiri Dienstbier, quoted in *International Herald Tribune*, 3 May 1991; and Josef Fucik, quoted in *Hospodarske Noviny*, no. 20 (1991).

[62] *Mlada Fronta Dnes*, 11 Jan. 1993.

[63] Dlouhy, in *Noviny*, 29 May 1992; and Deputy Minister of Defence Ivan Balas, 'Zrusime zbrojni vyrobu? [Will we liquidate armaments production?], *Vojensky Profesional* [Military Professional], no. 7 (1992).

[64] *The Guardian*, 22 June 1992.

investors (who could have helped it to modernize and return to the lucrative military markets) than its Czech counterparts.

As the size and nature of their industry were different, conversion problems were also different in the two parts of the country. Slovakia—where the military sector was more concentrated, less diversified and developed—was hit more severely by the crisis than the rest of the Federation. The decision to halt production and exports of tanks and APCs was made by the Federal Government in 1990. After long constitutional disputes about the competence of the respective republics, the Slovak Government (led by Jan Carnogursky) regained control over military production in early 1991. It decided to continue a limited amount of tank production and exports in order to ease growing social tension caused by the massive lay-offs.

At the same time the Slovak leadership became actively involved in conversion. In January 1992 it published its own document 'On conversion of arms production in industrial enterprises in Slovakia' which attempted to lay out a comprehensive strategy to deal with the problem. The idea apparently gained support among regional and local organizations as well. Municipal authorities, mainly in Martin and Dubnica, tried to work out proposals to resolve the problems caused by the defence industry crisis in cooperation with factories, regional developers and representatives of the emerging private sector.

The Czech Government did not deal with the question so intensively. Their situation was certainly much less dramatic. According to Josef Fucik, there were only two seriously affected companies in the Czech lands—the ammunition factory in Bojkovice and the Adamovski enterprise in Brno. Czech sources did not report significant job losses as a result of conversion, claiming that alternative civilian production had absorbed the redundant workers.[65]

Federal institutions were unable or unwilling to deal with conversion. The labour, regional, market and industrial policy dimensions of the problem were not addressed. There were no policy decisions on direct or indirect economic means that could have facilitated conversion, like preferential credits, tax allowances or specific wage regulations. Conversion and the whole set of related issues had no 'patron' to promote and monitor the process once the original decision was made. Managing the process was a responsibility distributed among several federal and regional ministries and government agencies. In the end no one was clearly responsible for it or able to handle its specific requirements and immediate consequences.

The conversion problem and the conflicts it triggered were used as a pretext to fuel separatist ambitions on the Czech and the Slovak side. Although it was hardly ever expressed openly, there was some resentment on the Czech side about the large sums of federal money being spent on Slovak military producers. The fact that conversion did not show any immediate progress further alienated Czech partners. Dlouhy's statement on 'fake' conversion obviously referred to Slovak enterprises.

[65] Interview with Josef Fucik (note 19).

According to the Slovak interpretation, Prague was eager to promote conversion in Slovakia but allowed Czech and Moravian industries to survive—having had in mind possible NATO membership (which would require a strong, modern army) from the very beginning.[66]

In the meantime the emerging Slovak nationalist opposition, led by Vladimir Meciar, used conversion as a general scapegoat for all the dramatic consequences of the unfolding economic crisis. Enterprises were described as being 'hit by conversion' and the state was called upon to protect them from it. Since the Federal Government was unable (and somewhat reluctant) to do this, the argument ran, the genuine national movement would undertake the task. The serious industrial problems and Prague's continued insensitivity to Slovak problems convinced many Slovaks that the breakup of the country would resolve their economic hardships. Before June 1992, in an absurd electoral end-game, arms production and exports became the symbol of Slovak national sovereignty, worth defending at any cost.

The narrow-mindedness of the Czech leadership—which was rapidly shifting towards a neo-liberal economic policy from its original social democratic positions—refused to take into account growing social and national tensions and began to see Slovakia as an unwanted handicap which was not only expensive but also slowed down the much desired union with the West. Czech decision makers also recognized that they had significant arms export opportunities, which further reduced support for conversion, increasingly seen as an undesirable hold-over from the original government agenda.

After the divorce both sides revealed that separation was seen as a historical chance to fulfil deep aspirations that the 'other side' seemed to hinder.

In one of his first interviews Vladimir Meciar, the new Prime Minister of Slovakia, declared that 'arms production will be resurrected wherever possible'.[67] The arguments presented were not exclusively economic. In a meeting with representatives of the Ministry of Defence he promised that 'the Slovak Army will have enough means to guarantee its efficiency, even if these means will have to be provided at the expense of other budget items'.[68]

Although the cold war had come to an end, new security threats emerged and the military industry was required to meet the new needs of the armed forces. The fact that during the WTO years all members had the same internal operational system and equipment also created new arguments for rebuilding the military industry. It had to contribute, for example, to the establishment of a new air-defence system since this capability had been provided by the Soviet Union. According to the new policy guidelines the resurrection of the military industry was not only needed to generate export earnings, but also because the

---

[66] According to one view, 'The current plan of defence industry conversion is widely resented and interpreted as an insidious plot to stab the Slovaks in the back. Allegedly it is the greatest catastrophe that the Slovak people had to endure since the Turkish invasion of the country in the 17th century'. *Forum*, 10 Apr. 1991, quoted in Ulc (note 49), p. 24.

[67] *Rude Pravo*, 6 Jan. 1993.

[68] *Lidove Noviny*, 5 Jan. 1993.

new Slovak national army faced threats from neighbouring Hungary.[69] However, after Meciar's belligerent statements, major actors—including Peter Magvasi, Director of the ZTS Martin Military Division and President of the Union of Engineering Industry of the Slovak Republic, the management of ZTS Dubnica (the other mammoth of the Slovak military industry) and Ludovit Cernak, Minister of the Economy, declared that a massive investment in reviving the defence industry would be a futile and impossible exercise. Independent of further decisions on military production, the Slovak Government provided 500 million Slovak korunas for ongoing conversion projects.[70]

For his part Vaclav Klaus, the new Prime Minister of the Czech Republic, declared that the 'Visegrad process'—regional cooperation between Hungary, Poland and what used to be Czechoslovakia—was an artificial Western invention.[71] After separation from the less developed Slovakia, the Czech leader distanced himself further from the East European heritage—seen as an obstacle to rapid integration into West European structures. As far as military issues were concerned, according to the new Minister of Defence, Antonin Baudys: 'What we [the Visegrad armies] have in common is the necessity to rearm. It is open, however, how cooperation can help this issue'.[72]

The new Czech Republic did not wish to follow a specific conversion policy because the new leadership considered that support provided by the former federal state was sufficient. In the new market environment, factories were expected to cope with their difficulties by themselves. In extraordinary cases they could apply to the Ministry of Industry for specific funds which would be provided on an individual basis. Similarly, if military producers had viable (and hopefully exportable) development projects, they too could ask for state-granted loans.[73]

The breakup of Czechoslovakia set back development in both the Czech and Slovak lands. It created significant and unnecessary losses and pain for the population and economies on both sides of the border. It also gave a boost to the build-up of national armies and therefore a rationale for rescuing what was left of the respective defence industries. These consequences are sinister enough to underline the importance of a well-founded, convincing and properly implemented conversion project in the countries of Eastern Europe.

---

[69] *Liberation*, 6 Jan. 1993.
[70] Interview with Karol Droppa (note 34).
[71] *Le Figaro*, 8 Jan. 1992.
[72] *Mlada Fronta Dnes*, 25 Jan. 1993.
[73] Interview with Ladislav Nemec (note 38).

3. The Czech Republic

I. The heritage of the breakup of the Czechoslovak Federation

Czechoslovakia was the country that began its radical transformation in 1989–90 with the most favourable macroeconomic conditions of the countries in the East–Central European (ECE) region. After the disintegration of the Czechoslovak Federation on 1 January 1993, the new Czech Republic was in a decidedly better position *vis-à-vis* its Federation partner, Slovakia: the level of general economic development and the living standards were higher in the Czech Republic and it had significantly less unemployment and fewer structural problems than Slovakia.[1] In addition, the bulk of the relatively modern industrial base was located in the Czech lands, as were most of the foreign contacts and foreign investment that followed the 'Velvet Revolution'. In 1993, at the time of the breakup, unemployment had reached 11 per cent in Slovakia but only 3 per cent in the Czech Republic. In 1990–92 the Czech lands had received an estimated $1.6 billion in foreign direct investment, in contrast to $270 million that went to Slovakia.[2]

The Czech Republic also benefited from a stable macroeconomic environment that was unique in the region and represented a considerable advantage. The macroeconomic stabilization programme launched in 1990 was carried out more or less consistently, even if there was a serious back side to the entire transformation process—including slow micro-economic adjustment, widespread corruption and ill-treatment of the Gypsy minority[3]—but in the broader context these developments did not seem to greatly disturb the generally positive economic picture.

The new country had a very positive image abroad; its stability and significant development potential were acknowledged from the beginning, although it was only in 1994 that the international press began to depict the Czech Republic as the genuine success story of the ECE transformation. The two public figures who characterized the new period—President Vaclav Havel and Prime Minister Vaclav Klaus, former Federation Minister of Finance—enjoyed international recognition, although in different circles and for different reasons. Havel was appreciated for his dissident past and for the high intellectual and moral stand he aimed to embody, and Klaus for his free-market ideology and professional competence.

[1] For a discussion of developments in Slovakia, see chapter 4 in this volume.
[2] *Financial Times,* 6 Mar. 1993.
[3] For details, see *Financial Times Survey: The Czech Republic,* 19 Dec. 1994; and 'Exclusive: corruption: à qui la faute?' [Exclusive: corruption: who is to blame?], *Tribune de Prague,* no. 4 (Dec. 1993/Jan. 1994).

The breakup of the Czechoslovak Federation caused a serious setback for both of the new states. New customs and trade regulations, different currencies, new institutional arrangements, judicial problems and controversies over the privatization vouchers that had already been distributed all made their economic contacts complicated and sometimes impossible. The level of all the major economic indicators fell dramatically in the first half year of independence in the Czech Republic and in the first two years in Slovakia.[4]

As far as the military inheritance from Czechoslovakia was concerned, the rule of thumb was a 3:2 proportionate distribution of the armed forces personnel, weaponry, equipment and other military establishments between the two new republics;[5] the Czech armed forces would number 93 000 and the Slovak 47 000.

Defence production capacities were also separated by the new borders into two lopsided military industrial bases—with more but smaller factories in the new Czech Republic and fewer, but mostly large-scale establishments in Slovakia. After the breakup, Slovakia inherited approximately 40 billion korunas in capital assets of the former Federation defence industry and the Czech Republic 26–28 billion korunas.[6] Structurally, however, the Czech lands were in a much more advantageous position: they inherited industry which produced aviation technology, small arms, and the bulk of the sophisticated optical, communications and electronic instrument production. In Slovakia heavy military production predominated.

Industrial ties that had been built up for decades were broken. Before the breakup about 60 per cent of the Czech companies depended on Slovak subcontractors and 75 per cent of the Slovak firms were dependent on deliveries from the Czech lands.[7] Apart from their interdependence regarding supplies of raw materials and spare parts, there were other difficulties owing to the fact that the former Czechoslovak enterprise structure was fairly rigid and overcentralized. Unlike the Polish or Hungarian economy, it had not been 'softened' by gradual reform efforts. Originally, most of the defence enterprises were organized in two immense conglomerates—ZTS (Heavy Engineering Works) and ZVS (General Engineering Works). The ZTS united companies produced land systems and the ZVS united companies provided support equipment, ammunition, small arms, and so on. Diverse enterprises which were located relatively far apart, such as Adast Adamov, PS Policka, VS Slavicin and ZVS Dubnica, belonged to the same united company. A similarly diverse group of enterprises belonging to Tesla and Meopta were also spread over the whole of the former Czechoslovakia. After 1989 serious decentralization efforts were made and most of the institutional dependencies were abolished. However, functional

[4] *Financial Times*, 6 Mar. 1993; and *International Herald Tribune*, 24 Mar. 1993.
[5] *Jane's Defence Weekly*, 30 Jan. 1993.
[6] Cechak, O., Selesovsky, J. and Stembera, M., 'Czechoslovakia: reductions in arms production in a time of economic and political transformation', ed. H. Wulf, SIPRI, *Arms Industry Limited* (Oxford University Press: Oxford, 1993), p. 249.
[7] Cechak, Selesovsky and Stembera (note 6).

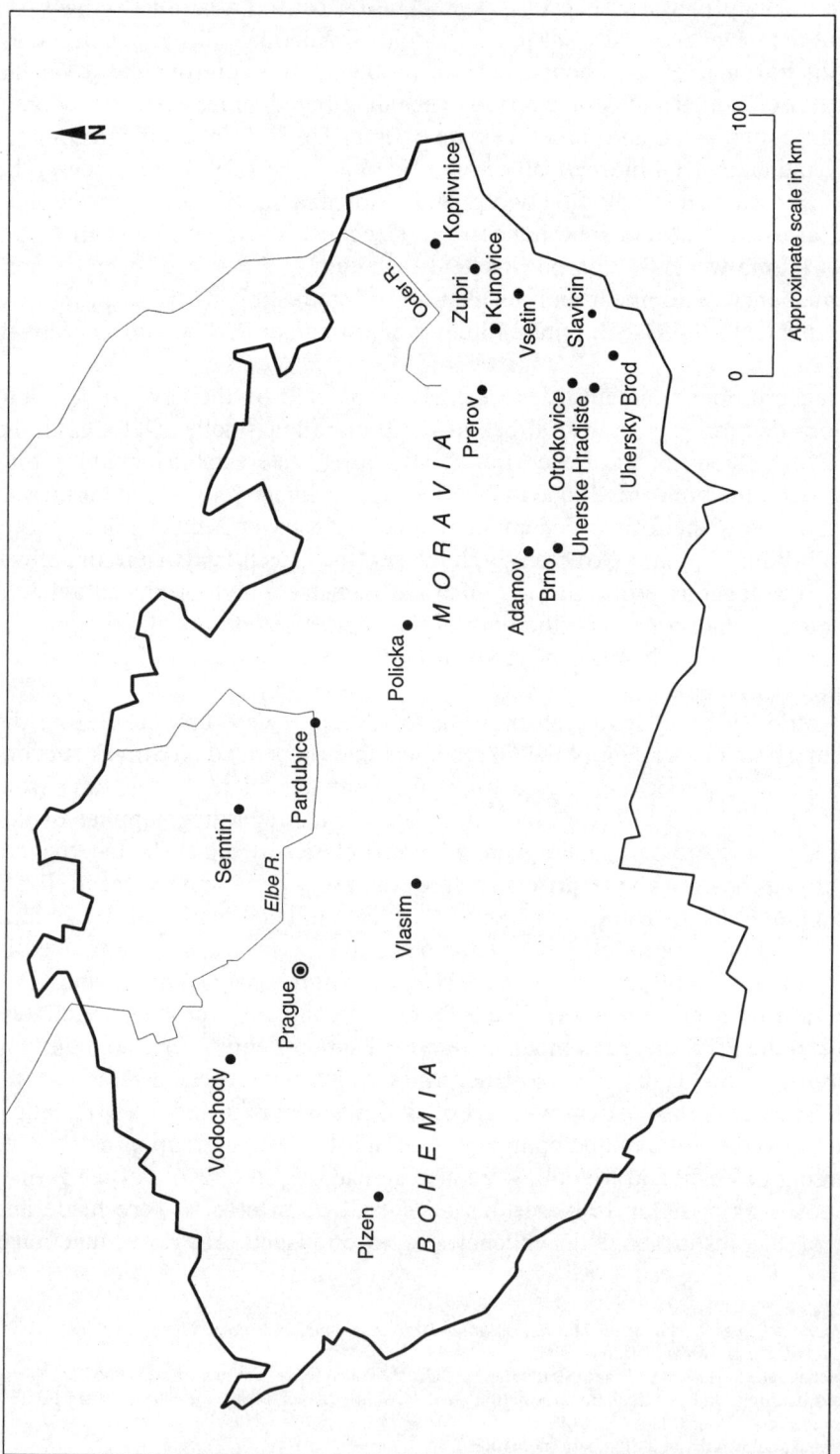

Figure 3.1. Location of defence enterprises in the Czech Republic

connections remained and these ties, too, were abruptly cut or became problematic with the breakup of the Federation.

For some time, and principally in cases of minor importance, cooperation continued over the border between the Czech Republic and Slovakia. However, since cooperation was not encouraged officially on either side and since emerging administrative obstacles made transactions slower and more costly, most of the former partnerships gradually withered away, particularly where crucial or large numbers of items and spare parts were involved. Relatively soon after the breakup, both countries began to try to complement their residual military production to substitute for lost suppliers, which led to fierce competition between them within two years.

In the Czech region of Bohemia, many companies terminated their former Slovak partnerships and looked for substitute partners. Since it would have been too expensive to rely on Western suppliers, partners were sought in the other former Warsaw Treaty Organization (WTO) countries or industries were rebuilt in the Czech Republic. For example, some new trade and cooperation relations were set up between the Czech firm Gumarny and the Hungarian firm Comasec-Respirator and between the Czech Aero and the Hungarian Dunai Repulogepgyar firms.

The second strategy adopted was more common. Even without serious financial backing, the technical needs of the Czech defence industry necessitated a reorganization. Defence industrialists began to search for production capacities that would allow a renewal of military production based on domestic resources. Companies that had previous experience in the field revived their capacities—for example, this is how heavy weapon production was restarted at Skoda-Plzen.

The new policy on arms industry and trade

After independence, the Czech Republic embarked on the most consistent and radical transformation policy of the region. The programme of 'velvet shock therapy' was followed by a far-reaching privatization programme. By early 1994 defence enterprises that had been involved in the first round of privatization in 1992 had a new organization and ownership structure. Most of these enterprises became shareholder companies, with majority shares owned by a state organization—the Ministry of Trade and Industry, the Ministry of Defence, the National Property Fund or state-owned banks. The rest of the shares were divided among coupon-holding citizens, most of whom entrusted their coupons to major investment funds.

Some of the enterprises that did not take part in the first wave of privatization were scheduled for the second one, which started in March 1994.[8] At the same time it was decided that some of the enterprises, because of their strategic

---

[8] Including the rest of Skoda-Plzen's shares and those of the former Synthesia in Semtin, the producer of the Semtex explosive.

importance, would be kept in state hands under the supervision of the Ministry of Trade and Industry.[9]

After mid-1992, but principally after 1 January 1993, when the breakup of the Federation became official, arms exports ceased to be regarded as immoral by senior members of government and this was considered an extremely lucrative type of foreign trade which the state had to control indirectly, by licensing exports according to international guidelines. The official policy concerning defence enterprises also changed completely. Arms production was in theory regarded as a branch of the economy subject to the same general economic rules that were valid for any other sector. Military-related enterprises lost all their former privileges and had to function under the same conditions as their civilian counterparts. Conversion subsidies have not been granted since 1993.

In its implementation, the general economic policy approach contained con-tradictions, at least as far as the defence industry was concerned. While the rhetoric and elements of policy were neo-liberal in their tone, they were com-plemented by state intervention both in industry and in the welfare system. As noted in chapter 2, arguments in favour of reviving the Czech defence industry were articulated even before the breakup. After the breakup this became the official policy.

The most spectacular manifestation of the reversal of policy came from Presi-dent Vaclav Havel, who symbolized the pacifist and moral stand associated with the first 'Velvet Revolution' government. Asked whether he personally opposed the production of tanks in the Czech Republic (as he had declared regarding production in the former Czechoslovakia), he answered that he had been opposed only to 'the production of outdated military technology and its export to dangerous areas'.[10]

The state never completely withdrew its support to the defence industry or for arms exports. Few military-related enterprises halted arms production and even fewer closed down. Since the situation of the defence enterprises was worse than the industry average, some measures must have been implemented to keep them functioning. In one case of macroeconomic importance, the state bailed out the Skoda Works—writing off 2 billion Czech korunas in bad debts and facilitating its privatization.[11] Similar treatment was expected in the case of the CKD Praha concern, another huge, heavy industrial enterprise which had a military-related branch. Other candidates for a large-scale government bail-out included some major construction companies. In the largest of them, Vojenska Stavby, 70 per cent of its activity was military production before 1989; by 1994 this share had dropped to 20 per cent.[12]

In June 1993, when the RDP (Research, Development and Production) Group—a private consortium to promote the Czech defence industry—was

---

[9] A sign of the change in official policy towards the defence industry was that after 3 years in which the author regularly interviewed ministry representatives and managers of state-owned defence enterprises, from Apr. 1994 permission was not granted.

[10] *Lidove Noviny*, 8 July 1994.

[11] This decision was taken in Oct. 1992 and carried out in early 1994.

[12] *Prague Post*, 5–11 Oct. 1994.

established in Prague, Minister of Defence Antonin Baudys and then Minister of Trade and Industry Vladimir Dlouhy participated in the first meeting of the RDP Group, which was evidently interpreted as a sign of government approval of the project. After the meeting Dlouhy stated: 'I believe that at least one member of the government should be on RDP's board of directors, since the government can provide support', confirming the hopes of defence industry managers that the new state administration would provide some backing for their activities.[13]

The other field where the state continued to intervene was in promoting arms sales. A coordinated announcement of a change in policy (similar to the simultaneous revision of conversion policy and easing of arms export policy) was made in June 1993. In the week when Skoda-Plzen announced that it was going to restart military production and launch the RDP Group, Dlouhy declared a revised arms trade policy, calling the old, restrictive policy 'naïve', and imposed on the country by Western powers who 'preached to us to drink water, while they were drinking wine'.[14]

As pointed out in chapter 2, after the end of the cold war the export control system of Czechoslovakia underwent significant revisions. The dissolution of the Federation led to further changes in the successor states. In the Czech Republic, discussions about the future elements of an export control system and the policy to be pursued by the government were particularly intensive in 1993. During this year arms export policy towards specific countries was being formed and the discussion of the advantages and disadvantages of sales to some destinations—notably Iran—was particularly intensive because of the commercial incentives to continue what had historically been an important arms transfer relationship. Dlouhy himself admitted that he had difficulties with representatives of the defence industry who tried to convince him to change the evaluation of some countries for the purposes of arms export policy.[15]

There were also problems in implementing existing regulations. Several Czech defence-related companies were implicated in sales of goods to Croatia and Slovenia, while government officials continued to discuss possible arms transfers with Iranian authorities. Several examples illustrate the problems of enforcing the export regulations. In 1992 Ceska Zbrojovka (CZ, located in Uhersky Brod) was investigated by the Czech police when it exported goods worth 30 million korunas more than the value stated on its export licence.[16] In 1993 the Ministry of Industry and Trade approved the sale of 25 000 assault rifles to the armed forces of Panama but, after the overthrow of General Manuel Noriega in 1989, the agency listed as the purchaser of the shipment no longer existed.[17] There were diverse views about what could be considered a weapon. In a controversy concerning the delivery of six 23-mm calibre aircraft cannons

---

[13] *Central European Business Weekly*, no. 75 (24 Dec. 1993–6 Jan. 1994).
[14] *Prague Post*, 16–22 June 1993.
[15] *Noviny*, 29 May 1992; and *Prague Post*, 16–22 June 1993.
[16] *Lidove Noviny*, 1 Jan. 1993.
[17] *Prague Post*, 1–7 Sep. 1993.

from Aero Vodochody to the Thai Air Force in June 1994 that was stopped by Austrian customs officers, it became clear that cannons disassembled from aircraft were considered as spare parts.[18]

As mentioned in chapter 2, after 1989 the former state-owned monopolist arms trade company Omnipol was stripped of its exclusive rights and had to diversify its activities—which came to include trade in civilian products and travel services. Several new private and state-owned trading companies compete fiercely on the market.

In addition to the state and private companies that were licensed to trade in weapons, government agencies and officials engaged in a search for new deals. Official visits by Minister of Industry and Trade Dlouhy, Minister of Defence Baudys and Prime Minister Klaus were sometimes followed by a contract for sales of major weapons or military cooperation or at least initial contacts between potential buyers and Czech military producers. This mediating activity by state officials was not acknowledged openly, since the official guideline was to let the defence industry either survive on its own or collapse. For example, on 1 April 1994 Baudys announced that no state assistance for military exports could be expected.[19]

Trying to find lucrative markets, representatives of the Czech Republic tried to set up contacts with several African, Asian and Latin American countries. The most publicized deal was the drawn-out affair with Iran regarding sale of the Tamara systems. After a US protest against the sale, Dlouhy visited Iran to try to negotiate other, purely civilian deals, for example, for building a large aluminium plant, an electric power station and other heavy industrial complexes. This visit raised suspicions about possible military-related deals and possible assistance to the Iranian nuclear industry. Dlouhy stressed that the Czech arms export policy was 'clear and accepted by the international community'.[20] In another controversial affair General Augusto Pinochet, the former Chilean dictator, visited the Czech Republic on what Klaus and Havel claimed was a private visit at the invitation of a Czech company. The company was Omnipol and the visit followed a trip to Chile by Klaus.[21]

Other possible markets for Czech weapons were the new states of the former Soviet Union. Representatives of the Czech Republic began negotiations with the Baltic states, as a result of which Latvia and Lithuania expressed their wish to buy Czech arms.[22]

In 1994 the new 'Act No. 38/1994 of the Code of 15 February 1994 to regulate trade in military material with foreign countries' was intended to reinforce government control over the arms trade and at the same time facilitate officially approved deals. According to this legislation no company trading in weapons could have more than a 49 per cent share of foreign participation. Any

[18] *Lidove Noviny*, 15 June 1994; and *Lidove Noviny*, 16 June 1994.

[19] *Hospodarske Noviny*, 1 Apr. 1994.

[20] *Defense News*, vol. 8, no. 27 (12–18 July 1993); *International Herald Tribune*, 28 Dec. 1993; *International Herald Tribune*, 4 Jan. 1994; and *Prague Post*, 24 Sep.–5 Oct. 1993.

[21] *Süddeutsche Zeitung*, 31 May 1994; and *Heti Vilaggazdasag*, 4 June 1994.

[22] *Baltic Independent*, 1–7 Oct. 1993.

individual involved in the arms business must be a Czech citizen, over 21 years of age and successfully pass the '*lustrace*' procedure.[23] Exporters needed to apply for licences from the Ministry of Industry and Trade, presenting end-user certificates and copies of agreements with the buyers. Licences had to be approved by the Ministries of Foreign Affairs, Defence and Interior, which could cancel the deal at any time during the authorization process if misleading information was provided. In cases where the political, economic and national security interests of the Czech Republic were threatened, fines of up to 50 per cent of the overall customs value could be levied.[24]

The change of government policy and well-publicized successes of the new Czech arms industry apparently had an impact on public opinion. According to a poll carried out by the Institute of Public Opinion Research in July 1994, 86 per cent of the respondents (of a sample of 1097 citizens over 15 years of age) saw no reason to stop military production, against 34 per cent who considered it immoral; 49 per cent thought that the defence industry should expand and 52 per cent agreed on a policy of exporting arms. The support for military production increased with the level of education and decreased with age, namely, people over 60 years of age.[25]

II. Restructuring the defence industry

The breakup of Czechoslovakia implemented the structural adjustment of the defence industry in that the most problematic branches remained in Slovakia. What remained on the Czech side seemed like a viable and rather promising arms industry, requiring more limited restructuring and modernization.

The crisis of military-related production in the Czech lands left at most four or five enterprises unable to maintain either military or civilian production. The rest kept their heads above water, if only because of the lack of a valid bankruptcy law. According to an estimate of the Ministry of Industry and Trade in early 1993, about 30 per cent of the defence enterprises would collapse once such a law was implemented. It was generally considered that by the spring of 1993 the decline had reached the bottom and the sector could slowly consolidate. At that time no more then 20 000 people were employed by the military industry.[26]

After the bankruptcy law came into force at the end of April 1993, no significant enterprise failures were reported in the military sector. This might have been because of the general laxity of the bankruptcy law. However, most enterprises seemed to have learned to survive with some state assistance.

---

[23] This procedure involved the screening of government officials for involvement with the secret police or other political involvement under the former regime.

[24] Act No. 38/1994 of the Code of 15 Feb. 1994.

[25] *Lidove Noviny*, 4 Aug. 1994.

[26] Interview by the author with Ladislav Nemec, Head of the Department of Technical Policy, Federal Ministry of Industry, Prague, 8 Apr. 1993.

An important new element in the Czech restructuring was a regrouping of the military enterprises. In June 1993, half a year after Skoda Works was relieved of its bad debts, Lubomir Soudek (the general manager of Skoda) and Jan Vlcek (the former director of a trading company, X-Trade) set up the RDP Group as a private consortium. X-Trade had been established by the armed forces with the task of selling surplus military hardware. The company was dissolved before June 1993 to put an end to what Minister of Defence Baudys had earlier called its 'not always transparent and very legal activity'.[27]

The Skoda Works was one of the oldest factories of the Czech lands.[28] Once among the major arms producers of Europe, by the 1960s it was principally a civilian company, with some spare parts production for Slovak enterprises. According to Jan Plzak, then head of the military department of Skoda-Plzen, the last orders for ZTS Martin were filled in February 1992 and the company did not have plans to continue military-related production in 1993.[29] The enterprise produced a wide range of civilian products including engines; vehicles; steam, water and gas turbines; nuclear equipment; and transformers. During the cold war it was one of the biggest Czechoslovak firms, with over 39 000 employees. The crisis of the state socialist system in Czechoslovakia and across East–Central Europe had a severe impact on the company. By 1992 the workforce had dropped to 21 000 and sales had diminished by 22 per cent and exports by 44 per cent. The value of unsold stocks equalled more than a year's turnover and the company was also desperately in debt.

In the course of the rescue operation, the Czech Government wrote off 2 billion korunas worth of debts and the concern was transformed into a holding with over 30 independent constituents. One of them, Skoda-Plzen, specialized in military-related production. Several economically problematic departments were liquidated. In the privatization agreement, Soudek's private firm, Nero, became the proprietor of 20 per cent of the shares, valued at 320 million korunas. The major creditors, Komercni Banka and Investicni Banka, each exchanged their claims for 7 per cent of the shares while 25 per cent remained directly state-owned. The rest of the shares were distributed through the coupon method, after which 18 per cent was controlled by investment funds.

Since this privatization method did not bring the necessary new capital and markets for the company, the Skoda Holding launched a search for foreign cooperation partners and investors. By 1994 it had several joint ventures with, among others, the German companies Dorries Scharmann and Bremer Vulkan, for drills and milling machines; the British–US Brown and Root, for engineer-

---

[27] X-Trade was probably dissolved in Feb. 1993, when the government issued a new regulation on the sale, rent and transfer of unused Ministry of Defence property. *Hospodarske Noviny*, 15 Feb. 1993; and *Hospodarske Noviny*, 24 Feb. 1993.

[28] The Skoda Works was founded by Count Wallenstein in 1859. Ten years later it was taken over by Emil Skoda, a Czech engineer, who employed 130 people. By 1914 Skoda was one of Europe's major arms producers, with 30 000 workers. After World War I the bulk of production was converted to civilian profiles with the help of French capital. During World War II Skoda became a military enterprise—mostly with Czech capital but as part of the Hermann Goering Imperial Works of Nazi Germany. By the end of the war 75% of the factory had been destroyed. *Figyelo*, 16 Sep. 1993.

[29] *Mlada Fronta Dnes*, 11 Jan. 1993.

ing and construction production; and the French state-owned SOFMA, for military products. There were long negotiations with Siemens of Germany about the establishment of a joint venture for turbine production. A 10-year agreement was signed in the spring of 1994 with the US company General Electric covering 'cooperation and strategic association in power generation projects'.[30]

The RDP Group was originally founded by 12 companies, among them Skoda-Plzen (located in Plzen; producing tank and heavy weaponry), Avia (Prague; trucks), Vlarske Strojirny (Slavicin; bombs, artillery ammunition), Liaz (Jablonec; wheeled vehicles), Mesit (Uherske Hradiste; aircraft instruments and radio communications systems) and Policske Strojirny (PS, Policka; ammunition). In April 1994 it had 40 members uniting most of the former, current and future arms producers, including the private and commercialized former state-owned enterprises. The 12 original members were joined by, among others, Meopta (in Prerov, producing optical instruments), Zbrojovka Brno (hand weapons) and Zbrojovka Vsetin (fuses and pyrotechnic devices).

The ratio of civilian to military production varied within the Group but on average military production represented 30–35 per cent of the activities. The combined workforce had approximately 180 000 employees. It is important to note, however, that the most successful military producers and exporters—the main companies of the aircraft industry united in the Aero Holding and Ceska Zbrojovka (Uhersky Brod)—did not join the consortium.[31]

RDP's aim was to coordinate its shareholders' activities, to mediate between them and state agencies, to assist marketing activities, occasionally to finance promising projects, and to promote military-related research and development (R&D). RDP's initial capital was provided by the member companies (each paid 1 million korunas). In late 1993, however, the Group set up a banking consortium uniting six small and medium-sized banks to coordinate and if necessary finance group activities. By then RDP already had its own banking house—TOPFIN (Top Finance)—and was seeking wider cooperation with other commercial banks, including foreign banks such as the French Credit Lyonnaise. It also set up its own investment fund, the First Investment Fund, to attract coupon holders to deposit their coupons during the scheduled second wave of privatization. RDP established a commercial company with permanent offices in France, Syria and the USA. The members had extensive sales networks, also in the former Soviet Union, where most of the shareholders had had significant trade links during the cold war.[32]

The fact that high-level government officials were present at the first meeting of the Group and expressed their approval gave the impression that the entire RDP project was officially backed. While government and RDP representatives insisted that RDP was a private consortium, completely independent of the

[30] *Prague Post,* 23–29 June 1993; *Figyelo,* 16 Sep. 1993; *Business Week,* 12 July 1993; *EastWest,* 27 Apr. 1993; and *Financial Times,* 27 Apr. 1994.

[31] CZ joined the RDP Group in Sep. 1993 and broke with it in Apr. 1994.

[32] Interview by the author with Pavel Cech, Technical Manager, and Milan Faltus, Commercial Director, of the RDP Group, Prague, 20 Apr. 1994. *Central European Business Weekly,* no. 75 (24 Dec. 1993–6 Jan. 1994).

state, both the wider public and representatives of the defence industry inside and outside the Group were convinced that the state would provide some kind of assistance to the holding. This conviction gave defence industry managers a more optimistic perspective on the future.

According to Pavel Cech, Head of the Technical Department of RDP, after the collapse of the defence industry in Czechoslovakia the only chance for the remaining industry was to establish new projects and cooperation with foreign partners. Since the internal market was restricted, projects needed to have an export potential. The goal was to increase and modernize military production in parallel with technical innovation. All the projects had to have both a civilian and a military purpose and all the gains from technological innovation were expected to be spread to the civilian sector.[33]

The first major project of the RDP Group was to modernize the Soviet-licensed T-72 tank by refitting it with a new engine, transmission, and fire control and night vision system, most of which were designed and produced by the member companies. The tank was principally developed for export, but the Group hoped that the Czech Army would also be interested in it. The project was carried out in cooperation with Western, mainly French, partners, including SAGEM. The prototype of the modernized T-72 tank was presented at a large arms fair, the second International Defence Technology Fair in Brno held on 1–4 June 1994, although there had been no time to conduct field trials.

According to Cech, the Czech T-72 project cost 2 billion korunas to reach the stage of mass-production. Since most of the companies involved in the project had very limited investment resources, TOPFIN provided some additional resources. Some of the holding's commercial revenue was used, along with contributions from the Ministry of Defence and some of the foreign cooperation partners. Modernization of the T-72 tank became part of the increasing competition between the Czech Republic and Slovakia. In mid-1993 Slovakia had proposed joining the two countries' military R&D efforts in the framework of the RDP Group. Among other projects, they suggested developing a modernized T-72 tank. Slovak Defence Minister Imrich Andrejcak argued that 'producing tanks in Bohemia just for the Czech Army or in Slovakia just for the Slovak Army will make them much more expensive',[34] but the idea was refused by the Czech companies. As a consequence both countries rushed to finish the project on their own and exhibit it as early as possible. At the Brno fair, the Slovak producers seemed to be further advanced.[35]

In the spring of 1994 the RDP Group ran 15 development projects. They included the development and production of a system for container transport for both civilian and military use and a dual-purpose jeep. According to *The*

[33] Interview with Pavel Cech (note 32).
[34] *Prague Post*, 6 Oct. 1994.
[35] *International Herald Tribune*, 8 June 1994.

Prague Post, by the time of the Brno arms fair they were working on 27 contracts involving foreign clients.[36]

One of RDP's major goals was to coordinate and mediate between its shareholders and, for example, the Ministry of Industry and Trade, the Ministry of Defence and the armed forces. The consortium was negotiating with the Ministry of Defence regarding plans for future equipment acquisition, trying to set up a precise time-schedule to help its shareholders to plan, taking into account the needs of the military.

The holding was not very successful in handling its public relations. The military criticized the Group for the slow pace at which its modernization projects were carried out. In June 1994 Minister of Defence Baudys declared that RDP mediation was not necessary for setting up contacts between individual firms and the Ministry.[37]

Other military-related enterprises attacked it for trying to build a monopoly as the supplier to the Czech armed forces, which could contribute in turn to enormous profits from exports. Apparently, Baudys personally forced RDP to withdraw its application for the licence necessary to engage in arms exports, without which its future prospects would be rather limited.[38] At the end of May 1994 Vlcek was replaced by Viktoria Hradska, a former official of the Committee for International Relations in the former Czech Republic (at that time still within the Federation).[39]

The RDP Group might turn out to be an ambitious failure. Company managers outside the Group claimed that it was only useful for those military producers which were unable to solve their structural problems—mainly capital and market issues—on their own. However, with its thorough and long-term development strategy, subtle state backing and the enormous possibilities that profits from the arms business create in a transforming economy short of development resources, it had the potential to become a major actor in the Czech economy.

Whatever the future of RDP, its activities have provided another important lesson. Its development strategy addressed the issues that an efficient conversion policy should have targeted: assistance with marketing and R&D, financing selected projects, and promoting inter-enterprise information flows and cooperation. It is unfortunate that all this was used for military purposes, but it might at least provide a lesson for decision makers about which problems are important to address when designing a new, comprehensive conversion policy.

[36] *Prague Post*, 15–21 June 1994.
[37] *Lidove Noviny*, 14 June 1994.
[38] *Prague Post*, 15–21 June 1994.
[39] *Lidove Noviny*, 27 May 1994; and 30 May 1994. The reasons for his dismissal were not published but must have been serious since the event happened at an unfortunate time—just days before the Brno arms show.

Signs of progress

Because of the generally promising performance of the Czech economy and the delicate, but real, official support for the defence industry, arms production and exports stopped declining in 1993 and increased slightly in 1994.[40]

In 1993 the value of Czech exports of military products reached $167 million. The main export items were hand weapons produced by Ceska Zbrojovka and L-39 Albatros jet trainer aircraft from Aero Vodochody (Odolena Voda), the aircraft representing 80 per cent of the total export value. By comparison, the 1992 export figure for the entire Federation was $150 million.[41] These figures were published in response to a claim published in the *SIPRI Yearbook 1994*[42] that in 1993 Czech military exports had reached a value of $482 million. In another response to the SIPRI figure, Bretislav Gregr, Head of the Committee on Arms Export Licences, said that 258 licences were issued in 1993, the largest deal being for pistols for the Turkish national police.[43]

In the first half of 1994 the Ministry of Industry and Trade issued 248 licences—152 for exports and 96 for imports. The value of Czech exports reached $60 million while that for imports was $14 million. Of the exports, aircraft and parts accounted for 77.4 per cent, technical services and repairs for 11.5 per cent, parts for armoured vehicles for 5 per cent, ammunition for 5 per cent and light weapons for 1 per cent.[44] The final value of 1994 exports was $194 million, 16 per cent higher than in the previous year.[45]

Both ministry officials and factory managers expected that the Czech defence industry would reach approximately 30 per cent of its 1988 record level of production by the time its reorganization was completed. Since such calculations in general took into consideration the Federal peak production level of an oversized defence industry created to cater to the entire WTO, these expectations were definitely less modest than they appeared to be.

One of the main exporters and most successful companies of the revived Czech military industry was Aero Vodochody, which operated a large and integrated complex for manufacturing jet trainer aircraft. After the collapse of the WTO the entire activity of the enterprise was analysed by the management. It was decided that major strategic changes were needed, both in updating the product portfolio and in the internal organization of the enterprise. On the basis of a thorough market analysis they decided to develop their jet trainer aircraft models partly on the basis of their own R&D and partly in cooperation with Western firms. In cooperation with US and Canadian firms (including General Electric) they modernized the L-39 jet trainer, 90 per cent of which had previ-

---

[40] Interview with Pavel Cech (note 31). According to Slovak sources the increase reached 10% in 1993. Czech sources did not confirm these figures.

[41] *Lidove Noviny*, 21 May 1994.

[42] Anthony, I. *et al.*, 'Arms production and arms trade', *SIPRI Yearbook 1994* (Oxford University Press: Oxford, 1994), table 13.8, p. 484.

[43] *Prague Post*, 29 June–3 July 1994.

[44] *Hospodarske Noviny*, 17 May 1994.

[45] CR TV News, 3 Feb. 1995.

ously been produced for Soviet markets. They identified new markets and began to approach them actively. They were for the most part developing countries, including Egypt, Nigeria, the Philippines and Thailand, and other, unspecified South-East Asian countries.

To improve its opportunities to sell, Aero Vodochody was keen to get an international quality certificate and to emphasize the introduction of Western standards in its production immediately after the radical socio-economic changes. It did not turn its back on former trade and cooperation partners either. A major project was the renewal and partial modernization of 20 L-39 trainer aircraft that Hungary received from arsenals of the former German Democratic Republic. One major comparative advantage Aero Vodochody had in the early 1990s was its ability to meet both Western and Eastern requirements, creating an amalgam of the two different production cultures. This could also be a major comparative advantage for other firms in the region that aspire to take part in the increasingly international sector.

One conclusion of the company's analysis was that the world market for military aircraft would gradually become saturated and that Aero Vodochody's market would shrink. Therefore, despite the fact that in the early 1990s practically all its output was military-related and highly lucrative, one strategic target was to diversify production through subcontracting and cooperation with major international civilian aircraft producers. The company set up contacts with major US and Canadian companies, including Boeing. Since future sales had a quantitative ceiling, the intention was to increase profits via cost reduction and increased productivity.[46]

Although the performance of Aero Vodochody as an individual enterprise was impressive, it was overshadowed by difficulties presented by the wider economic background, both 'above', at the higher level of industrial organization, and 'below', at the level of subcontractors. The parent company, Aero Holding, originally united 10 subsidiary companies, including the enterprises of the Czech aircraft industry, both civilian and military. Aero Holding was set up in 1990 and had a workforce of 29 000; in 1994 it had about 16 000 employees.

The Aero Holding management appeared to be incompetent and inefficient, to the extent that in January 1994 an opposition MP initiated a parliamentary investigation into the mismanagement and systematic deterioration of the holding's enterprises. Aero Vodochody complained that the holding functioned as an old-style redistributive state enterprise, using profits from successful companies to subsidize uncompetitive ones instead of forcing them to restructure.

After the first wave of privatization in 1993, most of the holding's shares ended up in the hands of Investicni Banka, but the bank did not prove to be a very good manager either. After a long period of designing various privatization and reorganization projects for Aero Holding, the Ministry of Industry and

---

[46] Interview by the author with Adam Stranak, Engineering Deputy President of Aero Vodochody, Odolena Voda, 21 Apr. 1994; Sutton, O., 'Czechoslovak industry re-orientates', *Aerospace World,* vol. 6 (June 1992); *Flight International,* 3 June 1992; *Ekonom,* 7 Feb. 1993; and *Jane's Defence Weekly,* 17–24 Sep. 1994.

Trade decided that it should be restricted to four companies: Aero Vodochody, Letov, Technometra Radotin, and the Research and Development Institute (VZLU). These were predominantly military producers and the most successful elements of the holding. The parent holding company and the state—through the National Property Fund—insisted on keeping their majority shares in these companies. As far as Aero Vodochody was concerned, the company management was not happy about a solution that left the majority of its shares in bank and state hands, rather than in the hands of strategic partners that could contribute fresh capital and markets to the company. At the same time they did not mind some state ownership, since foreign partners considered it a guarantee.

On the side of the subcontractors to Aero Vodochody, they were far less successful. Letov, which produced wings, tails and flight simulators, was having serious financial difficulties and was desperate to find partners in order to diversify its product range and ease its dependence on Aero Vodochody. Technometra Radotin fabricated the very specialized wheels for jets and was also in need of a major financial infusion. Adam Stranak, Vice-President for Engineering of Aero Vodochody, confirmed that the company generally had to provide financial and technical support to its subcontractors, which pushed up production costs. Since most of the subcontractors were in poor financial shape, they often asked for at least 50 per cent advance payment—a serious disadvantage in a cash-stripped economy. Possible solutions for Aero Vodochody were to take over subcontractor activities or try to find other, more stable partners.

In addition to its export markets, the fact that the Czech armed forces were among its buyers also gave Aero Vodochody a privileged position. However, this seemed to be in doubt in late 1994, when controversies emerged over a tender to convert the L-59 jet trainer into an L-159 multi-role combat aircraft. Tensions surfaced between the company's General Manager, Zdenek Chaloupnik, and the Ministry of Industry and Trade and Defence, in 1990—the worst time of defence industry recession in Czechoslovakia. Aero Vodochody signed a contract for the sale of 36 L-39 Albatros trainer jets to Thailand and 48 L-59 aircraft to Egypt (the latter resulting from the mediation of the Israeli Elbit Corporation). The Israeli partner provided technical assistance and a loan. In this deal Aero Vodochody sold the L-59 at a unit price of $1.3 million to Elbit, which refitted them with modern electronics and delivered them to Thailand for $4.3 million.[47] The two companies maintained close links and, when it came to deciding on a foreign partner for the L-159 project, Chaloupnik insisted on Elbit, in spite of the resistance from ministry officials. In the end the Ministry of Defence announced that the US company Rockwell had been chosen as the cooperation partner.

This case illustrated the external vulnerability that characterized even one of the most successful defence industry firms in the region. It also provided insight into the decision-making process at both the enterprise and the ministry level. The enterprise management was torn between professional arguments and loy-

---

[47] According to *Prague Post*, 14–20 Sep. 1994, Elbit paid $1.3 million per unit, added about $600 000 worth of electronics and sold the aircraft for roughly $4.5 million each.

alty to Elbit. Minister of Industry and Trade Dlouhy said that the foreign partner selected would be able to provide 'maximum NATO compatibility', and Ministry of Defence sources noted that their first preference was 'maximum export potential' followed by maximum NATO compatibility.[48]

The other highly successful export items of the Czech Republic were the light weapons produced by Ceska Zbrojovka. CZ was a rare success story of a reconstructed ECE defence enterprise without significant foreign participation, either in the form of direct investment or in the form of cooperation. The company was one of the oldest weapon factories in Bohemia.[49] During the cold war an average of one-third of its production was military-related, one-third consisted of hydraulics for tractors and one-third consisted of spare parts (transmissions and suspensions) for civilian aircraft. Between 1950 and 1990 CZ had developed 10 different models for the Czechoslovak Army. In 1990 it finished supplying the army and immediately shifted its production to civilian sport and hunting weapons. CZ also gradually reduced its other civilian profiles to concentrate on its main activity—producing arms for civilian customers— which, by mid-1993, represented 85 per cent of its total production.

About 90 per cent of CZ's output was exported. The plant had trade contacts with 70 countries, its main clients being Austria, France, Germany and the USA. In 1992, after the liberalization of regulations concerning arms in Czechoslovakia, the local market grew to 20 per cent but quickly became saturated. Immediately after independence, the Slovak market was also important— until a new, strict arms licence regulation removed it. CZ was one of the few defence enterprises that produced profits practically from 1992 and reinvested a considerable part of the profits in technological improvements. At the beginning of the transformation CZ also received development loans from a local bank. Most of the machinery they used was relatively up-to-date and Western. The production process involved a considerable amount of manual work as well, and about 50 per cent of the workforce were skilled workers.

According to Miroslav Duda, the company's General Director, CZ did not have any major difficulties in converting to civilian production because it used basically the same technology and skills. The workforce diminished by only 3 or 5 per cent after 1989. This also meant that they were able to meet military orders quickly if required to do so. Such was the case of the Lada kit that CZ and the Czech central military R&D institute Prototypa began to work on in 1983. The original plan included a whole range of infantry weapons, a pistol, a carbine, an assault rifle and different types of machine-gun. At the beginning the project was lavishly financed from central budget resources. Jiri Misinsky, Technical Director of CZ, said: 'The development costs for the Lada were tremendous, but they were mostly paid by the government'.[50]

---

[48] *Hospodarske Noviny*, 18 and 25 Aug. 1994; and *Prague Post*, 14–20 Sep. 1994.
[49] CZ was established in 1936 to provide arms for the Czechoslovak Army. During the war it was taken over to produce for the German armed forces.
[50] *Prague Post*, 15–21 Sep. 1993.

After the Velvet Revolution the project to mass-produce the system for the WTO and the Czech armed forces was abandoned. In 1990, however, the State Defence Council decided to refit the system to NATO standards. The management of CZ succeeded in acquiring the contract to continue development of the project, which was then principally financed from the enterprise budget. The new models—a submachine-gun, an assault rifle and a lightweight machine-gun—were ready by 1993 but, because of prolonged insecurity about the modernization programme of the Czech armed forces, mass-production was not launched either for domestic use or for export.[51]

The condition of the less successful branches of the Czech defence industry was similar to that of most of their counterparts in the region—burdened by bad debts, lack of markets and financial resources, over-capacity and over-employment. A typical case was truck production, once a stronghold of Czechoslovak military production. All three main conglomerates where production was concentrated—Liaz (in Jablonec), Avia (Prague) and Tatra (Koprivnice)—were producing losses, faced serious production and marketing difficulties, and had serious managerial problems.[52]

Responding to the possible revival of the defence industry, many enterprises that carried out a more or less thorough conversion programme between 1989 and 1992 at least partially resumed defence-related production—which was once again seen as a neutral and progressive activity. Apart from Skoda-Plzen and Ceska Zbrojovka, Adast (Adamov) appeared to be fully converted and a rather successful producer and exporter of printing machines and oil pumps in 1993. However, after some hesitation, it joined the RDP Group in mid-1994.

Another case of 'reverse conversion' was Zbrojovka Vsetin. The company was a major producer of fuses, triggers and other pyrotechnic devices. Before World War II it was a fairly successful arms producer that sold machine-guns and other products to Afghanistan, China, Iran, Romania, Sweden and the UK. After the war military production decreased radically and electric sewing, weaving and knitting machines, mining detonators and drilling tools were introduced instead. At this time the share of defence-related activity was officially 3 per cent and, according to the factory's managers, it was not profitable because of the distorted price system. For example, the Czechoslovak Army bought equipment at fixed prices that did not reflect the exchange value of the article bought.

After the cold war ended, the collapse of the Soviet civilian market caused major difficulties for the company. Exports fell drastically, and even successful deals presented many problems. Barter arrangements frequently caused payments to be late and complicated. Since the technology used to produce sewing-machines made it possible to fabricate weapons without major transformations

---

[51] Interview by the author with Miroslav Duda, President and General Director of CZ, Uherski Brod, 17 June 1993; *Prague Post*, 15–21 Sep. 1993; *Prague Post*, 5–11 Oct. 1994; *Lidove Noviny*, 8 Oct. 1993; and *International Defense Review*, vol. 26, no. 6 (June 1993).

[52] The best-known case was Tatra Koprivnice, where a US team of managers failed to restructure the company, which sank even deeper into crisis. *Prague Post*, 1–7 June 1994; *Prague Post*, 14–20 Sep. 1994; *Prague Post*, 5–11 Oct. 1994; and *Prague Post*, 21–27 Dec. 1994.

and since foreign arms markets appeared to be responsive, in mid-1993 the management was considering a return to defence-related production. Director-General Karel Dancak explained the reason for returning to military-related production as: 'Weapons are paid for promptly, unlike textile machines'. Relying on its positive reputation, the company began to offer machine-guns, detonators and other products for export.[53]

By the autumn of 1994, the company had managed to expand its export markets to Germany, Italy, Spain, Sweden and the USA with electrical detonators for mining. It also entered the Croatian and Slovenian markets, which had lost their Bosnian supplier. The UN Security Council committee responsible for implementing the UN arms embargo against the former Yugoslavia investigated the company's export activity. According to Dancak, the protests came from competitors which tried to push them out of the market. Zbrojovka Vsetin became a member of the RDP Group, was given an arms export licence by the Ministry of Industry and Trade, and signed a cooperation contract with Omnipol and the Merkuria foreign trade company. It also planned to revive the production of machine-guns, which had been halted for over 15 years .[54]

In the Czech Republic, as in the other countries of the region, there were self-destructive or passive defence-related companies that continued to cause major losses at the enterprise and at the macroeconomic level. However, the Czech military sector proved to be the most successful in the region, seen from the perspective of efficient industrial restructuring. One of the important elements of this success was the reliance on local R&D. The sector's most promising new products—such as modern jet trainers, Lada light weapons and the Tamara surveillance system—all made use of the intellectual capital of the country. This was partly because of the strong historical traditions of the defence industry in the Czech lands and partly because, even though most military-related research institutes were in poor economic shape, the general smoothness of the Czech transformation did not force closures and preserved some core expertise and all documentation.

Another very important factor was that, even in the high times of conversion zeal, the Federal Government had supported and partly financed military development projects. In an interview in 1991, Josef Fucik mentioned several spheres where local development had resulted in interesting products—the modernized L-39MS; flight simulation systems; passive radar surveillance systems of Tesla Pardubice; protection devices against nuclear, biological and chemical (NBC) weapons produced by Gumarny (Zubri) and Slovenske Lucobne Zavody (SLZ, Hnusta); and night-vision instruments developed in the State Glass Research Institute (Hradec Kralove) and Krizik (Prague).[55]

In a 1992 interview with a specialized military journal, Deputy Minister of Defence Ivan Balaz confirmed that state-run military-related research would continue on the basis of select projects combining high-level military perfor-

[53] *Lidove Noviny,* 17 Sep. 1994.
[54] *Lidove Noviny*, 17 Sep. 1994.
[55] *Hospodarske Noviny*, no. 20 (1991).

mance with commercial advantages. The main task was to develop technologies for certain defence needs and to find civilian employment with commercial prospects for these new technologies as a 'side product'. Another aim was to reduce the cost and material intensity of the military production process.[56] A similar approach was adopted by the RDP Group that emphasized military development with possible civilian use.

The Tamara surveillance system and the Lada light weapon were the two Czech successes of the June 1994 Brno arms fair.[57] The Tamara surveillance system, which is mounted on 12 trucks, is a passive system that intercepts electronic signals emitted by aircraft and analyses the signal to determine the location of the aircraft which emitted it. Although it is presented as non-lethal equipment, if it is connected with other military technology it can help to guide a missile to aircraft when they are detected. The system was considered to be capable of detecting even Stealth planes.[58]

The Tamara was developed and produced by the Tesla Pardubice company. Until the late 1980s, 50 per cent of Tesla Pardubice's output was military-related, the rest being airport and air traffic-control systems serving principally the Soviet markets. The collapse of the WTO and the Council for Mutual Economic Assistance (CMEA) meant that the company abruptly lost 80 per cent of its markets. Between 1990 and 1993 the workforce decreased from 6500 to 2500 and output from 2.2 billion to 400 million korunas. In the spring of 1993 the enterprise was in typical 'privatization agony'. No crucial reorganization decisions were taken in advance of government decisions about privatization. In addition, the experienced general manager was about to retire.[59]

In June 1993 Tesla Pardubice was bought by a newly established private company, High Technology Transfer (HTT), headed by Oldrich Barak, the former head of procurement of the Czechoslovak Army. Tesla was acquired for 155 million korunas ($5.2 million) with a debt burden of 1.4 billion korunas. The new owners committed themselves to invest 620 million korunas, for which they had already received some long-term loans from Czech banks. The main hope for the company's revival was that it would sell the Tamara system on the world market; the management hoped that it would be reclassified for licensing purposes as a non-lethal defensive system.[60]

Another important sign of the restructuring successes of the Czech Republic was that, unlike most of the defence-related companies in the region, several enterprises were in a solid financial state, able to get new loans and (perhaps most important) to reinvest some of their profit in future development. Aero Vodochody, Sellier & Bellot and Ceska Zbrojovka were among the few enter-

[56] *Military Professional*, no. 7 (1992).

[57] Development of both the Tamara and the Lada began in Czechoslovakia but was completed by the Czech Republic, and both were presented as Czech products.

[58] *Lidove Noviny*, 8 July 1993; and *Defense News*, 12–18 July 1993.

[59] Interview by the author with Josef Opocensky, Chief Executive Officer of Tesla Pardubice, Pardubice, Czech Republic, 16 June 1993.

[60] *Lidove Noviny*, 15 June and 8 July 1993.

prises that accomplished such major investments during the lean period of defence industry development of 1990–94.

These strong and prospering enterprises were functioning in branches that, in addition to their profitability, might have positive backward linkages in the Czech economy. The aircraft production of Aero required a major set of suppliers while each Tamara system produced would require 12 trucks.[61] Instead of the over-employment that troubled most companies of the sector, many—for example Adast, Aero Vodochody and Sellier & Bellot—actually needed new, qualified workers for their renewed production.

Two visits by the author to the same factory gave a sense of the nature and direction of the changes that had been taking place in the sector.[62] Policske Strojirny, in Policka, had been a major ammunition producer in the Czechoslovak Federation. An interview with General Director Bohumir Pospisil in 1992 produced a rather desperate picture of the enterprise. In 1989 more than 80 per cent of its production was military but in 1990 it did not receive a single order from the armed forces. By mid-1992 about one-third of the workforce had left or been made redundant. At least half of the workshops were closed and the company had grave liquidity problems. The main source of its indebtedness was a large investment in the late 1980s which was completed but never used in production. There were large unsold stocks and reserves. Negotiations about forming a joint venture with a Spanish company that promised large new markets in Spain and eventually Latin America went sour.[63] They were running several conversion projects and had many potential product lines—from fireworks to household devices—that were proving difficult to sell. Worst of all was the general feeling of loss and desperation that pervaded in the company. As the General Director put it, with no major intervention by the authorities the future looked fairly catastrophic.

A year later, in an interview with Petr Lajzner, Economic Deputy Director, the picture was much more optimistic.[64] PS Policka was still among the worst-off companies of the Czech Republic, but its fate did not seem to be as hopeless. By 1993 they had made a selection from the conversion projects and concentrated their efforts on petrol station equipment, principally gas-pumps and filters, in cooperation with Adast.[65] The recent foundation of the RDP Group suggested that in the future military production would be able to continue, even if on a smaller scale than before. In April 1994 the company won a tender announced by the Ministry of Defence to destroy old ammunition. Among their

---

[61] The macroeconomic usefulness of military production that generates more military-related production is another question. Moreover, the Tamara could be mounted on any large truck and need not produce any follow-on sales for Tatra.

[62] The author visited Policske Strojirny, in Policka, in 1992 and 1993.

[63] The civilian Spanish firm was technologically at a lower level and wanted to pay less than the assessed value for shares in PS Policka.

[64] Petr Lajzner, who was an economist and not an engineer, may have been able to see signs of general improvement better than the director.

[65] It was fairly common practice throughout the region that former (or present) military-related companies kept cooperating on new civilian projects as well.

other plans was a partial return to ammunition production that was hindered by financial difficulties.[66]

At the time of writing, mid-1994, it was still too early to draw any conclusions about the impact of foreign direct investment and foreign cooperation in the military sector in the Czech Republic. There were examples of both positive and negative influences.

A case in which foreign capital took over an existing establishment and workforce—leaving the Czech company with remnants that had few good prospects—was Tesla Praha. Tesla Praha had been one of the main components of the Tesla group, with an important civilian telecommunications production profile in addition to its military-related products. The defence division had been allocated more human and technological resources. In the spring of 1993 the company formed a joint venture with the US firm AT&T, which bought the workshops and equipment used for military production. The best workers left for the joint venture. The remaining divisions of Tesla were still struggling for survival as of mid-1993.

On the other hand, there were cases in which cooperation with foreign firms was used in order to learn Western methods of enterprise and production process organization that were applied across the entire company. There were definitely such benefits for Aero Vodochody and Vlarske Strojirny (Slavicin), for example.

As far as privatization was concerned, as mentioned above, the majority of the Czech defence firms were privatized in the period 1990–94. However, most of them were eventually controlled by primarily state-owned banks or investment funds, which in turn were also often in the hands of a state bank or agency, for example, the National Property Fund. Banks did not turn out to be significantly more successful owners than ministries, as the case of Aero Holding demonstrated. However, the freedom of enterprise management increased considerably and general economic conditions pushed towards even further management changes that did improve the performance of many enterprises.

One justification for revamping the Czech defence industry was to modernize the new national armed forces, responding to new security threats but mainly in the hope of rapid admission to NATO. However, this seemed slightly hypothetical in the light of the restricted defence budget and unclear procurement plans. The defence budget for 1993 was 22.988 billion korunas, of which 7.5 billion korunas was allocated for purchases.[67] The 1994 budget was 27 billion korunas, with a similar share for purchases, of which only approximately 100 million korunas was for buying new weaponry.[68] The defence budget in 1993 and 1994 was slightly less than $1 billion and was expected to increase to $1.1 billion in 1995—roughly the same amount taking into account inflation.

---

[66] Interview by the author with Bohumir Pospisil, General Director of Policske Strojirny, Policka, Czech Republic, 15 Apr. 1992; Interview by the author with Petr Lajzner, Economic Deputy Director of Policske Strojirny, Policka, Czech Republic, 16 June 1993; and *Hospodarske Noviny*, 20 Apr. 1994.

[67] *Hospodarske Noviny*, 24 Feb. 1993.

[68] *Lidove Noviny*, 12 July 1994.

However, it was not self-evident that this meagre allowance was to be spent on Czech-made weapons. The original idea in late 1992 and early 1993 (expressed by among others Oldrich Barak, at the time head of procurement of the Czech Army, and General Stanislav Chromec, of the Ministry of Defence) was that cooperation between the Visegrad countries' defence industries would provide the means for modernizing the armed forces.[69] This could have been the cheapest and most reliable solution as far as intra-regional cooperation and common security measures were concerned. Unfortunately, increasing diversification and competition between the ECE countries quickly ruled out this option. The emphasis shifted to rebuilding national defence industries and, if possible, importing from the West.

Despite the rather successful reorganization of the Czech defence industry, there were signs that the Czech armed forces aspired to purchase Western weapons. Although there were long negotiations with the RDP Group and directly with the military producers about introducing some of the new products of the revived Czech defence industry, the Ministry of Defence was giving signals that it would not necessarily rely on Czech products. Negotiations have been held with a number of West European, US and Israeli firms.

During the long period in which modernization of the Czech armed forces was in the making, defence industry managers were hoping that it would include procurement of their products. They were encouraged by several official declarations. For example, Antonin Baudys, then Minister of Defence, declared that 'the army's modernization project could be a source of state orders for a number of companies'.[70] In late August 1994 the Ministry of Defence finally published its plans to rearm the Czech armed forces. The plan requested a defence budget equal to 2.5 per cent of the gross national product (GNP).[71] This would mean a defence budget of approximately $1.07 billion for 1995, of which about 30 per cent would be spent on procurement. The armed forces opted for three major upgrade projects for T-72 battle tanks, MiG-21 fighter aircraft and L-59 jet trainers.[72]

Later in 1994, in a meeting with representatives of industry, the recently appointed Minister of Defence, Vilem Holan, declared that the Czech armed forces would not buy light weapons produced by Ceska Zbrojovka. This was interpreted as a signal to the other representatives of defence-related firms who were hoping that the army would include their products in its modernization. While expressing disappointment, Soudek, on behalf of the RDP Group, confirmed that they would continue developing and producing new products for export. He also declared that military production would represent only 5 per cent of Skoda-Plzen's activities.[73]

---

[69] *ATM* [Armadni Technicky Magazin], vol. 24, no. 10 (1992); and *Mlada Fronta Dnes*, 11 Jan. 1993.
[70] *Hospodarske Noviny*, 1 Apr. 1994.
[71] In 1993 GNP was $30.3 billion; it was expected to reach $37 billion in 1994 and was forecast to be $42.9 billion in 1995.
[72] *Prague Post*, 31 Aug.–6 Sep. 1994.
[73] *Lidove Noviny*, 26 Nov. 1994.

4. Slovakia

I. The heritage of the breakup of the Czechoslovak Federation

In contrast to the Czech Republic, Slovakia had to struggle from the beginning of its independent statehood with a negative international image.[1] Slovakia was often featured as the 'ugly duckling' in analyses of the East–Central European (ECE) region principally for two reasons. The first was the more traditional pattern of life and values that made the country take its time in accepting and accomplishing socio-economic changes.[2] The belligerent and authoritarian statements of Prime Minister Vladimir Meciar were the second factor.

Living standards and levels of economic development were lower in Slovakia than in the Czech lands and, after independence, they dropped further with the loss of direct Czechoslovak Federal Government allocations and crucial production and exchange contacts. Between 1970 and 1989 an annual Federal Government subsidy of 10 billion Czechoslovak korunas—in total about 190–195 billion korunas—was paid to Slovakia to develop infrastructure, support agriculture, raise living standards and balance the republic's budget.[3]

After the introduction of market-oriented reforms in the Czechoslovak Federation, progress not only was slower in Slovakia than in the Czech lands but also manifested some important negative tendencies. The growth of the private sector, especially industry, and the introduction of new market institutions were far slower and more complicated in Slovakia, and industrial output, productivity and profits fell to a greater extent. Insolvency was paralysing most of the enterprises.[4]

The additional negative effects of the breakup of the Federation made these problems worse. Crucial projects of the macroeconomic stabilization and reform programme, principally privatization, balancing the state budget and eliminating mutual enterprise indebtedness, were halted or seriously distorted. The gross domestic product (GDP) of the Slovak Republic in 1992 was

---

[1] For a discussion of the Czech Republic, see chapter 3 in this volume.

[2] The different historical patterns and mentality of the Slovak people are described in Butorova, Z., 'A szlovak demokracia nehez szuletese' [The difficult birth of the Slovak democracy], *Tarsadalmi Szemle*, vol. 47, no. 8–9 (Aug.–Sep. 1992); Butora, M., Butorova, Z. and Gyarfasova, O., 'Nemzeti kerdes a poszttotalitarius Szlovakiaban' [National question in the post-totalitarian Slovakia], *Mozgo Vilag*, 2 Feb. 1993; and Radicova, I., 'Privatization: the case of Slovakia', *History of European Ideas*, vol. 17, no. 6 (Nov. 1993).

[3] *Hospodarske Noviny*, 31 May 1991.

[4] Gabrielova, H., 'Analysis of transformation processes in enterprises in the Slovak Republic', eds Z. Kominkova and B. Schmognerova, *Conversion of Military Production: Comparative Approach*, Papers presented at a conference organized by the Slovak Academy of Sciences and the Friedrich Ebert Foundation (Slovak Office of the Friedrich Ebert Foundation and the Institute of Economics of the Slovak Academy of Sciences: Bratislava, 1993); and Karasz, P., 'Main macro-economic features of the Slovak economic development for 1994', Unpublished manuscript, Institute for Forecasting, Slovak Academy of Sciences, Bratislava, 1993.

484 billion Slovak korunas and in 1993 it was 465 billion korunas (a decrease of 4 per cent).[5] Other economic indicators showed negative trends: industrial production fell by 13.5 per cent in 1993 (repeating the 1992 fall), while inflation, unemployment, trade and budget deficits kept climbing.[6]

As far as strictly military-related production was concerned, Slovakia had an indisputably heavy heritage since the defence industry played a predominant role in the economy. The industry was very concentrated both regionally and in the sense that the production of heavy weapons was over-represented in its structure. The enterprises themselves had received considerable new investment in the 1980s in the framework of a large-scale modernization campaign.

According to Slovak sources, military production reached its peak in 1988 (a year later than in the Czechoslovak Federation) and Slovakia contributed 19.3 billion korunas—over 60 per cent of total output—while its population represented only 33 per cent of the national total.[7] Most military-related production was concentrated in the heavy engineering and electronics sectors. In 1988 arms manufacturing represented 24 per cent of the total output of these two branches (the corresponding share in the Czech Republic was 7 per cent).[8]

Although employment figures varied widely, it is likely that at its 1988 peak the Slovak defence industry employed around 70 000–80 000 people directly and another 55 000 indirectly.[9] Because of the crisis, employment decreased dramatically but certainly much less than production. This created the further tensions of overemployment and financial burdens for the companies.

In the Czechoslovak Federation, the share of military output in total production in 1988 was higher than 20 per cent in only one-third of the military-related companies, while it was higher than 20 per cent in a full 56 per cent of the companies in Slovakia.[10] Between 1980 and 1990, 60–90 per cent of all investment in these enterprises was dedicated to military purposes. Most of the Slovak defence enterprises were large-scale establishments: in 1988 the average production of Slovak firms was about 600 million korunas per year (the corresponding figure for Czech firms was 290 million korunas). The average employment of a Slovak enterprise was 12 000–14 000.[11] In 1991 ZTS (Zavody Tazkeho Strojarstva) Martin, the largest Slovak enterprise, produced an output

[5] World Trade Organisation Trade Policy Review Body, 'Slovakia counts on trade to continue economic reforms and growth', Press release TPRB/19, 29 Nov. 1995.

[6] *Financial Times*, 16 Dec. 1994.

[7] The figure 19.3 billion korunas, quoted by the Slovak authorities after the break-up, is higher than that quoted by the Federal Ministry of the Economy (14.4 billion), cited in table 2.1, chapter 2 of this volume.

[8] Droppa, K., 'History of the armament production in Czechoslovakia', Kominkova and Schmognerova (note 4), p. 7.

[9] Stanek, P., 'Problems of employment related to the conversion', Kominkova and Schmognerova (note 4), p. 95. However, other sources mention figures as high as 160 000.

[10] The key role in military production was played by 16 factories where the share of military production ranged between 30% and 65%. Stanek (note 9), p. 95.

[11] Outrata, R., 'Conversion and industrial policy in the Slovak Republic', Kominkova and Schmognerova (note 4), pp. 84–85.

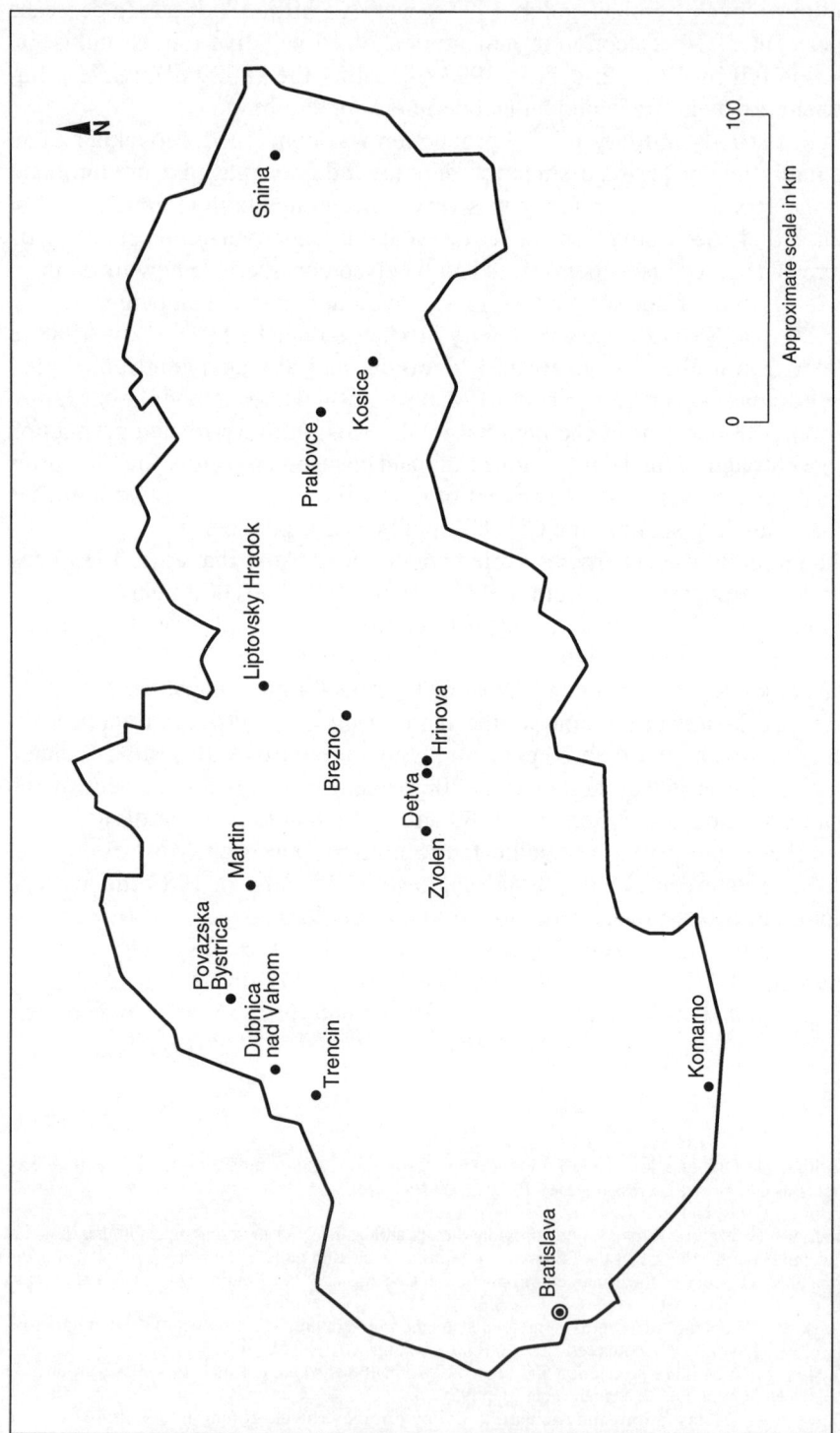

Figure 4.1. Location of defence enterprises in Slovakia

of 1.5 billion korunas, while the largest Czech firm, Tesla Pardubice, produced an output of 150 million korunas.[12]

The Slovak defence industry depended on a wide and complex network of subcontractors. One tank, for example, required several thousand parts. Slovak sources in general cited 25 major arms manufacturers in the country. Federal statistics listed 36. In 1988–89 there were 5 major end-producers, 9 main suppliers, and 22 companies providing components and semi-finished products.[13] When the crisis came in the late 1980s and early 1990s, this network of suppliers was the first to collapse.

The Slovak defence industry suffered to a significantly greater extent than its Czech counterpart. According to Karol Droppa, head of the Armament and Reconversion Division of the Ministry of the Economy of Slovakia, between 1988 and 1991 defence industry output fell from 19 billion to 3.5 billion korunas. By 1992 output was a mere 1.8 billion korunas, or 9.3 per cent of 1988 peak production. The crisis caused the loss of 30 000 jobs in the sector.[14] Arms exports suffered a similar decline. Between 1976 and 1988 average annual sales reached a level of about 7 billion korunas but in 1991 and 1992 amounted to only 3.7 billion korunas. The direction of sales also changed considerably. The share of former East-bloc country recipients dropped from 57 per cent in 1976–88 to 28.5 per cent in 1991 and was expected to fall to 4 per cent in 1992. The developing countries, which represented 21 per cent in the first period, reached 56.3 per cent in 1991 and were expected to reach 77 per cent in 1992.[15]

In addition to the problems emerging from their special profile, Slovak defence firms had to struggle with difficulties stemming from the state of the economy. The fact that the crisis unfolded in conditions of a general decline made it more difficult for Slovak enterprises to adjust. It was much more difficult to find new jobs for the redundant workforce, to replace former suppliers or to get credits for development projects from either the state budget or local banks. The general underdevelopment of the economy made enterprise-level improvements difficult and sometimes impossible.

Another serious obstacle to development was posed by political uncertainties. Even though Meciar was celebrated as the champion of independence immediately after the breakup of Czechoslovakia, general disenchantment followed rather quickly. His personalized and inconsistent style made policy unpredictable. In the spring of 1994 Meciar's cabinet was ousted and a new government was formed, led by Josef Moravcik, the former Minister of Foreign Affairs. The new administration made a heroic and rather successful attempt to stabilize the economic situation and address major development bottlenecks.

[12] Cechak, O., Selesovsky, J. and Stembera, M., 'Czechoslovakia: reductions in arms production in a time of economic and political transformation', ed. H. Wulf, SIPRI, *Arms Industry Limited* (Oxford University Press: Oxford, 1993), table 12.5, p. 244.

[13] Statement by Peter Magvasi at the joint Helsinki Citizens' Assembly–Institute for EastWest Studies meeting on conversion within the framework of the Foundation for East–West Development Initiatives (FEWDI), Martin, Slovakia, 29–30 Mar. 1993.

[14] Karol Droppa, Presentation at a meeting organized for defence industry representatitves of Central, Eastern and Southern Europe, under the auspices of NATO, Paris, 1–11 Feb. 1994.

[15] Outrata (note 11), pp. 88–89.

However, the time was too short for many important changes to be implemented and when the interim government's mandate ended in November 1994 the voters returned Meciar and his allies to power.

II. The policy on military production and export

In the Czechoslovak Federation, the Government of the Slovak Republic acted with some independence in respect of questions of defence industry, conversion and arms exports. The original decision of the Federal Government to halt the production and export of tanks and armoured personnel carriers was a major blow to the Slovak economy and the reaction was twofold.

On the one hand, the Slovak Government tried to soften the blow. Slovak politicians exerted pressure on the decision-making institutions of the Federation to continue arms sales and thus at least limited production. It was mostly because of their influence that the Czechoslovak regulations were gradually loosened and the republic won some time to continue military deliveries. On the other hand, the Slovak authorities intended to address the negative effects of the rapid decrease in military production, looking for solutions. In its January 1991 Decree No. 1991, the Slovak Government published its own policy guidelines for state assistance to enterprises involved in military production. The document also envisaged addressing problems like unemployment and regional imbalances caused by the decay of the industry. According to Slovak sources, it was under the influence of their government that the Federal Government began to provide state subsidies and other forms of financial aid to troubled companies in the sector. In the liberal economic policy declared by the Federal Government at the beginning of the transformation process, no special industrial or regional policy considerations were envisaged. No targeted economic measures, specific tax, credit or budget regulations were implemented to facilitate conversion or diminish its negative side-effects. Since macroeconomic regulation remained within the competence of the Federal state agencies, the most Slovak authorities were able to do was to provide additional financial support to the military-related enterprises from their own budget.[16]

After the breakup of the Federation, Meciar was eager to confirm that the defence sector enjoyed undisputed priority in economic policy. In his first months in office he often stressed that his government would 'create the necessary conditions so that the army could get everything for its activity and the defence of the Slovak Republic'.[17] However, there were many dissenting voices, even among representatives of the sector. Peter Magvasi, Director of the Special Division at ZTS Martin, declared that it was impossible to revive the production of some of the military equipment suggested by the prime minister, particularly in the short time he called for.[18] Ludovit Cernak, Minister of the

---

[16] Mikusova, K., 'Fiscal and credit policy of the government: impact on the conversion of military production', Kominkova and Schmognerova (note 4); and Outrata (note 11).

[17] *Pravda*, 18 Mar. 1993.

[18] *Mlada Fronta Dnes*, 9 Jan. 1993.

Economy, declared that Slovakia was not considering modernizing its arms industry since world arms markets had suffered a major slump.[19] However, this initial discord was soon settled or at least put aside for some time to come.

In the first two years after the breakup, all the major political actors—the nationalist–populist Vladimir Meciar as well as his main opposition, the centre–left Peter Weiss and liberal Josef Moravcik—seemed to agree that Slovakia would continue to produce and sell arms, but there were differences regarding details of policy: regarding what scale and which branches of the sector should be preserved and under which conditions. In the spring 1994 election, representatives of the government and its challengers—led by Peter Weiss, head of the Party of the Democratic Left (PDL)—both stood for reviving and modernizing the Slovak defence industry.[20] In August 1994 Moravcik signed an agreement with India on sales and cooperation in the military sector and expressed his hope 'to expand bilateral defence cooperation and sell Slovak hardware to the Indian military'.[21]

Apart from the (changing) government circles, the main representatives of both employers and employees also lobbied unanimously for continued arms production and state support. The Union of Engineering Industry of the Slovak Republic, uniting state-owned and private enterprises involved in military-related production, tried to exert pressure on state agencies to regulate the conversion process more and to re-establish a level of arms production in harmony with the country's needs and possibilities.[22] Very importantly, the KOVO trade union, representing employees in the metal and engineering industry, fought from 1990 to modify government policy towards a gradual, slow conversion process (with the reduction in orders by the state not exceeding 8–15 per cent per year) while maintaining military production to produce the revenue necessary for conversion.[23] The union stressed that they understood the humanitarian approach of former President Vaclav Havel, but 'it was not in harmony with the humanitarian position of our citizens. . . . This implementation of "humanism" is unfavourable for our trade unionists. The right to export arms is given to large and powerful states, but denied to small and economically weak states'.[24]

Multiple arguments for rescuing the sector were presented. The most obvious was the urgent, short-term need for hard currency in the fairly precarious state of the Slovak economy. The sale of arms was presented as an absolute economic necessity in order to create resources for the future conversion or modernization of the sector and to generate the hard-currency income that was badly needed for overall economic restructuring. In contrast to their Czech counterparts, who used principally economic arguments to justify the revival of the

[19] *Ekonom*, no. 5 (16 Jan. 1993).

[20] *Financial Times*, 24 May 1994.

[21] *Prague Post*, 10–16 Aug. 1994.

[22] The union's starting-point was that by the end of 1992 the 'conversion of the Slovak defense industry is terminated'. Magvasi, P., 'Approach of the Union of Engineering Industry to the process of conversion of armament production', Kominkova and Schmognerova (note 4), p. 134.

[23] Krumpolec, J., 'Attitude and views of the trade union KOVO to the conversion of arms production in Slovakia', Kominkova and Schmognerova (note 4).

[24] Krumpolec (note 23).

defence industry, the Slovak authorities often referred to welfare, nationalist and strategic considerations to convince people of the indispensability of the defence sector. In the election campaigns, arms production was often presented as a symbol of national independence. Revamping the military industry featured as a guarantee of external security in the face of the general insecurity of the 'new Europe', specifically the 'Hungarian threat'.[25] Continued arms production was presented as a guarantee of internal security since it offered the only means of economic survival for thousands of people and therefore prevented the major social and regional disturbances that would follow the closure of important enterprises in traditional centres of the defence industry.

These official arguments reinforced existing feelings about the necessity of continued military production. The defence industry in general was seen as one of the outstanding branches of the Slovak economy, since—because of the privileged position it had enjoyed for decades—its general level of development, technology and performance was higher than that of the average industry. It represented high-technology development in the context of the Slovak economy, and in an international comparison had significant competitive advantages because of its relative high quality and low costs. This is why military production could become a cause of national pride in political rhetoric and why both politicians and citizens found it difficult to part with.

In the times of the Federation, Slovakia carried out independent arms deals, even violating existing regulations. After independence in January 1993, the Slovak policy on arms exports was more desperate and bolder than the Czech policy, partly because Slovak products were more difficult to sell in the changing world market and partly because the country lacked trade infrastructure and expertise. Most of the experienced weapon dealers remained at Omnipol, in Prague, and the Slovak arms trade companies were not particularly successful. According to the Czech newspaper *Hospodarske Noviny*, 20 arms trade companies had been established in Slovakia by 1994 but their activities were not coordinated.[26]

In May 1993 the Slovak Government set up an Export Licence Committee consisting of representatives of the Ministries of Foreign Affairs, Defence and Economy and headed by the Secretary of State of the Security Council. A Secretariat was also established, working in the Ministry of Economy, to prepare materials for the committee. The Export Licence Committee was charged with issuing licences for each arms deal in harmony with UN resolutions. It also issued individual concessions for economic agents trading in arms.[27]

---

[25] The Hungarian issue was another example of lack of unanimity within government. Despite Vladimir Meciar's continuous efforts to stir up hysteria about the Hungarian threat, in his first interview given to the Slovak daily *Pravda* as Minister of Defence, Imrich Andrejcak stressed that there was no need to be afraid of the Hungarian armed forces as those of Slovakia matched them in force. *Pravda*, 18 Mar. 1993.

[26] *Hospodarske Noviny*, 18 May 1994.

[27] Droppa (note 8), pp. 10–11. In addition, strict internal regulations on light-weapon licences limited the Slovak civil market for such arms. This had serious effects on Czech arms makers, as became apparent from the interview with Miroslav Duda of Ceska Zbrojovka. *Prague Post*, 5–11 Oct. 1994.

In 1992 and 1993 Slovakia delivered the last of 250 T-72 tanks to Syria and began to negotiate new deals with Egypt, Pakistan and Syria and with other Arab countries. Arms trade links with several Arab countries were pursued despite the large irrecoverable claims that had accumulated in the past. In 1994 Slovakia had claims worth several tens of billions of korunas, 80 per cent of which stemmed from arms sales.[28] The value of arms exports in 1993 was 2 billion korunas, consisting mostly of spare parts.[29]

Despite strict control, it was difficult to avoid black-market deals completely. The most serious incident that became public was the disappearance of 1 tonne of Semtex explosive from an apparently poorly guarded storage place of the company Zylna located in Zvolen, in southern Slovakia. This was probably the old variety of Semtex that is practically impossible to detect.[30] More than a year later the results of a British police investigation were published, highlighting a Europe-wide network of illegal arms traffic aimed to arm Islamic fundamentalist groups. Arms were bought in the ECE countries and explosives specifically came from Bratislava.[31]

Immediately after independence, the future Minister of Defence, Imrich Andrejcak, declared that Slovakia would not seek membership of NATO since the organization evidently had no interest in the country. Cooperation with other European security systems, however, was envisaged.[32] This approach later changed and Slovakia joined the NATO Partnership for Peace (PFP) programme, considered the waiting-room for NATO membership. Slovakia's wish to join NATO was clearly confirmed in later declarations. Preparing to integrate the Slovak armed forces into Western security systems provided another argument for maintaining defence production since, according to the official view, the armed forces would rely on the domestic industry since Slovakia lacked the resources for imports.

The Slovak national armed forces were relatively well equipped at independence, when weapons and military equipment were divided in a 2 : 1 ratio between the Czech Republic and Slovakia, although in some areas—for example, aircraft—the ratio was 1 : 1. The Slovak Air Force later received another 5 MiG-29 fighter aircraft from Russia as a debt-swap, and its fleet grew to 15 aircraft.[33] According to Colonel Ivan Koblem of the Ministry of Defence, before 1995 the armed forces could plan for the maintenance of only their current equipment. Gradual modernization would begin after 1995, including the creation of a communications system within the army, refurbishment of the

---

[28] *Nepszabadsag*, 27 Aug. 1994; *Financial Times*, 2 Nov. 1993; and *The Economist*, 6 Nov. 1993.

[29] *Hospodarske Noviny*, 18 May 1994.

[30] *Nepszabadsag*, 1 Nov. 1993.

[31] *Liberation*, 4 Jan. 1995.

[32] *Mlada Fronta Dnes*, 14 Jan. 1993.

[33] The fighters were accepted, among other reasons, to compensate for a similar deal with Hungary that involved 28 MiG-29s. Later, some of these jets were used to offer private individuals test-flights on a commercial basis in cooperation with a British firm, at the airport of Sliac, near Banska Bystrica. *Financial Times*, 21–22 Jan. 1995.

existing aircraft inventory and navigation systems, acquisition of new helicopters and modernization of the air-defence system.[34]

III. Crisis and survival

The initial collapse of the Slovak defence industry in the late 1980s and early 1990s was followed by a slower decline in production.[35] Under the daunting difficulties faced by the entire economy and the military sector in particular, the long agony of defence enterprises dragged on. In the midst of institutional insecurity, lacking markets and resources to modernize military production, follow up conversion projects or maintain production, the situation of Slovak defence enterprises became more desperate. By early 1993 most of these enterprises were in a virtual state of bankruptcy and faced dim future prospects.[36] By early 1994 the workforce had diminished by at least one-half, causing unemployment rates of up to 30 per cent in some heavily affected areas.[37] If the promised bankruptcy law had been introduced and enforced, approximately 50 per cent of the companies would have faced immediate liquidation.[38]

Since the policy on terminating military production and promoting conversion had a 'stop–go' nature, enterprises tended to implement only the necessary minimum changes in the hope that Draconian political decisions would sooner or later be reversed. Despite heavy redundancies, most defence firms intended to keep their core military workers in anticipation of a future recovery. Most of the dismissed workers were re-employed in spin-off companies created as independent enterprises from former divisions of industrial conglomerates. Another large group included people forced into early retirement and women, who were encouraged to stay in the home.[39] Many, principally the most entrepreneurial, employees left voluntarily to join the private sector at the beginning of the crisis. In Martin, where the ZTS Martin leadership complained about the enormous losses of workers that allegedly made it impossible for them to introduce further reorganization measures, local unemployment in 1993 was below the regional average.

The three former strongholds of traditional Slovak arms production located in the 'military triangle' of central Slovakia were in the worst situation. Because of their importance, their crisis and potential collapse threatened to destabilize

---

[34] *Heti Vilaggazdasag*, 6 Aug. 1994.

[35] A detailed study of the Slovak defence industry prepared by a British–French consultancy firm for the EC PHARE project gives an in-depth picture of the first, dramatic collapse of the sector on the basis of the situation of 13 select companies, which represented 83% of total military output in 1989 and 80% of the residual military employment in 1991. From the author's notes on: SEMA Division Conseil, in cooperation with the Technica group and Sofres, 'The situation of the Slovak defence industry', Unpublished manuscript, [1992].

[36] Interview by the author with Karel Droppa, 1 Apr. 1993.

[37] According to *The Economist* this meant laying off 60 000 people. *The Economist*, 6 Nov. 1993. Average unemployment in Slovakia was 14% in early 1994, in some regions reaching 20%. *Le Monde*, 5 Apr. 1994.

[38] Interview by the author with Karel Droppa, 14 Feb. 1994.

[39] Although the arms industry is fairly male-dominated in general, branches like ammunition, precision- and optical-instrument making and light-arms production have a considerable share of female employees.

the entire Slovak economy. Between 1988 and mid-1994 the workforce in ZTS Martin decreased from 13 000 to 6000, in ZVS Dubnica from 14 000 to 7000 and in PS Detva from 12 000 to 3000. The average wage in these factories was lower than the national average, reversing the historical experience.[40]

The situation at ZTS Martin was representative of the Slovak defence industry. The facility was designed to produce heavy military equipment, principally tanks. It had an annual capacity of 250–300 tanks but in an emergency output could reach 600 units. At peak production in 1988 total output was 14 billion korunas and profits reached 1.6 billion korunas. In 1992 the value of production was 6 billion korunas, with a gross profit of 32 million korunas. Military-related production represented 10.3 billion korunas in 1988 but had dropped to 2.7 billion korunas by 1992.[41]

As a reaction to the decreasing export demand in the late 1980s, the company became involved in several diversification projects that aimed to increase the share of civilian production. New production profiles included tractors, engines, construction and road-building machinery to be produced under Western licences. In 1988 the enterprise signed a contract with the German company Hannomag to produce tractors and construction machinery using Hannomag licences and technology. In 1989 a similar deal was made with the Italian firm Lombardini for small diesel engines.

In 1990, to combat mounting financial and production problems, four major independent enterprises were created from enterprise divisions. According to Jozef Hanzel, the official company spokesman, in 1993 the share of special (military) production was only 5 per cent of total company output, consisting mostly of spare parts supplied under previous contracts.[42] This statement contradicted other declarations by company managers. In early 1993 the management announced that in that year military-related output would represent 40 per cent of total output, a reduction of 10 per cent from 1991–92, when it reached a level of 50 per cent.[43] Although the importance of civilian products undoubtedly continued to increase, military production remained the most profitable division partly because of the nature of the arms market. According to Jan Fillo, Strategic Director, 'it takes 86 tractors to equal a single tank. And the world market for tractors is soft'.[44] It was not surprising that ZTS Martin was actively engaged in a programme for modernization of T-72 tanks.

To maintain the high profitability of military-related production and continue exporting, the company would sooner or later require modernization of its military division. According to Western experts, restructuring ZTS Martin would require major capital investments since the firm did not have most of the automated equipment used in similar factories in the West.[45]

[40] *Magyar Hirlap*, 27 Aug. 1994.
[41] *Financial Times*, 2 Nov. 1993.
[42] Interview by the author with Jozef Hanzel, Communications Manager of ZTS Martin, Martin, Slovakia, 16 Feb. 1994.
[43] *Hospodarske Noviny*, 10 Feb. 1993.
[44] *Prague Post*, 24–30 Nov. 1993.
[45] *Hospodarske Noviny*, 10 Feb. 1993.

Civilian product profiles also exhibited the old-style attitudes towards management. The Lombardini project resembled the planning mechanisms of the past. Assuming the existence of an almost unlimited market, the original plan was to manufacture 60 000 engines per year, but after a later modification the division was set up to produce 40 000 units. Under the licence agreement the engines could only be sold on East European markets. This led to serious problems after the former East-bloc markets collapsed. In 1994, in the most ambitious sales plan since 1991, when the project was launched, the enterprise hoped to sell 12 000 units. Despite these difficulties the enterprise management did not even try to improve its marketing activities and use such sales techniques as barter or leasing.[46]

Despite its early attempts to cope with the challenge of decreasing military production and a considerable amount of attention and some assistance on behalf of international agencies, the enterprise did not succeed. Neither the conversion projects nor the decentralization and reorganization measures prompted a genuine change in the attitude of the management. The multi-level, rigid hierarchical organization inherited from the past remained largely unreformed. Enterprise divisions had very limited freedom of decision and individual accountability. Most of the strategic and operational decisions had to go through the company general management. Despite some important changes (e.g., the creation of spin-off companies and some elemental rationalization measures) minimal changes were introduced in the actual production process to enhance efficiency and productivity.

The company management in turn continued to wait for decisions concerning privatization and state support for military production, which prevented them from carrying out internal restructuring. Between the author's two visits in early 1993 and early 1994, in a crucial period for enterprise restructuring, only minor changes were carried out at the company. Significant personnel changes were made in the senior management (although in February 1994 the implications of these changes were still unclear). A Labour Foundation had been established to address unemployment and retraining questions, and ZTS Martin provided it with office space, equipment and 'some management'. An official spokesperson for the company had been appointed to handle enquiries from journalists and researchers.[47]

The other ZTS manufacturing giant in nearby Dubnica nad Vahom did slightly better, mainly because of its more open and flexible managerial attitude. This company, too, was hit hard by the collapse of the defence industry. Between 1989 and 1993 the workforce was reduced from 16 000 to 7500 and revenue fell from $164 million to $89 million. In 1987 nearly 75 per cent of the output was military-related but by 1993 the share of military production in out-

---

[46] At the 1993 visit it was learned that a former ZTS employee had set up a small private company that successfully sold ZTS products using these techniques.

[47] Round-table discussion with Peter Magvasi, Financial Director; Jan Fillo, Director of Strategic Management; Juraj Kovacik, Manager of the Engines Division; and other members of the management of ZTS Martin at the joint Helsinki Citizens' Assembly–Institute for EastWest Studies meeting (note 13); Interview with Hanzel (note 42); *Hospodarske Noviny*, 10 Feb. 1993; and *Financial Times*, 2 Nov. 1993.

put fell to about 5 per cent and the revenue it yielded dropped from $89 million to $23 million. The factory took up several conversion projects from 1990.

The original conversion plans envisaged mechanical gearboxes and machinery for rubber, chemical and food production. The enterprise searched for potential business partners who could provide capital, know-how and markets for the new civilian products. Of the many potential foreign investors who contacted the factory, in the end only Reda Corporation (Oklahoma, USA) signed a contract to transfer technology for drilling pumps. The intention was to sell the pumps to Russia in exchange for crude oil. In order to buy the licence and technology the company needed a guarantee from the National Bank and the backing of a bank consortium. The plan envisaged sales of 3000 units per year, but in 1994 the company management was pleased to be able to produce and sell only 500 units.

This project ran into major difficulties because of the unexpected collapse of the former Soviet market and protectionist measures introduced by the Russian Government as regards the oil sector. Other civilian projects, such as construction machines, some hydraulic equipment, small multi-purpose vehicles (e.g., snow bulldozers) and lightweight building materials produced principally for the internal market, fared better. However, their share in total production was limited. These civilian products were all developed by the company locally or in cooperation with the R&D institute in Zvolen that had serviced the entire ZTS complex. Despite these efforts, it was clear that a major improvement of the company's situation was envisaged through renewed military orders and possible arms exports. The enterprise developed and produced the Zuzana self-propelled artillery system, which was considered to have possibilities as an export item.

Some decentralization and reorganization efforts were also carried out. Strategic decisions remained in the competence of the central management but enterprise divisions gained more freedom in their daily management. The administrative staff employed at the centre was reduced from 3000 to 200. However, these efforts were restricted by its state-owned enterprise status and structure; for example, administrative regulations made it impossible to sell company property valued at over 25 000 korunas, which restricted the possibilities to obtain quick cash for internal reorganization. Similarly, the centralized accountancy system made it very difficult to introduce division-based accounts and strict efficiency criteria. Since functional decentralization and privatization efforts initiated by the enterprise were systematically thwarted by official decision makers, the management experimented with new methods that aimed at creating market-like conditions among the enterprise divisions; for example, they created an internal bank where the divisions kept separate accounts and tried to imitate independent financial management.

As part of the internal reorganization effort, the central sales department was dissolved and each division set up its own marketing department. The only division which served the whole company was a recently established strategic marketing division that concentrated on future markets and cooperation opportunities throughout the world. To facilitate trade with the former Soviet republics a specialized company, Trade, was set up to manage forms of exchange like barter.[48]

State control versus enterprise freedom

The dynamic of the Slovak situation was determined by two conflicting tendencies. On the one hand the state and its agencies tried to reassert control over the defence industry and provide resources for its development. On the other hand enterprises that had learned lessons from their relative independence during the years of crisis and conversion were aware that even if they received state help it would not be enough for the entire enterprise to survive. Therefore, their policy towards state agencies fluctuated between reviving old-style close cooperation, including financial backing, with their superior authorities and fighting for more independence of manoeuvre.

The government tried to reassert its control over the military sector through new institutional arrangements and financial support. The principal means to preserve direct influence was by maintaining ownership. At disintegration of the Federation, a small group of Slovak defence enterprises had already been privatized in the first Czechoslovak privatization wave. Under Vladimir Meciar's first government, privatization became a major issue of internal political struggle and led to several cases where it was suspected that privatization had been accompanied by illegal activity which, in combination, eventually led to the fall of the government. The entire process, in particular where large-scale enterprises were concerned, became paralysed.

Josef Moravcik's cabinet tried to revive the process and suggested that weapon factories would also be sold, with the state keeping only 2–3 per cent of the shares.[49] A month later, however, a high-ranking official declared that arms-producing companies would not automatically be included in the (planned) second round of privatization, but would be dealt with on a case-to-case basis.[50] The Moravcik Government did not manage to pass the new privatization law and, as of 1994, most of the Slovak defence enterprises were still state-owned, under the direct supervision of the Ministry of the Economy.

In addition to direct control exerted through ownership, the Slovak Government started to create new organizations to coordinate and promote defence industry production more efficiently. In early 1993 the authorities established a state-owned trading company, ARMEX, to promote exports. However, according to *Hospodarske Noviny*, it did not manage to close a deal until May 1994. In November 1993 a new, completely state-owned company was created to ensure

---

[48] Interview by the author with Miroslav Macko, Marketing Manager, and Rudolf Cyprian, Public Relations Manager, ZTS Dubnica, Dubnica nad Vahom, Slovakia, 17 Feb. 1994; *International Defense Review*, vol. 24, no. 8 (Aug. 1991), pp. 799–801; *International Herald Tribune*, 2 Feb. 1992; and *International Herald Tribune*, 13 Feb. 1993.

[49] *Lidove Noviny*, 18 Apr. 1994. This proposal was formulated by Peter Magvasi, Minister of the Economy.

[50] *Hospodarske Noviny*, 18 May 1994.

the maintenance of state influence in coordinating, promoting and controlling military production and exports. Five ministries—the Ministries of Defence, the Economy, Transport and Public Works, Finance and Interior—represented the state and put together the initial capital of 10 million korunas. According to the original plan, major defence enterprises were to join the company later.[51]

The government also tried to continue to provide financial support to the crisis-stricken enterprises of the military sector. Official guidelines concerning the new national security and defence policy, including military production, were far from clear. In practice, however, effective official promotion and support were given to defence enterprises. In 1993, 500 million korunas were scheduled for ongoing conversion projects; by the end of the year, as an emergency measure, the government provided 2 billion korunas to write off the military enterprises' bad debts.[52] According to the Bratislava correspondent of the Hungarian daily *Magyar Hirlap*, the sum was transferred from the Slovak Privatization Agency, the National Property Fund.[53] In 1994 the Moravcik Government decided to allocate another 245 million korunas for conversion projects.[54] In June a decision was taken to help about 30 companies with another 300 million korunas to resolve the problem of their bad debts.[55]

These funds covered a small percentage of the enormous needs of the companies. Losses stemming from the sudden halt of heavy weaponry production were high, and the following years of general economic insecurity and crisis created further erosion and decay of the productive assets of the military-related firms. This pushed up the cost of both conversion and military production.

The generally bad shape of the economy made defence industry restructuring costlier in several ways. An emerging active small and medium-sized enterprise network, the steady slow growth of service industries, and a renewed and more efficient public sector were present in the Czech Republic and made defence industry restructuring easier and smoother. These were absent in Slovakia, which made defence industry restructuring there more difficult and costly. Many large-scale Slovak companies not only kept their diverse profile but in some cases saw themselves as obliged to extend it. It was very difficult, sometimes impossible, to reconstruct the wide supplier system that had been available for defence-related factories. Many enterprises decided to re-establish these activities within their own factory gates. In the early 1990s one common argument against further decentralization of the mammoth defence enterprises was that without their extended and varied range of activities they would be unable to carry out production.

---

[51] *Pravda*, 31 Jan. 1994; and Interview with Bohumil Gerinec, Head of the Export Licence Committee, Ministry of Defence of Slovakia, Bratislava, 18 Feb. 1994.

[52] Interviews by the author with Karol Droppa, Head of Department of Special Production, Slovak Ministry of the Economy, Bratislava, 1 Apr. 1993 and 14 Feb. 1994; *Pravda,* 31 Jan. 1994. Two billion korunas must have been the 'magic number' for 1993, since in official data defence industry output, government subsidies and export all had the same value.

[53] *Magyar Hirlap,* 27 Aug. 1994.

[54] *Lidove Noviny,* 18 Apr. 1994.

[55] *Lidove Noviny*, 22 June 1994.

Despite their best intentions, state organizations were unable to provide more assistance to military-related enterprises since the country was in a deep recession and the state budget seriously in deficit. However, the government was reluctant to widen the freedom of action of state-owned defence enterprises or privatize them. Worse than the standstill in the privatization process, enterprises had to cope with an environment in which they had lost their traditional framework of operations but in which they were still prevented from operating according to the principles of the market. The old systems for regulation broke down but the recently introduced ones did not function properly yet.

One important positive element, however, was that many former defence industry managers, used to a completely different background and working conditions, simply gave up and took early retirement or chose some other form of economic activity. The new breed of managers was more dynamic and creative than the old guard. They wanted to guarantee the survival of their firms, if necessary by renouncing military production.

At the enterprise level, managers sought for survival strategies and a huge gap opened between macro- and micro-level policies. In interviews carried out in early 1994 the main concern expressed by managers was macroeconomic instability and the impossible requirements of the political centre.

Trapped between the remaining central regulations that limited their range of decisions, pressure from above to maintain and if possible increase military production, and the inevitable pressures of a quasi-market economy in deep crisis, they resorted to various forms of 'economic acrobatics' to try to ensure the future of their enterprises. Many state-owned companies tried to imitate market conditions in order to improve internal company performance. Within the framework of official limits they tried to differentiate wages and introduce different internal accounting procedures and incentive systems.

Development in crisis

The restricted economic resources and the generally poor shape of the economy meant that, when deciding about the future of military production, high-level Slovak decision makers had a very limited range of choices. There was an option to invest limited resources in further conversion efforts, but the modest success of ongoing conversion projects and political and social pressure to continue arms production and exports made this choice rather hypothetical. Some support was given to ongoing conversion programmes that were then programmes more for diversification than for genuine conversion. Conversion funds and incomes deriving from conversion projects represented an additional source of revenue to compensate for the fluctuations in the military market. Even though the average share of civilian production in enterprise output increased significantly, in the majority of cases this output was treated as a supplement rather than a viable alternative to military production.

If it was decided to continue military production and sales, only very limited development on a narrow range of projects could be afforded. Enterprises relied mainly on what they had—large-scale capacities to produce heavy weapons and large stocks of unsold military hardware. This defined the circle of possible cooperation partners and clients. It seems that the strategic decision was made (or it occurred without an explicit decision) to concentrate efforts on finding potential trading partners in the developing countries, focusing on those with an inventory of former WTO weaponry who would be interested in upgraded versions. The promise of these markets could attract Western producers to cooperate on modernization projects. In this way the enormous costs of development could be shared and the limited resources of the Slovak Government would not limit further military-related R&D and production.[56]

By mid-1994 there were signs that this policy was viable, at least in the short term. In June 1994 Ivan Kovacik, Director of the Machinery and Electronics Department of the Slovak Ministry of the Economy, declared that by the end of 1995 the large heavy-weapon producers of the country could come out of their deficit production if their debt problem were properly arranged. This was the first openly optimistic official declaration concerning the Slovak military sector since 1989.[57]

This timid optimism was probably based on new export deals that the Slovak manufacturers managed to strike during the year. After the Zuzana self-propelled gun and the modernized T-72 tank were exhibited at the 1994 Brno arms fair, Prime Minister Moravcik, accompanied by the Ministers of Defence and the Economy, visited Asia. (The Czechoslovak Dana 152-mm calibre self-propelled artillery system was fitted with a 155-mm calibre gun and renamed the Zuzana. The system was built on automotive components from Tatra.) Negotiations took place with India about, among other things, the sale of Zuzana guns, T-72 armoured recovery vehicles and other types of heavy weaponry. Subsequently, contracts were signed with India for the transfer of armoured recovery vehicles and military trucks.[58] Viet Nam also expressed interest in purchasing parts and equipment for its existing WTO-based arsenal. According to Western observers, in 1994 nearly 80 per cent of the Slovak output continued to be exported.[59]

By 1994 the Slovak economy also showed a surprising improvement, with a rise in GDP in both 1994 (to 480 billion korunas, a growth of 4.8 per cent over 1993) and 1995 (518 billion korunas, or $17.2 billion—a growth of 7.4 per cent).[60] Industrial production also began to recover, as did exports and private

---

[56] As an indicator of the costs involved in starting new production of major equipment, the T-72 programme established in the Czech Republic after the separation required investment of 2 billion korunas. The costs of a similar programme might have been lower in Slovakia because some of the capital assets needed for production were already in place. Interview by the author with Pavel Cech, Technical Manager, and Milan Faltus, Commercial Director, of the RDP Group, Prague, Czech Republic, 20 Apr. 1994.

[57] *Lidove Noviny*, 22 June 1994.

[58] *Jane's Defence Weekly*, 23 July 1994; and *Defense News*, 18–24 July 1994. According to plans, the Tatra trucks will be co-produced with the Slovak firm Sipox—the only part of the Tatra group located in Slovakia. After independence, the Czech members of the Tatra group rebuffed efforts by the Slovak company to maintain cooperation.

[59] *Prague Post*, 10–16 Aug. 1994; and *Heti Vilaggazdasag*, 6 Aug. 1994.

[60] 'The Slovak Republic and the integration process in the world economy, Slovak Chamber of Commerce and Industry', Paper delivered at the Fourth OSCE Economic Forum, Prague, 27–29 Mar. 1996.

consumption. At the same time inflation, the budget deficit and the trade balance were under control.[61] These first signs of economic recovery, however modest, must have created a more positive environment for the defence industry as well.

One reason why the Slovak defence industry managed to make a partial recovery was that it had preserved the military-related R&D centres in the country. In contrast to the generally held view that the Slovak defence industry was only able to produce under licence and/or under the guidance of the more developed Czech industry, there were several R&D centres in the country and indigenous research activity produced some interesting results. There were R&D institutes attached to practically all the major military enterprises and the independent Central Research Institute based in Trencin. In 1988, 4000 people were employed by these institutes.[62]

In 1991, in a list of promising Czechoslovak projects prepared by Josef Fucik, former head of the Department of Special Production in the Federal Ministry of the Economy, the only Slovak item was the DV-2 jet engine developed and produced at PS Povazska Bystrica. In an interview conducted in 1992, Ladislav Nemec mentioned that Konstrukta Trencin had developed modernization projects for the T-72 tank, a mine-dispensing system, a mortar and an ambulance. It also developed the Dana self-propelled gun, truck modifications, armoured bridges and other support equipment.[63] The Slovak need to export was closely connected with the urge to develop new systems. Bohumil Gerinec, head of the Security and Defence Committee of the Slovak Government, explained that since Slovakia was confined in the past to producing WTO-licensed weaponry the future of the defence industry depended on R&D.[64]

In both military R&D and the introduction of new equipment, there was close cooperation between the defence industry, the armed forces and the Ministries of the Economy and Defence. For decision makers in government it must have been clear that the promotion of this activity was central to the chosen macro-economic adjustment strategy. For enterprise management it was equally clear that even if the bulk of their activities were unassisted by the central authorities new, promising military-related products could count on central financing. As such they could act as a safety-belt for the whole enterprise. As Samuel Kodaj, Director of Special Production of ZTS Dubnica, put it: 'We have an association of defence industries that works to solve questions of coordination of development work and planning. We have very close cooperation with the army.'[65]

After independence the Slovak Republic was the first former WTO country to produce NATO-compatible artillery. The first Zuzana gun prototype was completed in ZTS Dubnica in December 1992 and firing trials took place soon afterwards in cooperation with, among others, Western firms.[66] The system was

[61] *Financial Times*, 16 Dec. 1994; and *Figyelo*, 3 Nov. 1994.
[62] Outrata (note 11), p. 86.
[63] Borovicka, M., 'The renaissance of arms trade?', *Noviny*, 29 May 1992 (in Czech).
[64] *Magyar Hirlap*, 27 Aug. 1994.
[65] *Prague Post*, 10–16 Aug. 1994.
[66] *Jane's Defence Weekly*, 6 Mar. 1993.

displayed at the 1994 Brno arms fair and in a similar exhibition in Trencin on 5–8 October 1994.[67] It was a sign of the cooperation between the national armed forces and industry that the Zuzana gun and the T-72 tank were selected by the armed forces. Some Zuzana systems were ordered for testing and eventual introduction into the army was expected.[68]

The Slovak version of the Soviet T-72 tank, produced by ZTS Martin and ZTS Dubnica, was developed in cooperation with the Belgian company SABCA, two French companies and the British GEC Marconi. According to Pierre Pellegrin, marketing manager of SABCA, the Slovak partners proved 'much more realistic and much more aggressive than the Czechs in producing an upgraded tank for the world market'.[69]

There was a large potential international market for both products. The T-72 could be marketed in Asia and South America and in the ECE countries that could not afford Western products with more or less similar performance.[70] According to Pellegrin, the modernized Slovak T-72 would cost one-fifth to one-tenth the price of a similar Western tank. This market is crowded, however, since the Czech Republic, Poland, Russia and Ukraine all offer versions of the T-72 and newer models of T-80 and T-84 tanks have entered the market. In addition, many second-hand US and European tanks have been available for export since the end of the cold war.

Competitor products to the Zuzana gun are produced by China, France, Germany, Israel, Italy, Russia, South Africa, the United Kingdom and the United States, and Argentina and Sweden have similar systems ready for production. After the Brno show several Asian countries contacted Slovak military producers and Prime Minister Moravcik signed an agreement concerning the possible sale and joint production of armoured vehicles and artillery with India.[71]

Apart from participating in promising military development projects, foreign capital played a rather modest role in the Slovak restructuring process. Foreign direct investment was small compared to the country's potential and compared to the amount its neighbours received. By the end of 1994 Slovakia had attracted $400 million, in contrast to $4 billion received by the Czech Republic and $6 billion by Hungary.[72] Of this sum a minimal amount was spent for providing conversion projects with much needed financial infusions. In 1991–92 only 152.9 million korunas worth of foreign capital was invested in conversion, a mere 3.1 per cent of the programme costs. Of 101 ongoing projects foreigners were involved in only 11.[73]

[67] The Slovak military show was accompanied by a conference on conversion. The city of Trencin organized a concert for peace and a photo exhibition on the Yugoslav War. There was also an anti-war demonstration organized by civil society movements.

[68] *Hospodarske Noviny*, 24 Jan. 1994; and *Nepszabadsag*, 3 Nov. 1994.

[69] *International Herald Tribune*, 8 June 1994.

[70] Altogether an estimated 20 000–25 000 T-72s had been produced by the end of 1992 and they were used in more than 25 countries. Anthony, I. (ed.), *The Future of the Defence Industries in Central and Eastern Europe*, SIPRI Research Report No. 7 (Oxford University Press: Oxford, 1994), p. 103.

[71] *The Economist*, 22 Oct. 1994; *Prague Post*, 10–16 Aug. 1994; and *Heti Vilaggazdasag*, 6 Aug. 1994.

[72] *Liberation*, 19 Dec. 1994.

[73] Droppa (note 8), p. 9.

Tesla Liptovsky Hradok was one of the few Slovak companies that succeeded in forming a joint venture with foreign capital. However, the results resembled those of Tesla Praha in the Czech Republic. Tesla Liptovsky Hradok was privatized in the first round of the Czechoslovak coupon programme. In 1991 the company created a joint venture with a German subsidiary of the French company Alcatel to produce civilian telecommunications technology. Tesla provided the land, buildings, infrastructure and a well-trained workforce; Alcatel provided the technology and capital. By early 1994 the companies were completely separated, the only link between them being the 30 per cent shares of Alcatel Tesla received. While Alcatel fulfilled its aim of entering the Central European and possibly the East European markets, Tesla was struggling to find new markets and new production profiles for its technology. In the past, 60–65 per cent of production was military-related and the destiny of the machines, special equipment, workshops, factory space and workforce used in this production was not decided. The best Tesla workers left to work for Alcatel.[74]

The positive developments from the Slovak case can be illustrated by the performance of PS Povazska Bystrica and Martin Diesel.

PS Povazska Bystrica was another huge military-related enterprise in central Slovakia which had produced engines for jet trainer aircraft and parts for rocket launchers and tank guns and had an extensive civilian profile of production of tractors and agricultural machinery. The company employed 12 000 people in 1989 but only 6000 by 1994. Output fell by 50 per cent between 1989 and 1993 and the share of military-related production fell from 35–40 per cent to 10 per cent, and another 10 per cent of production was engaged in producing military components. These figures exclude engine production, which was the most promising branch of enterprise activity. According to Milos Kraus, General Director, it was not worth continuing classic military production; in order to compete on the world market the enterprise would need enormous investments, while market prospects were not promising.

The company created a wide range of civilian products to make up for the loss of former civilian and military markets. They produced agricultural machinery, glass-cutting and -grinding machines, machinery for the food processing industry, pumps, small motorcycles, bearings and other engineering products. The workshop that in the past produced ammunition now produced fire-extinguishers. They concluded significant cooperation agreements with major Western firms, for example gear-box production with a US–German firm, and had several negotiations in progress. The most important of these was a possible agreement with the Canadian company Pratt and Whitney, a branch of the US United Technologies, about a joint venture to modernize and produce the DV-2 engines.[75] Thanks to its successful reorganization and relatively quick

---

[74] Interview by the author with Anton Murgas, President of the Executive Board, and Ivan Orenak, General Director, Tesla Liptovsky Hradok, Liptovsky Hradok, Slovakia, 15 Feb. 1994.

[75] The Canadian firm originally bid for Motorlet, one of the Aero Holdings companies that produced similar engines. After over a year of hesitation and changes by the Czech Government and the Aero Hold-

profile diversification, the company was in a relatively sound financial state by early 1994.

During its transformation and privatization process, PS Povazska Bystrica changed its internal structure. Production divisions that were not crucial for the core production profiles were separated from the main company and worked as independent enterprises. The remaining divisions worked with full financial and managerial autonomy. Major strategic decisions and marketing were coordinated at the enterprise level, with an emphasis on R&D and innovation. About one-half the number of recently introduced civilian products were developed internally, the rest being produced under Western licences. The company's own R&D institute engaged in creating new products and some more far-reaching technologies were preserved. One of the main management concerns was to generate additional financing to maintain the institute.[76]

Despite Kraus's clear vision of the futility of military production, the ties with the military were not completely cut. After privatization, a representative of the army remained on the company board of managers, and in January 1994 the board decided on a partial return to military production. In May 1994 the company unveiled its new product, the PS 93 Parabellum, a 9-mm hand gun that was expected to be produced from the end of the year.[77]

The case of the Martin Diesel company was clearly an unusual success story as far as conversion and restructuring were concerned. The company was created as a spin-off from ZTS Martin with the separation of the engine-producing division at the end of 1992. A year later the enterprise became a joint stock company with 100 per cent of its shares in the National Property Fund. Martin Diesel produced engines for tractors and other agricultural machines, construction equipment, ships and other vessels. About 80 per cent of its output was exported to China and Poland, and prototypes were tested in Bulgaria and Lebanon.

After separation from the parent company, the management of Martin Diesel carried out a thorough review of the current and potential markets in order to define new programmes in the light of market cycles and opportunities. The fundamental restructuring of company activities was carried out in line with medium- to long-term development projects. The production profile was based on a selection of four main product lines. Workshops were reorganized both functionally and aesthetically, so work in them could be organized more efficiently and would become more pleasant. Instead of the previous vertical hierarchy, project-based teams were formed that organized and controlled their own work. A strict personal quality-control system was introduced for workers

ing management, Pratt seemed to have had enough and decided to look across the border. In 1993 a joint venture agreement was signed with Povazska Bystrica. The only possible problem for this was the Russian Air Force, which had already selected the DV-2 for its trainer aircraft and carried out negotiations about a major deal with PS Povazska Bystrica. *Prague Post*, 5–11 Oct. 1994.

[76] Interview by the author with Milos Kraus, General Director, and Miroslav Jalc, Strategy Manager, PS Povazska Bystrica, 17 Feb. 1994.

[77] *Lidove Noviny*, 12 May 1994.

at all levels. There was a differentiated wage and material and non-material incentive system related to individual and team performance.[78]

The management of Martin Diesel intended to improve performance further in order to acquire international quality certificates. They hoped that the company would be privatized as soon as possible, partly because formal state ownership did not suit their potential foreign partners but also because they expected to gain more independence of action. Plans were in hand to create a joint venture with a British partner that was expected to contribute fresh capital and know-how.

One major goal was to transform the enterprise from a production-oriented to a consumer-oriented company that could provide customers with goods tailored to their requirements. They realized that quick and reliable delivery with after-sales service was sometimes more important than price in a competitive situation.

In a deal with China, a cooperation framework agreement was decided in May 1993 and by November the engines were being field-tested in China. The contract was signed in January 1994 and deliveries began in March. Since the analysis of activities had shown that the demand for agricultural tractors was likely to decrease, the company's tractor engines were expected to encounter problems. There was an effort to develop products in other areas, for example, mobile generators and other industrial machinery.

In early 1994 Martin Diesel had two major problems: privatization and dependence on ZTS Martin—still the major customer, but struggling with its own serious liquidity problems. The problem of suppliers was resolved by diversifying the supply network to avoid dependence on any single supplier and by creating a demanding requirement and reward system for their partners.

Early morning meetings of the entire Martin Diesel management were an accelerated lesson in strategic management. Although the representatives of Martin Diesel were dressed in the same poorly designed grey suits as their counterparts in ZTS Martin and although their conference room was much shabbier than ZTS Martin's, they exhibited a completely different mentality. Their dynamic, radical managerial approach aimed at long-term success instead of day-to-day survival; they confronted their internal problems, attempted to solve them quickly and tried to build long-term external cooperation in harmony with the internal goals of the company.

---

[78] For example, the company employed a full-time English teacher who, in addition to keeping contact with Western business partners, taught English to enterprise employees, from the workers to the managers.

5. Hungary

I. Introduction

In the euphoric years 1989–90, rapid social and economic transformation—including radical demilitarization and conversion programmes—promised to be the easiest in Hungary of all the countries of East–Central Europe. It seemed that the transition from a watered-down version of state socialism to a liberal society with a functioning market economy would be rather smooth.

The country's post-war history was marked by revolt, reform and compromise—the political establishment learned to find compromises even among deeply antagonistic political forces. Although Hungary was burdened by major economic and social problems, they did not seem likely to lead to disintegration, explosive ethnic conflicts or paralysing economic crisis. Hungary had the smallest armed forces within the Warsaw Treaty Organization (WTO) and the army never played as crucial a political and social role in Hungarian history as it had in, for example, Poland. The Hungarian defence industry was never as economically important as that of Czechoslovakia or Poland. Defence-related production was concentrated in the electronics sector, which was, in theory, the easiest sector to convert to civilian production.

However, as so often in Hungarian history, the reality turned out to be very different from the predictions. In the first five years after the fall of the Berlin Wall the country became entangled in a sluggish and contradictory process of transformation. Despite many important improvements in economic and political life, Hungary was unable to overcome its deep structural crisis and embark on sustainable economic development. Although it was not thrown into turmoil by the permanent changes of government, unpredictable changes within government made political life highly volatile.

The first post-communist coalition government, led by the centre–right Hungarian Democratic Forum (MDF), which came into power in 1990, remained stable on the surface but in reality was absorbed in constant internal struggles. These conflicts manifested themselves in the emergence of several power centres, whose infighting was marked by frequent changes in policy concerning key issues of transformation—such as the role of the state in economic life, privatization and the future of the defence industry. During its four troubled years in power the MDF Government became increasingly authoritarian and nationalist, antagonizing most of the Hungarian population and creating tensions with neighbouring countries. The MDF-led coalition lost the election of 1994, when a new coalition of the reformed Communist Party (called the Hungarian Socialist Party) and the Free Democrats (a party formed by the former opposition to the communists) was created. Despite changes in major

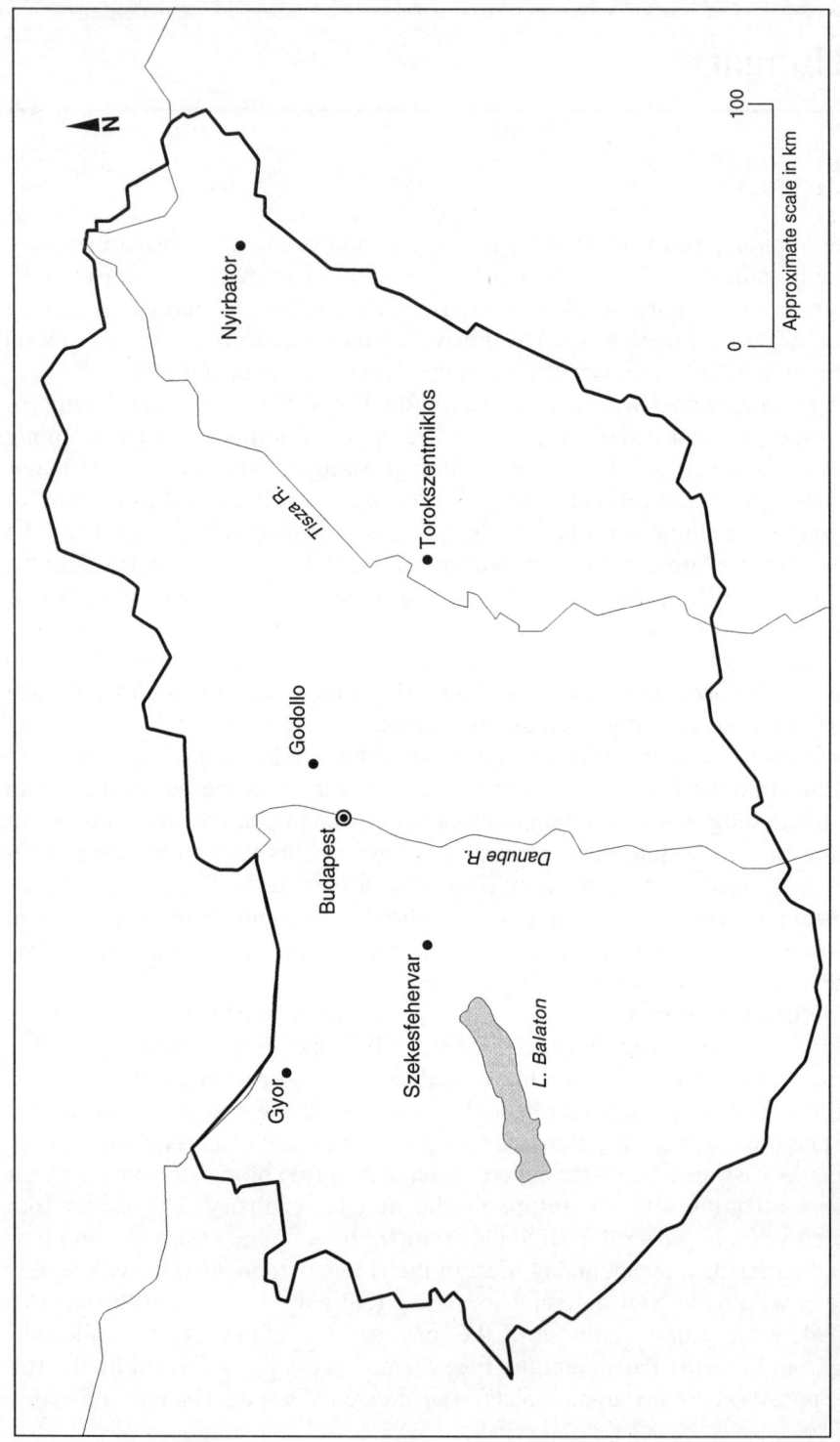

Figure 5.1. Location of defence enterprises in Hungary

policy areas, this coalition has been characterized by the same indecisiveness, unpredictability and internal power struggles as its predecessor.

Economic developments became embroiled in these political complications. The country had a fairly advantageous starting position for the introduction of a genuine market economy, and in 1990–94 it enjoyed the highest level of foreign capital inflow of the East–Central European (ECE) region. Nevertheless, the major projects of macroeconomic stabilization as well as economic transformation policy were plagued by serious delays and inconsistencies. The gross domestic product (GDP) declined by 4.3 per cent in real terms between 1991 and 1992, to 2883 billion forints, and then declined by 2.3 per cent (in real terms) between 1992 and 1993. In 1994 GDP grew at a rate of 2 per cent, a level which was sustained in 1995. In the area of industrial production the reduction was even steeper. Industrial output fell by 30 per cent between 1989 and 1993, before growing by 9 per cent in 1994.[1] By the end of 1994, although industrial production and investments showed some signs of recovery, privatization had still been only partially implemented and was prey to permanent political struggles. External and internal indebtedness increased alarmingly and the state budget was dangerously unbalanced. Despite the favourable conditions, the restructuring and eventual conversion of the defence industry were also stalled. Instead of a success story, the Hungarian case became a lesson in how expensive the spontaneous disintegration of the military–industrial sector and the lack of conversion can become.

The Hungarian case is also of interest because of its variety. By 1994 defence enterprises presented a diverse, colourful but slightly chaotic picture. There were newly established private companies, cases of complete or partial privatization of former state-owned enterprises (with both domestic and foreign capital), the emergence of different types of corporation created from spin-offs from former state-owned enterprises and controlled by different state agencies, joint ventures created with both Eastern and Western partners, and remnants of 'classic' state-owned enterprises.

II. The main structural features of the defence industry

The Hungarian defence industry dates from the Austro-Hungarian monarchy, when some of the major arms factories were established. It has since then been expanded and modernized several times. The first major modernization project was accomplished in the framework of the infamous 'Programme of Gyor' of 1938 that aimed to arm the country, an ally of fascist Germany, in preparation for World War II. The second modernization took place between 1949 and 1955, marked by the crystallizing cold war and the creation of the WTO in 1955. The reconstruction of the defence industry became part of the forced industrialization programme launched by the Communist Party after it seized

---

[1] Erlich, E., 'The economy and some key fields of social and human dimension in Hungary', Paper presented at Economic Developments and Reforms in Cooperation Partner Countries: The Social and Human Dimension, Colloquium 1996, NATO Economics Directorate, Brussels, 26–28 June 1996.

power in 1948. The aim was to build up a powerful Soviet-type economy, based on heavy industry. Heavy metallurgy, chemical, machine-building and cement production became the backbone of the new economic structure. The third major modernization programme took place in the mid- to late 1980s, when several grandiose new investments and expansions of existing production capacities were accomplished as a reaction to the boom in exports during the decade.

In 1988, the most successful year for the Hungarian defence industry, some 70 factories were involved in military-related production. All but one had a mixed civilian and military profile. The exception, Godolloi Gepgyar, was specialized in armoured vehicle and weapon repair and its entire production was military. Ninety-three per cent of the country's military output was produced by 17 enterprises, the share of military production at these enterprises ranging from 7.1 per cent to 82.2 per cent of total production. Defence production represented over 50 per cent of the overall output in only five companies—MN Godolloi Gepgyar, Mechlabor, Finommechanika, Pestvideki Gepgyar (PVG) and Labor MIM (Labor Muszeripari Muvek, Laboratory Instrument Works).

According to data published in 1992, in 1988 total military output was 20 billion forints ($370 million), representing 3 per cent of Hungarian industrial production and approximately 1.5 per cent of the processing industry's output.[2] This meant that in 1988 it was approaching full capacity—quite a remarkable achievement taking into consideration that one structural problem of the Hungarian industry was a chronic under-utilization of its production capacity. In 1988 around 30 000 people were employed in the defence industry, approximately 2 per cent of the economically active population.[3]

After a 1968 reform of the information system, statistics for the Hungarian defence industry included only those end-producers whose direct output of weapons, military equipment and other military-related items represented at least 10 per cent of output. Subcontractors and enterprises that supplied the military with, for example, utensils, vehicles, uniforms, raw materials or food were generally excluded. The scope of these activities and their importance for the activities of the respective enterprises were also unknown.

In the late 1980s electronic communications equipment and precision instruments represented 75 per cent of total military output, weapons and ammunition 12 per cent, vehicle and aircraft repair 8 per cent, and other goods (e.g., chemical and textile products) 5 per cent.[4] The share of telecommunications and precision instruments grew from 22 per cent in the period 1961–65 to 57 per cent in 1976–80 and reached 80 per cent in the 1990 estimate.[5] The share of defence-

---

[2] *Heti Vilaggazdasag*, 28 Nov. 1992; and Babus, E. 'Felfegyverzo mosoly' [Arming smile], *Heti Vilaggazdasag*, 16 Feb. 1991.

[3] *Figyelo*, 14 Feb. 1991. Other sources cite figures between 20 000 and 35 000.

[4] *Figyelo*, 13 Apr. 1990. This list was unusual because light industry was not supposed to be included in calculations of the military sector. Another source quoted different percentages: 66.7% telecommunications electronics and precision instruments, 13.8% vehicles, 10.8% weapons, 6.9% 'other products' and 1.8% ammunition. Csobay, J., 'Valsagban van-e a magyar hadiipar?' [Is the Hungarian defence industry in crisis?], *Vilaggazdasag*, 21 Sep. 1990.

[5] *Figyelo*, 14 Feb. 1991.

related activities was 6 per cent for machinery production and 25–30 per cent for electronics and instrument production.[6]

The dominance of electronic communications equipment and precision instruments within the Hungarian defence industry could in theory have stimulated the production of civilian equipment, creating a positive impact on the development of the entire economy. While the military-related electronics industry absorbed the best engineers and workers and the best technology available, its achievements were not distributed throughout the economy. According to a 1991 report of the Ministry of Industry, the Hungarian electronics industry was characterized by strong vertical integration, weak inter-enterprise cooperation and an underdeveloped subcontractor system.[7]

After 1968—when the first economic reform programme was launched—the Hungarian economy went through multiple, although often contradictory, modifications that moved it towards economic liberalization. However, the defence industry remained almost untouched, a residual from the classic command economy. Its activities were secret. It was managed by detailed five-year plans that were disaggregated into yearly plans with obligatory targets. The fulfilment of the defence industry plan enjoyed priority over other economic goals. Even in periods of progressive reform, special regulations and allowances facilitated implementation of the plan.

After the reorganization of the military industry following the 1956 uprising, all the military producers were subordinated to the Ministry of Industry except for Godolloi Gepgyar, which belonged to the Ministry of Defence. The 20–25 most important factories were under strict state supervision, with managers appointed directly by the Minister of Industry. All other ministries whose activities were connected with military production had a special 'closed department' whose function was to ensure fulfilment of the requirements for military-related activities. These special departments may have had separate funds within the respective ministry's budget. (One common way of hiding military expenditure in the past was to integrate it into other departmental budgets.)

Enterprises engaged in military activity had access to special credits for investment and development with extremely favourable conditions—low interest or in some cases no interest. There were indications that they also received special subsidies to facilitate imports and exports. Military-related research and development (R&D) was lavishly financed by both the central state budget and special funds. Technological innovations and investments were also facilitated by tax allowances. Even in 1990, when the sector's decline had become visible and the entire economy had a serious lack of resources for new investment and R&D, Videoton (one of the largest military producers) still

[6] Kovacs, S., 'A magyar hadiipari tevekenyseg jelene & jovoje' [The present and future of the Hungarian defence industrial activity], Paper presented at a round-table discussion among defence industry producers and customers, Hungarian Ministry of Defence, Budapest, 25 Nov. 1993.

[7] *Figyelo*, 17 Oct. 1991.

applied for a preferential state subsidy for a new military investment.[8] From the early 1980s financial support usually took the form of state-backed preferential credits instead of direct state allowances.

A special heading in the state budget maintained 'cold capacities' in several enterprises—including non-military ones. Cold capacities were unused machinery, reserves and eventually labour that could be mobilized for military purposes at any time. There were no reliable data available for the range of enterprises, the size of the reserves or the costs involved. Another separate budget item of 'several hundred million forints/year' was to finance the maintenance of military reserves.[9] A 1990 regulation authorized the Ministry of Defence and the Ministry of Finance to grant individual authorization to enterprises that wished to sell or lease their unused military capacities, although only a few such transactions took place. The absence of a clearly defined defence doctrine also made it difficult to decide which military capacities and reserves were superfluous.

Military producers could count on stable and massive markets that were ensured by state-guaranteed contracts. These markets were not only predictable but also fairly lucrative, thanks to a particular method of price determination consisting of a personal bargaining process between representatives of the customer and producer. Regardless of costs and productivity, the producers' profit was automatically included in the price. The deal was 'ratified' by a special Military Price Setting Committee. As a whole, the military sector achieved an average profit margin that was 10 per cent higher than that of the civilian producers. This is why enterprises continued to compete for state-backed military orders in the 1980s, when participation in military production ceased to be obligatory.

Workers employed in military-related production received an average 10 per cent 'wage complement' and other privileges that were made possible through special state subsidies provided for the factories. In exchange, to safeguard the secrecy of production, the sector's core workers could not easily change jobs and were rarely allowed to travel to the West. Although administrative restrictions were waived after the 1968 reforms, most of the workers and engineers developed a special loyalty towards military production and were reluctant to leave, even when it was made an easy alternative. Their fidelity was partly due to the material allowances and partly to the extremely good working conditions that offered the possibility for versatile, creative work, which was far from common in the rest of industry.

Military production was partly based on local R&D.[10] According to *International Defense Review* about 30 per cent of production was based on local

---

[8] Although the Ministry of Finance rejected the proposal, the Videoton management mobilized support from the Ministry of Industry and in the end received the money from a commercial bank. Csobay, J., 'Megjegyzesek' [Notes], Unpublished manuscript, Ministry of Finance, Budapest, 1991.

[9] Csobay, J., 'A magyar hadiiparrol, penzugyi szemmel' [The Hungarian defence industry from a financial perspective], *Penzugyi Szemle*, no. 1 (1990).

[10] During the worst years of defence industry crisis most local experts tended to deny that there was any local R&D at all. Some sources claimed that there was no independent research but confirmed local tech-

R&D.[11] Enterprise managers generally confirmed that production was originally based almost exclusively on Soviet licences. Later, as specialization developed within the WTO, in spheres where Hungary was responsible for certain products (principally electronics), local developments became dominant. Modifications and improvements to WTO designs also became significant.

The most important local R&D centres were at enterprises that simultaneously carried out research and short-series production, such as Mechlabor, Tavkozlesi Kutato Intezet (TAKI, Research Institute for Telecommunications) and Merestechnikai, Informatikai, Kutato es Innovacios Reszvenytarsasag (MIKI, Research and Innovation for Measuring and Information Technology). A central research institute specialized in military technology that belonged to the armed forces, Magyar Honvedseg Haditechnikai Intezet (MH HTI, Hungarian Armed Forces Institute for Military Technology), developed a wide range of military products. In addition to electronics and information technology, projects for artillery, vehicle and ammunition production were elaborated as well. This institute was financed directly from the military budget, while the others received their contributions principally from the main state budget. Even in 1991, when the sector was already deep in crisis, the state budget allocated a certain amount of money for military technical development under the heading 'experimental research'.[12] Apart from specific central R&D sources, other agencies (principally branch ministries) financed military-related production and development as well. The Ministry of Industry, for example, had a special fund for allocations of 200–300 million forints per year to military development projects; in 1990 this source was used to finance conversion projects in the amount of 25–30 million forints per project.[13]

Hungarian military production was predominantly geared to exports. In the peak year 1988, 76 per cent of production was exported, 60 per cent of which to the Soviet Union.[14] Arms exports became increasingly important from the mid-1970s. The recipients of Hungarian weaponry were the WTO allies and some 'socialist-minded' developing countries. None of the deals was conducted on a commercial basis. Within the WTO a barter-like commodity exchange system functioned. In the case of Hungary, arms exports were paid for with arms imports, and the balance was made up of other goods—partly military-related and partly civilian.

Although most weapon exchanges functioned on a barter basis within the framework of the WTO, a smaller proportion of the sales gradually became an important source of hard currency. The main customers were countries in the

nological development. Csobay (note 8); Balazsy, S., 'Bekejobb a hadiiparnak' [Peace offer to the defence industry], *Figyelo*, 26 Sep. 1991; and Kovacs, A., 'A leszereles es a haditermeles konverziojanak hatasa a magyar gazdasagra' [The impact of disarmament and defence industry conversion on the Hungarian economy], *Aula*, no. 1 (1991).

[11] Sauerwein, B., 'Hungary's national defense: the taste of freedom', *International Defense Review*, vol. 23, no. 11 (Nov. 1990), p. 1223.

[12] Interview by the author with Jozsef Csobay, Head of Department, Ministry of Finance, Budapest, 30 Mar. 1992.

[13] *Figyelo*, 14 Feb. 1991.

[14] *Heti Vilaggazdasag*, 5 Nov. 1994.

Middle East. Later, because of the political and liquidity problems in that region, countries in the Far East and Western Europe were also targeted. Arms exports were extremely lucrative. In the 1980s in the military sector the forint-to-dollar ratio was 50–60 : 1, while even in the best industrial sectors it was 80–120 : 1.[15]

The requirements of the Hungarian military were met through military sales, mainly to the Soviet Union. Following the rationale of the barter system, prices were kept artificially low in the whole Eastern bloc because 'it was not in our interest to raise export prices, which automatically would have increased the prices of imports'.[16] However, since the volume of WTO exports was large compared to the size of the Hungarian economy, the country had a permanent surplus in its trade with the Soviet Union until the introduction of dollar-based accountancy in 1991. In that year, after long and complicated negotiations, the representatives of the two countries agreed on the size of the debt accumulated during the decades of WTO–CMEA (Council for Mutual Economic Assistance) cooperation. A commercial debt of $1.7 billion owed to Hungary by the former USSR was acknowleged.

Alongside the increasing export orientation of the Hungarian defence industry, the requirements of the local armed forces and the military sector became import-dependent. In 1952, 70 per cent of the needs of the Hungarian military were still covered by the local industry; from the 1970s this percentage dropped to around 30 per cent.

III. Crisis

After the peak in 1988, a drastic reduction in military orders came in 1989, the year considered to mark the end of the cold war. Because of the Hungarian military budget cuts, local consumption declined. Significant military expenditure cuts in the USSR meant a steep decline in orders from Hungary. The Soviet export demand fell from 230 million roubles in 1989 to 128 million roubles in 1990 and to the equivalent of 46 million forints in 1991.[17] Domestic industrial orders fell by 30 per cent in 1989, mainly as a consequence of the contraction of export demand, and decreased by another 50 per cent (from 20 billion to 10 billion forints) between 1989 and 1990.[18]

In expert circles there were discussions about whether it was the decline of the WTO military market or the internal military budget cuts that were mainly responsible for the crisis. Some claimed that the radical cuts in Soviet military orders were a reaction to diminishing import orders on the Hungarian side. The

---

[15] According to Gombos, the ratio was 8–10 times higher in the defence industry, but that seems to have been an overestimate. Gombos, J., *Hungarian Defence Industry: Past, Present and Future* (BITS [Berliner Informationszentrum für Transatlantische Sicherheit]: Berlin, 1994), p. 3.

[16] Interview with Karoly Janza in 'A vedelemgazdasagrol' [About defense economy], *Uj Honvedsegi Szemle*, no.10 (1991).

[17] Since 1 Jan. 1991 foreign trade has been carried out in hard currency among the former socialist countries. *Figyelo*, 14 Feb. 1991

[18] *Figyelo*, 13 Apr. 1989.

Table 5.1. Hungarian military expenditure, 1990–94

Figures for GDP, military expenditure and development are in b. forints, at current prices. Figures in italics are percentages.

	1990	1991	1992	1993	1994
GDP	–	–	2 805	3 320	3 955
Military expenditure	46.2	54.4	60.8	64.5	66.5
Share of GDP (%)	–	–	*2.16*	*1.9*	*1.6*
Development	9.8	6.4	6.8	4.9	5.9
Share of development (%)	*21.2*	*11.8*	*11.2*	*7.6*	*8.9*
Share of maintenance (%)	*78.8*	*88.2*	*88.8*	*92.4*	*91.1*

Source: Adapted from *Nepszava*, 11 Apr. 1994.

truth was probably that the combined effect of these simultaneous processes shook the sector. In addition, this took place together with the unexpectedly quick collapse of the civilian market of the CMEA, which made it difficult for military-related enterprises to compensate for losses with increased civilian production.

Military expenditure was radically reduced after 1990 as part of the macro-economic stabilization and demilitarization effort. Despite these cuts and serious efforts to promote transparency, there were still some additional sources of military expenditure: the state budget was readjusted each year in the period 1990–94, and each time additional funding was allocated to the military. In addition, part of the allocation in the defence budget was used for financial speculation which, until it was discovered, increased the expenditure for military purposes.

In 1992 a State Audit Office investigation revealed that between 1987 and 1990 the Ministry of Defence had accumulated unspent budget allocations in undeclared bank accounts and had used them for a variety of purposes.[19] In an interview with the Hungarian armed forces weekly publication, Gabor Moricz (then Deputy Chief Economist at the Ministry of Defence) stated that the ministry had also accumulated funds from sales of property (including arms) that had been used to purchase state bonds. These had been subsequently resold at a profit and the revenue distributed between the Ministry of Defence and the headquarters of the armed forces to provide, for example, additional food and clothing for employees and servicemen.[20]

Another element that pushed defence enterprises into the crisis was the abrupt withdrawal of what had been almost unconditional official backing. The most important change after 1989–90 was the reorganization of the sector's management. Until 1989 military production was supervised by a special Defence

[19] *Nepszava*, 28 Feb. 1992. According to FIDESZ (Fiatal Demokratak Szovetsege, or Alliance of Young Democrats) Member of Parliament Tamas Wachsler, this practice continued into 1991. Wachsler, T., 'A miniszter csak hallgat' [The minister is just silent], *Nepszabadsag*, 24 Feb. 1992; and Interview with Wachsler in *Beszelo*, 7 Mar. 1992.

[20] Interview with Gabor Moricz in *Magyar Honved*, 7 June 1991.

Committee. After the political changes a small Coordinating Bureau, responsible to the Council of Ministers, took over this function. The Price Setting Committee together with other institutions and special regulations that formerly guaranteed the military sector's privileged position were abolished. Ministries and other central state organizations that had formerly lavishly supported defence enterprises apparently became reluctant to provide them with backing and resources.

In 1989–90 minor changes began to take place in the performance of the sector and production became slightly more concentrated. In 1989 the 17 main producers provided 96 per cent of total military output (up from 93 per cent). However, individual enterprise performance suggested that 1989 was not (or was not considered) a crisis year for them. Two enterprises increased their military production while cutting back on civilian output, 4 decreased their military output by over 10 per cent, and 13 increased their civilian production, most of these enterprises by over 10 per cent.[21]

The slow reaction of enterprises was strange, considering that even their supervising authorities had urged a thorough adjustment of the sector in the mid-1980s. They expected a major restructuring within the WTO and growing competition among 'brother' countries that showed clear signs of dissent concerning the existing division of labour and specialization patterns. Defence enterprises might have predicted the approaching collapse of the CMEA markets as well, since they experienced signs of a crisis in the strictly military-related trade that was the core of CMEA activities.[22]

Apparently, defence producers did not feel or did not want to recognize that the external conditions were changing dramatically. Whether they still enjoyed protection (like most state enterprises in the absence of a genuine bankruptcy law) and hoped to continue or whether they were driven by sheer inertia is difficult to tell. By reacting promptly to the gathering signs of crisis, defence producers might have avoided the devastating crisis or at least smothered its effect. Their inability to react led to a dramatic collapse between 1990 and 1992 from which the sector never fully recovered.

The exact scale of the reduction in output is presented somewhat differently in different sources. According to data published in 1994, 40 enterprises had a military output of 21 billion forints and employed 30 000 people in 1988; this represented 2.5 per cent of total output from the processing industry. By 1990 output had dropped to 9.3 billion forints, of which almost 50 per cent was exported.[23] By 1993 production had fallen to a value of 6.7 billion forints, of which 1.4 billion forints was exported.[24] According to Istvan Szarka, then

[21] Csobay (note 9).
[22] *Figyelo*, 14 Feb. 1991.
[23] The total value of export was $60 million, or roughly 4.8 billion forints at the $1 : 80 forints exchange rate of the time.
[24] *Heti Vilaggazdasag*, 5 Nov. 1994.

Table 5.2. The main indicators of Hungarian military production, 1988 and 1991

	1988	1991
Output (b. forints)	20	3.6
Employed (1000s)	35	6.3
Enterprises (number)	45	45
Share of military production in the output of these enterprises (%)	20	4.7
Share of military production in industry (%)	3	0.5

Source: Data from the Military Industrial Office, in *Heti Vilaggazdasag,* 28 Nov. 1992.

Director of the Military Industrial Office (MIO), 95 per cent of the output of 6 billion forints in 1993 was exported.[25]

A report prepared for the Chamber of Commerce in 1990 stated that the then 38 core military enterprises had unfulfilled production obligations worth 10 billion forints (that were supposed to pay for development loans received previously), unused productive capacity and unsold products worth 1.5–7 billion forints, 6000 workers to dismiss and a total of 2.9 billion forints in debt. Two enterprises had already gone bankrupt and the rest faced dim prospects.[26]

A 1991 report concluded that the two largest military producers—Videoton (35 per cent military production, producing telecommunications equipment)[27] and Finommechanika (69 per cent, producing telecommunications and precision instruments)—which together were responsible for over 50 per cent of total military production in 1988, had already gone bankrupt and were in the process of liquidation. Three other major companies—Labor MIM (49 per cent, producing instruments), MN Godolloi Gepgyar (100 per cent, producing vehicles) and PVG (60 per cent, producing vehicles)—had recently gone bankrupt and were facing liquidation.

Three enterprises managed to avoid the crisis—Danuvia (14 per cent, producing hand weapons), Bakony Fem (11 per cent, ammunition) and Gamma (26 per cent, telecommunications electronics). They all cut back military production radically. The only enterprise that seemed not to suffer major shocks until 1991 was Mechanikai Labor (82 per cent, telecommunications and electronic instruments).[28]

The first dramatic drop in Hungarian military production was followed by a rapid erosion of the sector's productive assets. Between 1990 and 1994, while struggling with the consequences of the fall in production, defence enterprises

[25] Szarka, I., 'Fejlesztesi iranyok, konverzio es kooperacio a magyar hadiiparban' [Development trends, conversion and cooperation in the Hungarian defence industry], Paper presented at the Conference on Defence Industry Conversion and International Cooperation, Budapest, 26 Nov. 1993. Basic data on the military sector kept changing during the crisis years. In 1993–94, e.g., several officials in charge of the sector quoted record production of 30 billion forints for 1988.

[26] *Vilaggazdasag*, 10 Aug. 1990.

[27] The numbers in parentheses show the share of military output in the overall production of the enterprise in 1988 and their main sphere of activity.

[28] Eller, E., 'Volt, nincs hadiipar' [Has been, is no more], *Figyelo*, 14 Feb. 1991; and Csobay (note 8).

were thrown into chaos by administrative reorganization, decentralization and changes in their legal form. Most went through several stages of decentralization and internal reorganization and became partially commercialized or entirely privatized. Because of the institutional insecurity and enterprise inertia, it usually took a very long time to make basic decisions about restructuring and ownership changes. The prolonged 'privatization agony' and their insecure official status made most defence enterprises postpone other strategic decisions as well, thus contributing to their worsening performance.

In spite of the serious crisis, relatively few enterprises closed down and/or liquidated their military-related productive capacities completely. This led to an enormous waste and a rapid amortization of preserved but unused fixed assets. By the end of 1993 the sector was utilizing 20 per cent of its production capacities.

IV. The new policy on defence industry and arms exports

The dramatic collapse of the Hungarian defence industry was not 'conversion'. Conversion was suggested to companies by their supervising authorities, but it was not genuinely promoted officially. Modest amounts of funding were allocated by the Ministry of Finance that enterprises could apply for in order to complement financing of conversion projects. According to Jozsef Csobay of the Ministry of Finance, not even these funds were used by the enterprises, which did not have feasible conversion projects.[29] In the first years after the change of the political system the defence industry was simply not on the official agenda. Military enterprises were left to fend for themselves, without state guidelines about the direction they were supposed to take. Their insecurity was emphasized by the fact that key legislation—for example, the new Law on Defence, laws on the arms trade and modernization of the armed forces, and regulations concerning cold capacities and military-related reserves—took a very long time to enact.[30]

After a relatively short interval, signs of a new government policy appeared in late 1991. In May 1990 Minister of Defence Lajos Fur said in an interview that Hungary did not need an independent defence industry because it could satisfy national requirements with arms imports.[31] A year later he stressed the need for a modernized Hungarian arms industry that could supply the army.[32] At a September 1991 conference organized by the University of Economics in Budapest, representatives of the defence industry called for intense state intervention. They argued that at least 30 per cent of the requirements of the Hungarian armed forces should be met by local production. To be able to achieve this goal, among others, they asked the Ministry of Finance to write off their bad debts and the Ministry of Industry and Commerce to select and protect

---

[29] Csobay (note 8).
[30] The Law on Defence and the regulations about reserves and cold capacities were introduced in 1993.
[31] *Magyar Nemzet*, 30 May 1990.
[32] *Heti Vilaggazdasag*, 20 Apr. 1991.

8–10 defence producers and liberalize the arms trade. Detailed plans to set up a military–industrial holding were also presented.[33]

These demands demonstrated that the 'shock therapy' implemented through market forces did not teach the sector important lessons about adjustment. Instead of elaborating efficient restructuring or conversion projects, most enterprises were eager to reproduce the old model of a closed military sector characterized by captive markets, direct state protection and dependence. They could make good use of the government's increasingly nationalist ideology and its ambitions to re-centralize both economic and political life.

On 1 January 1992 Government Decree No. 85/1992 established the Military Industrial Office to coordinate and promote military production and related activities in Hungary. This independent, civilian agency was financed directly from the budget of the Prime Minister's Office, and its director, Jeno Laszlo, held the rank of state secretary. The office was expected to act 'above' the branch ministries, coordinating their activities in order to rescue the Hungarian defence industry.

One major MIO project was to establish a military industrial holding. The assets of 10 main military producers were to be transferred from the state supervisory agencies to which they belonged to a central state-owned military industrial holding, under the supervision of the MIO. The 10 chosen enterprises were to become the core of the renewed Hungarian defence industry. The entire project was to be financed directly from the state budget and from other, independent sources, such as the Fund for Technical Innovation. According to the MIO proposals, by 1994 military output was to have reached 10–20 billion forints and employment 20 000 people. At a later stage, according to Laszlo's ambitious plans, output was to increase to 200–250 billion forints.[34]

Even though this plan was hotly contested by experts and the broader public, according to Laszlo the organizational–structural conditions for establishing the holding had already been created and members in crucial positions in the cabinet had pledged their support for the plan. Before the project was carried out, however, the governing MDF Party went through a major internal crisis as a result of which it purged its most extreme right wing. Laszlo, who voiced the aspirations of this conservative, nationalist faction, was sacrificed in these internal power struggles and dismissed in June 1993.[35] The MIO, as an independent government agency, was dissolved, and some of its personnel and its functions were transferred to the Ministry of Industry and Trade. Although it preserved its title, it became a department of the ministry, with limited administrative power and financial resources.

The MIO recovered relatively quickly from this shock. By the end of the year it was the main organizer of a large-scale ECE defence industry exhibition and conference aimed at boosting Hungarian arms sales and cooperation with for-

---

[33] *Heti Vilaggazdasag*, 21 Sep. 1992.
[34] Interview with Jeno Laszlo, *Nepszava*, 21 Apr. 1993.
[35] He became a leading figure in the extremist nationalist 'Hungarian way'.

eign, principally Western and Russian, firms.[36] After further changes in leadership, the MIO seemed to fill rather efficient coordinating and lobbying functions within and for the Hungarian defence industry.[37]

In October 1994 a new project prepared by the MIO was published. The document asked for an emergency financial infusion of 15.5 billion forints to rescue the sector. By comparison, the entire military budget for the year was 66.5 billion forints. The document listed 59 enterprises that were involved in defence-related production and were proposed to receive special state protection—17 of these firms provided 77 per cent of total national military output and 93 per cent of military exports. Most of the companies were created from the vestiges of former core defence enterprises that split into several smaller units. According to the document, state-backed orders financed (partly or entirely) from the state budget could still save the enterprises from definitive bankruptcy. The authors claimed that the proposal was supported by the Ministry of Industry and Trade, the Ministry of Defence and the Ministry of Interior.[38]

After publication of the document, the project was criticized by several state agencies, including officials of the Ministry of Finance. Less than a month later MIO Director Janos Isaszegi was removed because he had 'lost the Ministry's confidence'. The MIO was again reorganized and the new Director, Bela Takacs, was transferred from the Ministry of Defence. According to Jozsef Hegyhati, Deputy State Secretary, who commented on the case, a programme on the reconstruction and development of the defence industry had already been prepared but had not been submitted to the government because the ministries affected had completely opposing ideas about it.[39]

While the efforts of the MIO to rescue and revamp Hungarian military production seemed to run into political and economic obstacles and its large-scale reorganization plans were systematically refused, a considerable amount of efficient work was devoted to preserving and rehabilitating what was left of the defence industry. Officials in the MIO as well as in the Ministry of Defence and the Ministry of Foreign Economic Relations were helping the sector's troubled enterprises to survive. The Ministry of Foreign Economic Relations tried to organize deals and represent Hungarian enterprises in international negotiations. However, coordination between these government bodies appeared to be somewhat obstructed and in several cases there was open hostility.

The strictly military power centres—the Ministry of Defence and the headquarters of the armed forces—seemed to follow their own agenda, notwithstanding other state agencies' ambitions and efforts. The Ministry of Defence

---

[36] The exhibition was originally organized together with a major conversion conference, but in the absence of interest in conversion the latter was converted into a half-day Seminar on Defence and Conversion Issues.

[37] The most awkward incident took place just before the exhibition opened, exactly as with the RDP Group in the Czech Republic. A scandal at the Technika Foreign Trade company, one of the major exhibitors, made necessary urgent personnel changes. Szarka was appointed director of Technika and Hamar was appointed director in charge of the MIO.

[38] *Heti Vilaggazdasag*, 5 Nov. 1994.

[39] *Nepszabadsag*, 18 Nov. 1994.

concentrated on its immediate needs without considering the interests of the defence industry as a whole. It united under ministry ownership five minor enterprises that were considered indispensable for the functioning of the armed forces. The selection seemed to be rather erratic. For example, PVG (the only aircraft and helicopter repair company) was not included. When foreign and Hungarian privateers wanted to buy the plant, the ministry 'woke up' and vetoed the deal. The controversy between representatives of the Ministry of Defence and other ministries surfaced in an apparently theoretical discussion about the economic importance of the defence industry. While the MIO and ministry officials tended to claim that military production was a crucial, dynamic production branch, representatives of the Ministry of Defence insisted that it was not and had never been so important.[40]

Facing increasing institutional chaos, it seemed that the Ministry of Defence found it important to keep military-related enterprises under state control. In the early 1990s it opposed privatization in the sector but was unable to prevent it. By the end of 1993 it consented to partial privatization, with the conditions that no major military supplier would become entirely foreign-owned, that companies established or taken over by the Ministry of Defence would remain state property, and that, even in cases of complete privatization, the successor firms would be obliged to fulfil inherited military obligations and maintain cold capacities.[41]

In addition to inter-ministerial conflicts, there were also tensions between enterprises and the Ministry of Defence. The major conflicts between military producers and the ministry were related to the facts that the ministry did not accept or pay for some products ordered, that the list of cold capacities was outdated and that the army failed to make public its detailed modernization programme. Enterprise managers found it offensive that, even with very limited resources, the military managed to purchase new equipment without having considered offers from the domestic industry and its opportunity to cooperate in maintaining and servicing the new weaponry.

A third power centre was represented by the state asset managing and privatization agencies and their allies that pushed alternately for rapid privatization and keeping the enterprises under state (i.e., their own) control. In the enthusiasm for privatization the only significant producer of heavy weaponry, Diosgyori Gepgyar (DIGEP), was sold at a rock-bottom price to private entrepreneurs of uncertain background. At the same time the efficient privatization of several companies was blocked because of the agencies' particular interests. In the case of PVG-Dunai Repulogepgyar, for example, the supervising company Allami Vagyonkezelo Rt (AVRt, State Property Management Ltd)—a state holding company set up in 1992 to manage enterprises that were not

[40] Kovacs (note 6); Szarka, I., 'Fejlesztesi iranyok, konverzio es kooperacio a magyar hadiiparban' [Development trends, conversion and cooperation in the Hungarian defence industry], Paper presented at the Conference on Defence Industry Conversion and International Cooperation, Budapest, 26 Nov. 1993; and Interview with Jeno Laszlo (note 34).

[41] Kovacs (note 6).

scheduled to be privatized in the medium or long term—obstructed genuine privatization, causing serious economic losses and cancellation of deals, while in the case of TAKI, AVRt seemed to act as a reasonable and efficient owner.

A major issue of clashing interests between state agencies was privatization. In the first enthusiasm for privatization immediately after the political turnover, defence enterprises were to be privatized quickly, without special considerations. One enterprise, the Gamma electronics factory, even appeared in the list of 20 state-owned enterprises included in the government's first showcase Privatization Programme in September 1990. Some time later it was decided that military-related firms would not be privatized immediately.

Because of the administrative and ownership changes they had gone through between 1990 and 1994, defence enterprises were supervised by different, sometimes new power centres that often had clashing interests. Some companies were transferred to AVRt while others were put under the jurisdiction of Allami Vagyonugynokseg (AVU, otherwise known as SPA, the State Property Agency), which was supposed to privatize them as soon as possible. The selection of firms to be privatized promptly or to be 'protected' by the state was fairly arbitrary, and enterprises and their supervising authorities engaged in intense bargaining over getting their names on or off the lists.

Since many military producers were bankrupt, they were put under the supervision of a liquidation agency—most often Reorg, a commercialized state-owned agency in charge of managing the liquidation process. As mentioned above, a few companies were taken over by the Ministry of Defence. By mid-1994 the only company under the supervision of the Ministry of Industry and Trade was the Matrafem ammunition factory, which was simply forgotten and remained a classic state-owned enterprise. Apart from this anachronism, the MIO could give advice and present proposals but did not have ownership rights.

Some enterprises were partly or completely privatized. There were cases in which privatization brought a formal change of legal status without major restructuring and other cases in which it led to genuine transformations. In some cases privatization was the means used to get rid of the then burdensome military production and in others it was a way to preserve military production in the hope of future orders and state support. In some cases state supervision through liquidation or privatization agencies blocked efficient decision making and prolonged the agony of the enterprises, while in others it guaranteed the company's survival and future restructuring.

Arguments presented in support of the defence industry

The protagonists in the Hungarian military sector engaged in fierce political struggles, but they all believed in the necessity to revive the defence industry. Some argued that Hungary needed modern and efficient armed forces to defend itself since it was located in the centre of a volatile region, emphasizing the 'Slovak threat' and the Yugoslav conflict. Another argument was that Hungarian membership of NATO required a modernized army. The economic arguments cited elaborate calculations of the high opportunity costs of revamping local defence industry as against importing weapons and the alleged positive linkages between the development of the defence industry and the wider economy. The defence industry was still considered an indisputable technological leader of economic development. It was supposed to create (or preserve) jobs in the high-unemployment Hungarian economy and was expected to help balance the state budget since its revenues would increase taxes.

Arms sales would provide the country with badly needed hard-currency income. In an interview held in late 1990, Minister of Defence Fur mentioned the possibility that the military industry could be revived in areas where profitable export products—for example, military vehicles—could be found.[42]

The political changes that took place in 1989–90 brought a re-evaluation of the arms trade by politicians and economic decision makers. According to the new view, arms are products like anything else on the market, independent of any moral or political considerations. One expert observed: 'Why should we not sell weapons to our neighbours if it is a profitable business? The income could be used for military development, which would strengthen us, and the buyers' need of spare parts would make them dependent on us'.[43] Parallel to the general liberalization of the economy, about 30 companies (both state-owned and private) were given a licence to trade arms. Technika, the state arms trading organization, was also undergoing a complicated process of decentralization and commercialization. According to Regulation No. 99/1990 of the Council of Ministers, every arms deal had to be approved by a special committee that included the highest-level representatives of the Ministries of Foreign Trade, Defence, Foreign Affairs and Interior, and the State Secretary of the National Security Office.

The proximity of Hungary to regions of ongoing conflicts, the inefficiency of the internal security forces and the high profitability of arms sales might explain why the illegal arms trade blossomed in the mid-1990s. Unofficial sources also point to the withdrawing Soviet forces as having been deeply involved in arms sales, following the tradition of selling food and other goods on the black market. Most of this business was run by private individuals who were difficult to stop or prosecute.

After 1989 'reform-minded' military budgets prescribed that a proportion of the maintenance of the armed forces should be self-financed.[44] According to an anonymous military expert, most of the income generated by the armed forces derived from arms sales. These sales were usually made using licences to export arms to distant developing countries (although it is suspected that in reality some sales were made to neighbouring countries). Moreover, civilian trading companies required expertise which could only come from the military.[45]

---

[42] *International Defense Review*, vol. 23, no. 8 (Aug. 1990), p. 833.

[43] Interview with Atilla Kovacs in *Magyar Hirlap*, 10 Oct. 1990.

[44] In 1989, e.g., 4.5 billion forints were expected to be raised from the armed forces' commercial activity. In that year, according to non-Hungarian sources, the country earned about $1 million from selling military products made superfluous due to the disarmament process. *Jane's Defence Weekly*, 14 July 1990.

[45] *Nepszava*, 19 Feb. 1992.

Several incidents revealed the difficulties with export licensing and executing export contracts in ECE countries during the early 1990s. In a case made public in December 1991, a significant shipment intended for Nigeria was stolen in the Polish port of Gdynia.[46] In another case, revealed by accident, a shipment of several million dollars worth of arms labelled as 'hospital equipment' and sent from Chile was detected at Budapest airport *en route* to an unspecified destination. According to the results of investigations, an international network of arms dealers was involved in the business.[47] The worst incident was the infamous sale of 10 000 Kalashnikov assault rifles to Croatian forces at the beginning of the war in Yugoslavia. The deal was concluded in spite of the 1990 regulation which forbade arms sales to countries at war or in crisis areas. To make the matter worse, high-level Hungarian state officials were involved in and tried to cover up the whole affair.[48]

Despite the fact that the Hungarian armed forces had very limited resources for new purchases, they received some major inputs. For example, during a visit to Budapest in November 1992 President Boris Yeltsin promised that Russia would assume the debts of the former Soviet Union. Part of the debt to Hungary would be paid with military equipment and spare parts, including 28 MiG-29 fighter aircraft, valued at about 66.3 billion forints—equivalent to almost the entire Hungarian military budget for 1992.[49]

Another major free military acquisition came from the arsenals of the former German Democratic Republic (GDR). Although these weapons were produced under Soviet licences, they were more advanced than those in the Hungarian Army thanks to the special status the GDR enjoyed within the WTO as a 'shop-window' for socialism. Hungary exploited the goodwill created by Budapest's role in the German unification process and requested arms from Bonn one month before unification. By November 1992, after several declarations and refutations, it was confirmed that Germany would present Hungary with an unspecified amount of unused military spare parts to improve the country's defence capabilities.[50]

V. Defence enterprises: the history of disintegration

The disintegration and partial transformation of the Hungarian defence industry can be followed through the history of individual enterprises. Table 5.3 lists the most important defence enterprises in Hungary in 1988–89 and the main changes in their activities by 1991 and table 5.4 the major enterprises in 1988, illustrating the discrepancies in official data.

[46] *Nepszabadsag*, 9 Dec. 1991.
[47] *Nepszava*, 6 Aug. 1992 and 25 Jan. 1993.
[48] *Tallozo*, 13 Feb. 1992.
[49] *Heti Vilaggazdasag*, 21 and 28 Nov. 1992.
[50] Radio Free Europe/Radio Liberty (RFE/RL), *RFE/RL Research Report*, vol. 1, no. 33 (21 Aug. 1992), p. 61, and vol. 1, no. 38 (25 Sep. 1992), p. 59; *Neue Zürcher Zeitung*, 18–19 Oct. 1992, p. 4; and *Süddeutsche Zeitung*, 16 Oct. 1992, p. 2.

By the end of 1994 all these companies had drastically reduced their military-related output and workforce. One—Labor MIM—had been liquidated, and two others—Bakony Muvek and Danuvia—had ceased all military-related production, selling or liquidating their capacities. Bakony became a specialist producer of spare parts for the automobile industry and was sold to the company's management and employees. Danuvia was divided into the parent company and a new joint venture with German capital. Both these successor companies, particularly the Hungarian parent enterprise, were facing serious difficulties in 1994.

The companies that retained a military profile and remained the same entity included both state-owned and private firms. Matrafem was still a classic state-owned enterprise. It was divided into a civilian division, which was privatized, and a military division, which was waiting for permission to be commercialized and to create a joint venture for military ammunition production together with a US company. After a lengthy reorganization and transformation, the weapon-producing division of Fegyver es Gazkeszulekgyar (FEG, Armaments and Gas Appliances Factory) was separated from the main enterprise and became a state-owned limited company. It was one of the most successful Hungarian military producers, principally producing for export. A successor firm that specialized in gas boiler and heating equipment was sold to Hungarian private entrepreneurs, while another, the foundry, became a German–Hungarian joint venture.[51]

Telefongyar formed a joint venture with Siemens in which the German company controlled 66 per cent of the shares. After a long and expensive liquidation process, Gamma had by January 1994 become a joint venture, with 30 per cent US and 70 per cent Hungarian private capital. TAKI was still 100 per cent state-owned under AVRt supervision. The other major telecommunications equipment producer, Budapesti Hiradastechnikai Gyar (BHG, Budapest Telecommunications Factory), was still in the process of restructuring and reorganization under AVU ownership.

Orion was an example of a company that managed to survive the collapse in military production but went bankrupt because of the abrupt import liberalization that crowded out Hungarian consumer goods from the shrinking domestic market. The enterprise succeeded in shifting to a civilian profile after losing its profitable WTO market. However, it was unable to compete with Western producers of television, video and other telecommunications equipment. In late 1993 it was bought with Russian private capital; the new joint venture became 83 per cent Russian property and was renamed Yuganskorion.[52]

[51] *Nepszabadsag*, 17 Apr. 1993; and Interview by the author with Istvan Kemencei, Managing Director of FEG, Budapest, 8 Oct. 1993.

[52] *Nepszabadsag*, 20 June 1991; *Heti Vilaggazdasag*, 11 Jan. 1992; and Kiss, M., *Orion: A Marketing Case Study* (Privatization Research Institute: Budapest, 1993).

Table 5.3. Military production as a share of total production in the main Hungarian defence enterprises, 1988–89

Figures are percentages.

Enterprise	Share of enterprise mil. production 1988	Share of total mil. production 1988	Share of enterprise mil. production 1989	Status in 1991
Artillery and infantry weapons: 10.8% (1988)				
DIGEP	29.3	6.7	18.9	Bankrupt
FEG	17.5	3.3	11.2	In crisis
Danuvia	14.0	0.8	–	Survived
Ammunition: 1.8%				
Bakony Muvek	10.7	0.9	–	Survived
Matrafem	8.2	0.9	–	In crisis
Telecommunications, precision instruments: 66.7% (1988)				
Gamma	26.2	1.9	9.8	Survived
MOM	12.2	1.2	–	In crisis
Finommechanikai	79.4	16.8	73.9	Insecure
Orion	13.1	0.4	–	In crisis
Videoton	35.3	34.9	28.8	Insecure
BHG	10.5	2.8	–	In crisis
Mechlabor	82.2	6.5	68.9	Solvent
TAKI	42.5	1.7	–	In crisis
Telefongyar	7.1	0.5	–	Bankrupt
Vehicles: 13.8% (1988)				
Labor MIM	49.1	1.9	–	Bankrupt
Pestvideki	59.7	4.5	40.6	Bankrupt
MN Godolloi	100.0	7.4	–	Bankrupt
Other companies: 6.9% (1988)				

Sources: For cols 2 and 3 (1988): Csobay, J., 'A magyar hadiiparrol, penzugyi szemmel' [The Hungarian defence industry from a financial perspective], *Penzugyi Szemle*, no. 1 (1990); for col. 4 (1989): Csobay, J., 'Valsagban van-e a magyar hadiipar?' [Is the Hungarian defence industry in crisis?], *Vilaggazdasag*, 21 Sep. 1990; and for col. 5 (1991): Eller, E., 'Volt, nincs hadiipar' [Has been, is no more], *Figyelo*, 14 Feb. 1991.

Among the companies in the process of liquidation and/or reorganization, the most unusual case was that of PVG. The enterprise enjoyed a monopoly position in Hungary, providing repairs for military aircraft and helicopters, and had the potential to cater to the entire East European market. PVG was located near a former Soviet military air base which could have been transformed into a civilian airport. The company had gone bankrupt by June 1990 and was scheduled to be liquidated by Reorg. In February 1991 Line Up, a British firm, won the tender to buy PVG but did not have the money to pay for it. In March 1992 the Eldorado Foundation, representing a group of private persons and

Table 5.4. Military production as a share of total production in the main Hungarian defence enterprises, 1988

Figures are percentages.

Enterprise	Production	Rouble exports	Dollar exports	Domestic sales	Share of mil. production in total turnover
Artillery and infantry weapons	*10.8*	*9.3*	*15.2*	*14.4*	–
DIGEP	6.7	9.3	1.8	0.0	26.4
FEG	3.3	0.0	11.9	11.3	22.8
Danuvia	0.8	0.0	1.5	3.1	15.8
Ammunition	*1.8*	*0.1*	*4.2*	*6.5*	–
Bakony Muvek	0.9	0.1	0.0	3.9	10.7
Matrafem	0.9	0.0	4.2	2.6	7.4
Telecommunications, instruments	*66.7*	*80.7*	*63.8*	*24.5*	–
Gamma	1.9	2.2	0.4	1.1	27.9
MOM	1.2	1.5	0.3	0.6	12.4
FMV	16.8	19.5	26.6	6.5	77.6
Orion	0.4	0.0	1.9	1.3	12.7
Videoton	34.9	46.4	14.2	3.5	33.7
BHG	2.8	1.5	9.4	4.9	13.6
Mechlabor	6.5	7.3	10.9	5.1	81.8
TAKI	1.7	1.9	0.1	0.9	45.2
Telefongyar	0.5	0.4	0.0	0.6	6.3
Vehicles	*13.8*	*9.9*	*3.9*	*27.6*	–
Labor MIM	1.9	1.2	0.0	3.8	44.0
Pestvideki	4.5	3.2	0.7	8.1	67.2
MN Godolloi	7.4	5.5	3.2	15.7	100.0
Other companies	*6.9*	*0.0*	*12.9*	*27.0*	–

Total employment:	30 713[a]
Employed in manufacturing (%):	2.7
Employed in instruments and telecommunications sector (%):	20

[a] Total number of full- and part-time employees.

Source: Hethy, L., Szabo, J. and Ungvar, G., 'Defence conversion and economic transformation in Hungary', Paper presented at the NATO Central and Eastern Europe Defence Conversion Seminar, Brussels, 20–22 May 1992.

entrepreneurs who came together to promote 'youth culture and sporting activity', won the new open tender for the company.

The Parliamentary Defence Committee and the Ministry of Defence protested against privatizing such a crucial military enterprise. When the Eldorado Foundation's financial assets were scrutinized, it turned out that it did not have sufficient capital and was probably acting on behalf of an unspecified foreign interest group. This deal was cancelled and, in June 1992, 572 of the former workforce of 945 created Dunai Repulogepgyar in order to manage the company until it was finally liquidated or sold. In the meantime, 25 per cent of the ordinary shares and a 2 per cent 'golden share' of the company's assets were transferred to AVRt, to preserve the state shareholding and its decisive influence over major decisions. By the end of 1994 Dunai Repulogepgyar had become a fairly successful private company, but business and legal difficulties with its state supervising agency, AVRt, and the parent company (basically an administrative centre) hindered its further development.[53]

The history of DIGEP showed how a combination of external and internal factors led to the bankruptcy and liquidation of Hungary's only heavy weapon end-producer and the risks of hasty, unfounded privatization policy. Because of the stricter economic regulations and higher production costs, the first economic difficulties of DIGEP had appeared by mid-1988, before the crisis in the military sector became visible. The firm issued bonds to generate resources for a civilian restructuring programme. In 1989 the contraction of Soviet export orders dealt a new blow and in 1989 military production at the enterprise shrank by over 40 per cent, although total production fell by only 2.5 per cent thanks to a 14.1 per cent increase in civilian output. Fighting bankruptcy, the enterprise management tried to issue more bonds and attract foreign capital. However, the loss of civilian export opportunities, the contraction of the domestic market and internal difficulties in the enterprise management led to bankruptcy in 1990.

After a two-year liquidation process, DIGEP was divided into a military division and several civilian divisions. The military division had no orders, but it was not liquidated and civilian production had to maintain it. The civilian divisions produced spare parts for, among others, Volvo, Fiat–Iveco and US firms. The company's military products included an automatic mortar which it had developed and which experts considered a potential export success.[54]

The enterprise's privatization was a stunning example of the contrasting interests of different government agencies. In March 1993 Reorg sold the military division to Hungarian private entrepreneurs without preserving the minimum 10 per cent state ownership in defence-related firms specified by the regulations at the time. In addition, the background of the buyers turned out to be insecure. Two entrepreneurs established a small private company with the minimum amount of capital necessary to take over DIGEP. They changed the name of the company to Army-Coop. The purchase price and the new investments promised were to be paid by their partners (owners of a dubious Russian–British joint venture). The deal and subsequent conflicts between the new owners and Hungarian officials caused serious controversies in military circles.

Since the enterprise's products promised an export potential, the Ministry of Foreign Economic Relations and the MIO tried to facilitate entry into the US market and organize one of the remaining ammunition companies to produce

---

[53] To make things more complicated, Dunai bought up a large part of the parent company's debts and became one of the owners of the enterprise, from which it leased its capital and workers. *Figyelo*, 23 Jan. 1992; *Figyelo*, 11 Feb. 1993; and Interview by the author with Dr Geza Peter Kovacs, President-Director of Dunai Repulogepgyar, Csepel, Hungary, 15 Apr. 1994.

[54] *Figyelo*, 13 Apr. 1989, 14 Feb. 1991, 23 Dec. 1992, and 4 Mar. 1993.

mortar ammunition. The MIO at the same time fought to get back at least a 10 per cent shareholding but seemed to be unable to mobilize the necessary resources. The Ministry of Defence declared that, as it did not need the company's products, it did not care about the fate of the enterprise.

The history of Videoton (which used to be the largest military producer in Hungary in terms of value added), located in Szekesfehervar, was another example of the partial re-emergence of the Hungarian defence industry. In the past, roughly one-third of the enterprise's output had been military, one-third consisted of civilian computers, and the rest was other consumer electronic products. Despite several warning signs of an approaching crisis in the late 1980s, Videoton increased its military output in 1989. Neither the enterprise management nor the supervising authorities were able to elaborate a viable company strategy. Videoton went bankrupt in 1991.

For over two years the policy was characterized by hesitation and capricious changes from privatization to decentralization, sell-off or direct supervision, during which time the company's assets eroded dramatically and the best of its qualified workforce left. In the tender announced in October 1991 the total sum offered for Videoton was 1.2 billion forints, although its book value was 14.5 billion forints. Its total debt was 25 billion forints. A consortium of Hungarian private entrepreneurs finally bought what was left of the company for 4 billion forints, with credits and majority participation of the largest state-owned commercial bank, Magyar Hitelbank (MHB, Hungarian Credit Bank). In 1991 it was declared that Videoton would halt military production but, according to later plans, at least 20–30 per cent of the total output would be military. The new owners planned to build up wide-scale international cooperation in assembly work. Partners included the countries of the former Soviet Union as well as several Western partners—principally Austria, France, Germany, Japan, Scandinavian countries and the USA. In 1994 the company employed 5000 and planned to employ several hundred more.

The restructuring of Videoton proved to be a success. In 1993 it produced a modest profit and had become so strong that it could commission Rendszertechnika to reorganize the remainder of the Hungarian military electronics sector. Videoton acted as a primary contractor and coordinated and financed large-scale military projects, mainly for export. According to a contract signed in 1993, Videoton-Rendszertechnika also became a certified supplier for the Hungarian armed forces. Among its large-scale plans were those to establish further joint ventures with foreign partners and to expand in both civilian and military electronics, in the telecommunications industry and possibly enter the transport sector as well.[55] By late 1994 the holding consisted of 23 limited companies, joint ventures and other forms of business corporations of which one, Rendszertechnika, was specialized in military production.

[55] Interview by the author with Megyeri Sandor, Managing Director of Videoton System-Technics Ltd, Szekesfehervar, Hungary, 8 Apr. 1994; *Heti Vilaggazdasag*, 14 Dec. 1991; *Beszelo*, 5 Oct. 1991, and 1 Feb. 1992; *Magyar Hirlap*, 22 Oct. 1992; *Heti Vilaggazdasag*, 24 Apr. 1993; *Heti Vilaggazdasag*, 14 Dec. 1991; and *Figyelo*, 10 Feb. 1994.

Videoton was a success for several reasons, one of which was the genuine restructuring efforts. The whole holding and all its individual enterprises were radically reorganized, and Western management and accountancy systems with tight financial control were introduced. Both workers and managers were motivated to work efficiently. Another reason for its success was its macroeconomic importance. Even after its demise, Videoton was a major Hungarian company that decision makers could not afford to liquidate in spite of the prevailing political ideology. When it was sold, the new owners benefited from the very low price, and—since the original company was liquidated—bad debts that had been accumulated in the past disappeared. Videoton could begin a new life with a clean balance sheet and with the residual capital assets, real estate, reserves, contacts and workforce of the former giant enterprise. Once the company was over the first period of convalescence it could capitalize on its macroeconomic importance in a small economy where monopolist structures were still predominant. Videoton was able to apply for and receive major credits using assets of the whole holding as collateral.

The third important reason for Videoton's success was the talent, ambition and political connections of its general manager, Szeles Gabor. Gabor was one of the few self-made entrepreneurs; he became the head of a small electronics firm in the 1980s. After the change in political system he enjoyed an astronomical economic and political career. In addition to being the general manager of Videoton, his original private company, Muszertechnika, formed a joint venture with Siemens and became a supplier to the new telephone network in Hungary. A former Videoton outlet, Kvattro, was bought by Gabor and some of his partners. The firm specialized in military-related electronics and telephone equipment. In 1994 the Videoton holding had different forms of cooperation (from assembly work to joint ventures) with major Western firms and was expanding in the countries of the former Soviet Union. During the splendour of the MDF-led government coalition, Gabor was a Deputy President of the party as well as the head of the Union of Entrepreneurs (GYOSZ), one of the new employers' organizations that was close to the government.

Finommechanikai Muvek fell apart and only a few of its successor companies survived. One, HM Radar Rt (Honvedelmi Miniszterium [Ministry of Defence] Radar Rt, in Torokszentmiklos), specialized in military-related development and production, was taken over by the Ministry of Defence and the state agency Allami Fejlesztesi Intezet (AFI, State Development Institute). The former MN Godolloi Gepgyar, which was previously totally engaged in military production under the Ministry of Defence, maintained its military profile under the supervision of a state-owned liquidating company, Penzintezeti Kozpont. In 1993 the company was taken over by the Ministry of Defence and was reorganized under the name Currus. The rest of the enterprise became independent and later formed a joint venture with the US company Caterpillar, concentrating its production in construction machinery.[56] Magyar Optikai Muvek (MOM, Hungarian Optical Works) was divided into several new companies. Three minor successor companies engaged in military-related production—two in Hungarian ownership and one with a majority German shareholding.

Mechlabor had been one of the most successful defence industry producers and was the only 'problem-free' company according to the 1991 survey of the sector. However, it went bankrupt by the end of 1992. During the long agony over the fate of the enterprise (before and after bankruptcy) Mechlabor shed all its activities and workforce except the mandatory cold capacities. This left 200 employees (down from 2400 in 1988, including over 100 highly skilled R&D engineers), 90 per cent of whom were engaged in military-related production. The company tried to survive with minor orders because its privatization was blocked by administrative complications and it could not get credit to meet a major export order. In the end, in 1994 the Videoton Holding bought up 50 per cent of Mechlabor's shares. The enterprise lost its formal independence but received a major capital infusion and was able to keep functioning as a subcontractor to Videoton.

In addition to the companies listed as the major military producers in 1988, several others had important military-related activities. In the 1993 proposal of the MIO (which presented the 10 most important companies that were to form the core of the revamped Hungarian military industry), the following companies were listed: Nitrokemia, TAKI, PVG, Technika, Mechlabor, Autoipari Kutato and Fejleszto Vallalat (AKFV), MIKI, DIGEP, Matrafem and FEG. The activities of these firms were considered indispensable to the Hungarian armed forces and the firms were still formally state-owned at the time. Videoton and Finommechanika, the two largest military producers, were already bankrupt and partially privatized. In the list of the enterprises which the MIO wished to preserve, three companies—Nitrokemiai Ipartelepek (located in Fuzfo, a petrochemical company), AKFV (Budapest, an R&D institute for the automobile industry) and MIKI (Budapest, an R&D institute for precision instruments)—had not previously been listed as military enterprises.

In late 1993 the MIO published a catalogue of the companies involved in military production which contained 43 private and state-owned firms. Among these companies were major enterprises such as Csepel Autogyar (located in Csepel, automobile production), Ganz Hunslet (Budapest, trains and other vehicles), Mechanikai Muvek Gyar Automatika Muvek Rt (MMG Automatika, Factory of Mechanical Appliances, Automatic Instruments Works; Budapest, precision instruments) and Raba (Gyor, engines and vehicle parts) which were crucial to the economy but had never before been listed formally among the defence enterprises.[57]

---

[56] *Nepszabadsag*, 5 Dec. 1992 and 15 Apr. 1993; and Interview by the author with Janos Acs, General Director, and Gyozo Czene, Economic Deputy to the General Director, Currus, Ministry of Defence Combat Vehicle Technique Company Ltd, Godollo, Hungary, 6 Apr. 1994.

[57] Unfortunately, the data presented in the catalogue were not very useful for statistical calculations or comparison since output, export and employment numbers were mixed. In some cases they referred to the strictly military-related activity, in others to the whole company. *Hadiipari es polgari termeles teruleten*

In 1994 the MIO presented a list of companies proposed for state support that was slightly different. It contained the names of 59 companies, of which 34 coincided with names in the 1993 catalogue. However, important firms such as Mechanikai Muvek, Army-Coop, Budapesti Vegyimuvek and MIKI were missing. The 'newcomers' were either small or medium-sized private companies, divisions of major industrial companies or institutions, such as the University of Technology in Budapest, Matav (the monopoly telephone company) and Ikarus (the bus producer).

The longer list of firms classified as defence-related showed the rapid decentralization and disintegration of what used to be a relatively coherent defence industry, even at the end of the 1980s. The new firms that had military connections were principally successor firms of former major military producers or companies emerging from the huge group of what had been subcontractors to the defence industry. Most of them had previously been divisions of military-related firms or were created by former employees, often using capital assets, know-how and network capital accumulated at the old company. There were no genuinely new establishments in the sector, and even those firms that were new to military production—such as a factory run by the local municipality in Nyirbator—had previously had informal ties with the sector.

The lists manifested the ambition of the MIO and related circles to rescue and keep under control the largest possible group of enterprises for military purposes. They also indicated how large the realm of defence-related enterprises could have been at the height of their production. The proliferation of defence-related firms also demonstrated a new tendency that will probably become increasingly important in the region: subcontracting by civilian firms for defence-related activities as opposed to concentrating military-related activities in some factories, protected directly by the state.

VI. Consolidation

By the end of 1994 the Hungarian defence industry still had not reached the worst point of its crisis. Military-related production was still decreasing or had stagnated at a fairly low level compared with 1988. However, because the state found several methods for helping defence-related enterprises indirectly and through the enterprises' own efforts, the situation was stabilizing.

As a general strategy, most military-related enterprises concentrated their energies on developing their civilian profile, awaiting a recovery in military orders and some form of state protection. The most dynamic companies—TAKI, Comasec, Dunai, Videoton and FEG—concentrated on increasing exports. The Technika Trade Company signed an agreement with Ukraine for the export of $6.4 million worth of military electronics in October 1994.[58] Hungary signed a memorandum of understanding with India that opened the

---

erdekelt magyar vallalatok rovid ismertetoje [Brief presentation of Hungarian companies active in the field of military and civilian production], (Military Industrial Office: Budapest, 1993).
[58] *Heti Vilaggazdasag*, 5 Nov. 1994.

possibility for defence industry cooperation between the two countries. Negotiations were held on the sale of electronic-warfare equipment, including radars
and spare parts, for Russian-made combat aircraft and tanks.[59]

In Hungary the best prospect for former military electronics and telecommunications producers was to become involved in the establishment of new communications networks. The Videoton empire, BHG and Telefongyar were
engaged in the expansion of the existing Hungarian telephone network, while
TAKI participated in the establishment of a new mobile telephone network.
Since these projects were under the heading of infrastructure development and
had an enormous business potential, some international agencies supported
them and foreign investors were keen to participate in them. The fact that most
of the Hungarian partners had a military-related activity did not bother any of
these outside parties. For former military-related companies, these new opportunities meant possible survival for the whole company, including the military-
related divisions that no one seemed to want to close down.

State resources for military-related production remained very limited but,
although the intense development of the sector never became part of official
policy, several enterprises received considerable help from state agencies. The
purchase of Videoton with credit provided by a state bank is mentioned above.
A purely military company, HM Radar Rt (one of the successor firms of the
former Finommechanika), was bailed out by the state at the request of then
Minister of Defence Fur.[60] In a major consolidation project announced by the
state in 1993, 13 major state-owned enterprises of 'crucial macroeconomic
importance' were selected to receive intensive state help in the form of debt for-
giveness and other protective measures. Six military-related enterprises were
among them.[61] A number of the military-related companies received fairly
advantageous credits for new development projects. Since preferential credits
were very difficult to get, most managers confirmed that the state guarantee
provided in view of the military aspects of their programmes was a decisive
factor in getting credits.[62]

Indirect support to the defence sector was provided through the promotion of
military-related R&D. In 1993 a special Defence Industry and Defence Technology Development Committee was set up within Orszagos Muszaki
Fejlesztesi Bizottsag (OMFB, National Committee for Technological Development)—the state agency in charge of coordinating and promoting R&D. Enterprises could apply for preferential loans from the special state budget reserved
for R&D to develop competitive new products: 50 per cent of the costs could be
interest-free state loans due to be serviced from eventual sales and the other half
of the development costs had to be provided by the enterprises. Projects in elec-

[59] *Defense News*, 12 Oct. 1994.

[60] *Heti Vilaggazdssag*, 3 July 1993.

[61] Karsai, J., 'A piszkos tizenharmak' [The dirty thirteen], *Kozgazdasagi Szemle*, vol. 40, no. 4 (1993);
and *Figyelo*, 2 Sep. 1993.

[62] Interview by the author with Dr Imre Spronz, Managing Director of Comasec-Respirator, Budapest,
16 Feb. 1994; and Interview by the author with Dr Istvan Erdei, General Director of the Research Institute
for Telecommunications, Budapest, 3 Dec. 1993.

tronics, vehicles, repair and service activities as well as those related to environmental protection and energy saving were encouraged, although an open competition was never announced specifically for conversion-related projects.[63] In addition, MH HTI and some minor military-related R&D institutes continued their development projects even in the worst years of the defence industry crisis.

Although military-related R&D never stopped, there was a large gap between development and production. Of the 40–50 strictly military-related projects developed at MH HTI between 1989 and 1993, only three or four products were actually supplied to the armed forces. This share had previously been much higher. A general concern of defence enterprise managers was that local production was two to three generations ahead of the equipment used by the national armed forces, partly because the Hungarian armed forces were not trusted within the WTO after the uprising of 1956 and were therefore given obsolete equipment and a marginal role in WTO strategy. As a result of the internal consolidation process that ensued after 1956, the army kept a relatively low social profile within the country as well. The Hungarian defence industry consequently became extremely export-oriented and the level of its production in some areas, principally in military electronics, far surpassed local demand. This was another source of tension between the defence industry and the military, because cold capacities often were obsolete productive capacities whose maintenance was considered complete nonsense by the industrialists.

While rival state agencies were unable to work out a clear defence industrial policy and mobilize significant resources for reconstruction of the entire sector, a private firm—Rendszertechnika, of the Videoton Holding—was quietly uniting and reorganizing what was left of the former core of the industry, military electronics. After Videoton confirmed its leading position in the ailing but surviving defence industry, the firm reached an exclusive supplier agreement with the Ministry of Defence. While the holding accomplished a professional and financial reorganization that was mostly limited to military electronics, the head of the holding, Szeles Gabor, undertook to structure an organization to represent the whole military-related sector. This association intended to unite all the military producers, both private and state enterprises, with the aim of coordinating and lobbying for the sector's special interests.

[63] Balotay, K., 'Recent tendencies in Hungarian R&D', Paper presented at a round-table discussion organized by the Hungarian Ministry of Defence, Budapest, 25 Nov. 1993 (Kalman Balotay was Head of Department in the OMFB [Hungarian Committee for R&D]); and Interview with Janos Medgyesy, Chief Adviser, Military Industrial Office, Budapest, 10 Feb. 1994.

6. Poland

I. Introduction: a pioneer country with problems

Poland is the largest and strategically most important country of the East–Central European (ECE) region. During the cold war its geopolitical location between East and West—constituting both a corridor and a buffer between the former Soviet Union and the divided Germany—gave it a special political importance. After the historical changes that shook the European continent in 1989–90, this delicate position became more complicated. When the political borders were redesigned in the aftermath of the cold war, Poland had five new states as its neighbours, including the united Germany and several unstable former Soviet republics. Two of the newly independent states, Ukraine and Lithuania, had long-standing historical grievances *vis-à-vis* Poland. Their volatile domestic political situation and the considerable Polish minorities living on their territories created a potential source of tension for Poland. Another neighbour—the region of Kaliningrad, belonging to Russia—was a major garrison with an inventory of modern weapons and equipment 50 times greater than Poland's military potential.[1] As one Polish political scientist has observed, Poland 'has a frontier location in between the predictable, yet hermetically closed West and the unpredictable and unstable East'.[2]

As a consequence of the Round-table Talks in 1989, Poland became the first country in the region to have a non-communist government, led by Prime Minister Tadeusz Mazowiecki. It also had the first government to introduce economic 'shock therapy', from 1990, to achieve macroeconomic stabilization and a rapid transformation to a market economy. The Polish economy suffered a dramatic collapse in the early 1990s but was also the first to show signs of recovery, from 1993. By 1994 the country was often referred to as the 'miracle' of the transition in the ECE region since it had achieved a 4 per cent growth in gross domestic product (GDP) and a relatively stable economy in only four years. However, in 1993 the GDP was 13 per cent lower than in 1989 and industrial output only 25 per cent of the 1989 level.[3] Other shortcomings in Poland's spectacular recovery were the stagnating investment and privatization processes, the slow transformation of the production sector—lagging far behind the spectacular boom in services—the high level of speculation and corruption, the rapidly increasing black and grey economy, and the extremely high social costs incurred in the economic adjustment process.[4]

[1] *Defense News*, 17–23 Oct. 1994.
[2] Kuzniar, R., 'The geostrategic factors conditioning Poland's security', *Polish Quarterly of International Affairs*, vol. 2, no. 1 (winter 1993), p. 15.
[3] *Defense News*, 10 Oct. 1994.

Figure 6.1. Location of defence enterprises in Poland

Permanent political instability was one side-effect of the transformation process in Poland. Between 1989 and 1994 five governments were formed with five different prime ministers. There were several major reshuffles within each of these governments, and parliament was dissolved three times in this period. This instability was caused by the immaturity of the political structures, the weakness of newly formed political parties and, to a great extent, the machinations of former President Lech Walesa. From being an outstanding freedom fighter, Walesa became a capricious and authoritarian political leader. Political

[4] See, e.g., Borzeda, A., 'Le tissu industriel polonais' [Polish industry], *Le courrier des pays de l'Est*, no. 387 (Mar. 1994); Brunner, H.-P., 'The recreation of Eastern European competitiveness: neither magic nor mirage', *European Journal of Development Research*, vol. 6, no. 1 (1994); Gebert, K., 'In Poland, reform has meant pain and division', *International Herald Tribune*, 5 May 1993; and Socha, M. W. and Sztanderska, U., 'Restructuring and industrial policy in Poland', *Moct-Most*, no. 2 (1994).

instability had direct consequences for the military sector. The Polish 'miracle' was possible in part because many enterprises and entire segments of the economy managed to isolate themselves from state interference and become independent from the 'political roller-coaster'. This was easiest for private firms and state-owned enterprises with significant foreign economic contacts. However, the defence industry was directly linked with the political establishment and suffered the effects of political instability.

Defence-related issues became the spark for political conflicts. President Walesa and his cabinet members clashed over control of the army. He was not content with having formal leadership of the country's armed forces but tried to exercise direct control over the general staff. He also tried to interfere directly in allocating the military budget.[5] Another area of conflict between the ministries and economic agencies was the regulation and eventual privatization of military production.

A specific feature of the situation in Poland was the central role played by the armed forces in Polish society. This was partly because of Poland's geopolitical position and partly a result of its painful history of a permanent struggle for independence or survival. The Polish Army was an integral part of the national identity. Even after the period of General Wojciech Jaruzelski's military emergency in the early 1980s, the prestige and relative coherence of the armed forces made it easier for them to represent their interests efficiently. Poland's new but vulnerable geopolitical situation made Polish citizens receptive to the military's needs. After several measures to purge, modernize and democratize the army were introduced after the political system changed in the early 1990s, the armed forces managed to recover most of their traditional prestige in Polish society.[6]

The main structural features of the Polish defence industry

The foundation of the Polish defence industry was laid after the country regained its independence in 1918. In the 1930s, in the framework of a major modernization programme, several new enterprises were established, primarily in the central region of the country. During the German occupation these enterprises were under military rule and produced equipment for the German armed forces. Most of this industry had been destroyed by the end of the war, and rebuilding it was part of the post-war reconstruction effort. After Poland joined the Warsaw Treaty Organization (WTO) in 1955, the existing facilities were modernized and several new factories were established. Additional facilities were built in the late 1970s and early 1980s.

During the three and a half decades of WTO cooperation, Poland was the third largest military producer of the WTO, after the Soviet Union and Czechoslovakia. Since the collapse of the Soviet Union and the breakup of the

---

[5] *Defense News*, 19–25 Dec. 1994.
[6] Ripley, T., 'The Polish armed forces in the 1990s', *Defense Analysis*, vol. 8, no. 1 (Apr. 1992).

Table 6.1. Major arms producers in Poland, 1991 and 1993

Branch/ enterprise (location)	Employment in 1991	Share of military production 1991 (%)	1993 (%)
Ammunition, small weapons			
Mesko (Skarzysko-Kamienna)	1 820	*46.8*	*25.3*
Lucznik (Radom)	740	*15.6*	*18.5*
Dezamet (Nowa Deba)	356	*52.5*	*15.6*
Niewiadow (Niewiadow)	252	*1.9*	*17.8*
Tarnow (Tarnow)	880	*34.7*	*30.1*
Optical and electronic instruments			
PCO (Warsaw)	1 100	*90.0*	*90.0*
Radmor (Gdynia)	420	*43.3*	*28.5*
Warel (Warsaw)	570	*81.1*	*45.1*
Radwar (Warsaw)	1 011	*84.0*	*55.0*
Armoured and other vehicles			
Bumar-Labedy (Gliwice)	1 520	*71.4*	*38.7*
Huta Stalowa Wola (Stalowa Wola)	1 876	*8.6*	*5.5*
Hydral (Wroclaw)	1 365	*58.9*	*19.3*
PZL-Wola (Warsaw)	1 010	*25.0*	*20.7*
Aircraft			
WSK-PZL Mielec (Mielec)	7 495	*53.8*	*40.5*
WSK-PZL Swidnik (Swidnik)	5 868	*81.0*	*82.0*
WSK-PZL Rzeszow (Rzeszow)	5 707	*66.6*	*30.5*
PZL Warszawa-Okecie (Warsaw)	704	*31.8*	*8.1*
Chemical production			
Nitro-Chem (Bydgoszcz)	379	*4.6*	*0.5*
ZTS Nitron (Krupski Mlyn)	40	*0.5*	*0.5*
Shipbuilding			
Stocznia Polnocna (Gdansk)	930	*94.7*	*83.0*
Other (spare parts)			
PZL-Warszawa II (Warsaw)	1 070	*68.8*	–

Sources: Perczynski, M. and Wieczorek, P., 'The disarmament dividend in the process of systematic transformation', *Polish Quarterly of International Affairs*, vol. 2, no. 1 (winter 1993), table 11.4, pp. 230–31; and Perczynski, M., Wieczorek, P. and Zukrowska, K., 'The current situation in Polish arms industry', Unpublished manuscript, Warsaw, 20 May 1994, table 4, p. 7 (data provided by the Ministry of Industry and Trade and various issues of *Polska Zbrojna*, 1991–92; in some cases data provided by enterprises differed from those provided by the Ministry of Industry and Trade).

Czechoslovak Federation, Poland has become the most important arms producer of the ECE region. Polish arms production reached its peak in 1988, with an output valued at 12.5 billion zlotys produced in the 128 core enterprises with a 'special status'. These enterprises employed 320 000 people, 75 000 of whom were directly engaged in military production.[7] The number of enterprises engaged in some way in military production, however, was larger than the core group of 128. By 1991—after the sector had suffered its first major collapse—350 enterprises were in some way still involved in defence-related production.

The Polish defence industry was organized in six major industrial branches: aviation; armoured vehicles and heavy weapons; electronics and optical instruments; ammunition and infantry weapons; specialized chemical production; and shipbuilding. The different characteristics of each sector made the impact of the crisis and the restructuring process complicated and multi-dimensional.

The aircraft industry was established in the aftermath of World War II to meet WTO requirements. Its principal products were small trainer aircraft and light helicopters, mainly produced by Wytwornia Sprzetu Komunikacyjnego (WSK), PZL-Mielec, Swidnik, Rzeszow and Warszawa-Okecie. Production of tanks, armoured vehicles and other heavy weapons had a long tradition in the main heavy industrial plants of the country. The major factories were KUM Bumar-Labedy (located in Gliwice), Huta Stalowa Wola (Stalowa Wola), Hydral (Wroclaw) and PZL-Wola (Warsaw). The main electronics and optical instrument plants—Przemyslowe Centrum Optyki (PCO), Radmor, Warel and Radwar—were established in Warsaw. The most important ammunition and anti-tank missile producer was Mesko (Skarzysko-Kamienna), while small arms were produced at Lucznik (Radom). Shipbuilding also had a centuries-old tradition and was concentrated in Stocznia Marynarky Wojennej and Stocznia Polnocna (both in Gdynia).

The share of military-related output in total production for the 32 major arms producers in 1991 ranged from under 5 per cent to 80–90 per cent. Low shares were characteristic of ammunition and explosives factories such as Gamrat (3.9 per cent), Nitro-Chem (4.6 per cent) and Nitron-Erg (0.5 per cent). The facilities with the highest share of military output were Radwar (located in Warsaw, producing electronics, with a share of 84 per cent), Bumar-Labedy (Gliwice, tanks and tracked vehicles, 71.4 per cent), PZL-Swidnik (Swidnik, helicopters, 81 per cent), Stocznia Polnocna (Gdynia, ships, 94.7 per cent and PCO (Warsaw, optical instruments, 90 per cent).[8]

Most of the facilities with the highest share of military production were large-scale enterprises. Of the 32 facilities, 12 employed more than 1000 workers in military-related production, the largest ones being PZL-Mielec (Mielec, aircraft, 7495 employees), PZL-Swidnik (5868), PZL-Rzeszow (Rzeszow, aircraft engines, 5707) and Mesko (1820).[9] Some of the facilities that had a relatively modest share of military-related output could be considered as significant pro-

---

[7] Zukrowska, K., 'Slimming down the world's industrial capacities: a threat or chance for arms producers from East–Central Europe?', Unpublished manuscript, Frankfurt, Germany, 1993, p. 18.

[8] In theory, in order to receive 'special production' status, companies had to have a minimum 20% share of military production in their output. Clarke, D. L., 'Eastern Europe's troubled arms industries: Part I', Radio Free Europe/Radio Liberty (RFE/RL), *RFE/RL Research Report,* vol. 3, no. 14 (8 Apr. 1994), p. 39.

[9] Perczynski, M. and Wieczorek, P., 'The disarmament dividend in the process of systematic transformation', *Polish Quarterly of International Affairs,* vol. 2, no. 1 (winter 1993), p. 251.

ducers, since they were large-scale industrial plants with multiple activities. Such was the case, for example, of Huta Stalowa Wola, which in 1989 had a 30 per cent share of military-related production, which had fallen to 8.6 per cent by 1991. However, the volume of output and the workforce (1876 employees in 1991) placed it among the most important Polish military producers.

In 1988 most of the Polish defence industry was state-owned and functioned under the supervision of the Military Department of the Ministry of Industry and Trade. Eleven enterprises, engaged in primarily repair and maintenance, were under the direct control of the Ministry of Defence.

The geographical distribution of the Polish defence industry had two special characteristics. The first was that some regions had an extremely high concentration of military-related production, most of which was located in the centre, in Warsaw and its surroundings and in the south-eastern part of Poland (in a region traditionally called the central industrial region). There were also important concentrations in the northern ports, where ships were built. The second geographical characteristic was that several enterprises were established in small or medium-sized cities; in about 20 such cities, the regional economy became completely dependent on the factory, which provided not only the main (often only) local employment opportunity but also a wide range of social services, from flats and hot-water services to financing the local fire brigade and soccer team.

Polish production was less geared to exports than that of Czechoslovakia and Hungary. Local orders absorbed 40–50 per cent of the output from the Polish defence industry until the end of the 1980s. In the early 1990s this share grew because exports were declining faster than demand from the Polish armed forces. Nevertheless, the circle of buyers of Polish military products outside the WTO was rather wide. A US Senate Committee document claimed that Poland 'sold arms to almost any nation that wanted them', including Austria, Ethiopia, Finland, Iran, Iraq, Kampuchea, Mozambique, Syria and South Yemen, and organizations such as the Contras in Nicaragua, the Palestine Liberation Organization (PLO) and the South West African People's Organization (SWAPO) in Namibia.[10] The Polish arms trade was conducted by Cenzin, the Central Board of Engineering in the Ministry of Foreign Economic Cooperation.

Between 1981 and 1990 the average annual value of Polish arms exports was 923.7 million roubles to members of the WTO and countries of 'progressive orientation' and $257.1 million to Western partners. The peak was reached in 1988, with 1138.6 million roubles in the rouble trade zone,[11] and in 1986 for trade with the West, with contracts worth $324.1 million. In 1991, after the

---

[10] Clarke (note 8), p. 42.
[11] Roubles were used to express the value of the trade within the Council on Mutual Economic Assistance.

countries of the Eastern bloc switched to US dollar accountancy, the aggregate value of Polish arms exports was $386.2 million.[12]

Arms exports were among the most lucrative of the economic activities that provided much-needed hard currency. In 1988 an investment of 200–300 zlotys was required to earn $1 if the item produced was an armoured vehicle. In the automobile industry it was necessary to invest twice as much and in the electronics sector three times as much in order to earn $1.[13]

In 1991 shipbuilding was the most profitable military-related production branch, while aircraft and armoured vehicles were the least profitable.[14] Unfortunately, it is not clear how profitability was measured in this comparison, and, if armoured vehicle production was indeed among the worst off, it either suffered a dramatic collapse or the other branches must have been spectacularly lucrative. The Director of Bumar-Labedy stated in an interview given in early 1989: 'Our exports are very profitable, at a rate of return approaching 40 per cent. In the last two years (1987–1988) about 80 per cent of our production was exported, mainly to the II payments area [outside the "socialist" bloc]. Income in terms of dollars and rubles was very high. In short, we earned so much that we were able to equip our armed forces for free'.[15] It is worth noting that the government's defence industrial policy, which emerged slowly, concentrated on preserving the production of the aviation industry and heavy weapon sector, while letting other branches—for example, shipbuilding—convert.

Despite the fact that members of the WTO predominantly produced equipment designed by the Soviet Union, considerable military-related research and development (R&D) was undertaken in Poland. There were 35–40 military-related research centres in the country attached to major enterprises, military schools and academies or industrial branches. Almost all the major military production sectors had a specialized research institute, and the Warsaw-based Aviation Research Institute developed (or coordinated the development of) several major military and civilian aviation products. In addition, several major enterprises had their own R&D centres.

Crisis

The crisis of the defence industry manifested itself later than the general crisis that afflicted the Polish economy from the early 1980s. Defence enterprises were far better off than their civilian counterparts in terms of their technological level, reserves and state protection. The crisis also came later and was less dramatic than was the case for the other Visegrad countries. Polish enterprises were slightly less export-dependent than others in the region, and the drop in

[12] Perczynski, M., Wieczorek, P. and Zukrowska, K., 'The current situation in Polish arms industry', Unpublished manuscript, Warsaw, 20 May 1994, table 5, p. 10; and Zukrowska (note 7), table 5, p. 34.

[13] Perczynski, Wieczorek and Zukrowska (note 12), p. 5.

[14] Zukrowska (note 7), p. 25.

[15] Clarke (note 8), p. 40, which cites Crane, K., The Economic Implications of Reductions in Military Budgets and Force Levels in Eastern Europe, RAND Note N-3208-USDP (RAND: Santa Monica, Calif., 1991), p. 30.

local orders was less extreme than in the other countries. However, once the sector did collapse, it did so more dramatically than for general manufacturing.

Between 1988 and 1991 military production fell by 67 per cent, while general industrial production fell by an average of 30 per cent. By 1991 defence industry output was valued at 4.13 billion zlotys. In 1991, 30 of the 120 final producers accounted for the bulk of the output of the Polish defence industry.[16] Of the 180 000 people employed in the sector, 40 000 were engaged in producing finished products.[17]

Total output from military-related enterprises fell by nearly 80 per cent between 1988 and 1993. Of the 180 000 employees working in the sector in 1988, roughly 50 per cent had lost their jobs by 1994. In 1988 defence production represented 1.5 per cent of total industrial output and in 1991 it still represented as much as 1.1 per cent. By 1994 this share had fallen to 0.5 per cent.[18]

The reasons for the crisis were, on the one hand, the collapse of the WTO as a market and diminished export orders from other (principally Middle Eastern) clients. On the other hand, the new political orientation of the country (while much less marked than the Czechoslovak reorientation) led to drastic cuts in military expenditure and a smaller share allocated to equipment procurement. Polish military expenditure fell in absolute terms each year from 1986. Compared to the 1986 peak, by 1990 it had declined by over 26 per cent and in 1994 by 56.5 per cent. Procurement represented 31 per cent of military expenditure in 1990 but only 11 per cent in 1993.[19]

In the framework of radical economic reforms aimed at establishing a market economy, defence enterprises were stripped of most of their traditional privileges. They lost their state guarantees of supplies of raw materials, spare parts and technology; access to preferential credits and other investment resources; remuneration allowances; and tax benefits. State subsidies to industry that were within the budget—previously a major source of special financial allowances for defence enterprises—were trimmed radically in the framework of the macroeconomic stabilization programme: from 10 per cent of GDP in 1989 to 3.7 per cent in 1993. By 1994 the only official state contribution which defence enterprises received as a direct transfer was to support unused capacities.[20]

By mid-1992 only 8 of the 32 most important producers had a financial position that was solid enough to allow them to apply for further credits; the rest were in financial bankruptcy. The aggregate profits produced by the 90 major military-related enterprises in April 1992 were estimated at 225 billion zlotys, while losses reached 1.6 trillion zlotys. The debt burden of the companies— from unpaid deliveries, unserviced bank credits and state-provided loans—was

[16] The numbers of final producers and later of those ones selected to be kept by the state, varied slightly in different publications and interviews.

[17] Perczynski and Wieczorek (note 9), pp. 226, 228. However, a different source identified 80 factories involved in military production, employing around 260 000 workers (7% of the economically active population) in 1992. *Jane's Defence Weekly*, 18 Jan. 1992.

[18] *Gazeta Wyborcza*, no. 35 (1992); and Perczynski, Wieczorek and Zukrowska (note 12), p. 5.

[19] Perczynski, Wieczorek and Zukrowska (note 12), pp. 2, 4.

[20] Socha and Sztanderska (note 4), p. 74.

120 trillion zlotys. However, 37 of the companies were still able to produce a net profit.[21]

One response to the crisis was to decrease the share of military-related production and increase civilian output. Between 1991 and 1993 there was a radical fall in the share of defence-related activity in overall activities at certain enterprises. According to a list of the 20 major arms producers produced by the Ministry of Industry and Trade, in 1993 three had increased the share of their military output and three had roughly the same percentage, while the rest had cut back defence-related activity radically—many by over 50 per cent.[22]

Another response was to cut enterprise overhead costs by decreasing the size of enterprises. The main methods used were the creation of spin-off companies and the lay-off of workers. In 1991 about 50 per cent of the defence-related firms employed fewer than 1000 people, 38 per cent (the medium-sized firms) employed 1000–3000, and 12 per cent employed more than 3000 workers.[23]

Since radical cuts in military-related production were not compensated by alternative civilian production, the entire sector had immense unused production capacities. In 1993 only about 20–25 per cent of the established military production capacities were being used.[24] Moreover, one estimate suggests that the cold war production capacity of the Polish defence industry was two or three times greater than needed for the requirements of the armed forces.[25]

II. The new Polish policy on defence industry and exports

During the political transition in Poland one question discussed at length was whether a specific policy for the defence industry was needed. Advocates of a radical free-market policy preferred to avoid any state intervention to protect or promote certain branches, including defence-related ones.

Another powerful group insisted that the state should maintain and help defence enterprises in a modified and restricted form. The arguments used to justify special treatment for the sector included economic calculations as well as external and internal security considerations. Advocates of state assistance held that strong national armed forces were needed to protect the country in volatile international conditions. Poland would need to be 'weaned' from its dependence on Soviet-origin military hardware. Polish equipment would have to be modernized before the country could realistically expect to join NATO, and the country lacked the resources to import military hardware. The relatively advanced technological level of the defence industry and its export potential were presented as economic arguments. Reviving the defence industry was also

---

[21] Zukrowska (note 7), p. 25. A year later apparently only 20 of the 42 most important firms had net profits. Perczynski, Wieczorek and Zukrowska (note 12), p. 5.

[22] Perczynski, Wieczorek and Zukrowska (note 12), table 4, p. 7.

[23] Zukrowska (note 7), p. 24. In terms of the other countries of the ECE region, the size of an average Polish enterprise was relatively large. What is considered a small-scale enterprise in Poland (employment under 1000) would be considered as a medium-sized or even large company in other Visegrad countries.

[24] Perczynski, Wieczorek and Zukrowska (note 12), p. 5.

[25] Borzeda (note 4), p. 53.

seen as a possible solution for some internal problems—for example, regional imbalances—and as necessary in 'one town–one factory' situations.

The first, 'hands-off', view was predominant in circles of the Ministry of Finance and the Ministry of Privatization, while the second was expressed by officials in and close to the Ministry of Defence and the Ministry of Industry and Trade. The fact that diverse currents were represented in the same government illustrated the erosion of monolithic structures and the emergence of multiple, competing power centres. Defence industrialists were now subject to multiple and often contradictory decisions.

In general, defence industrialists felt strongly discriminated against. They were pushed to pay additional taxes (most notably the *popiwek* tax that all state-owned enterprises had to pay above a certain wage increase), and their access to credit was limited. They also remained under much tighter official control than their counterparts outside the defence sector.[26]

In the meantime traditional supervising ministries tried to rescue defence enterprises from bankruptcy and help them to survive. With the prevailing budget policy and the general economic contraction, state organizations could provide only limited help before 1993. Another major difficulty was the fact that both governments and government policy were in a continuous process of change and redefinition. By the time a defence industrial policy was elaborated, a change in government had occurred and led to its postponement and reformulation.

The long saga of changing policy guidelines began in 1988 when the Ministry of Industry and Trade declared that military-related enterprises should switch to or significantly increase civilian production. In 1990 a commission was set up with representatives of several ministries to prepare a programme for restructuring the defence industry. Its proposals were never implemented. In October 1991 a new programme was designed around a study prepared by a Polish consultancy company, Proxy. The programme called for significant government support for restructuring and partial conversion of enterprises but the the recommendations were not followed because of a lack of resources. Only a minor portion of the amount requested was provided in order to ease the most pressing financial problems of the companies.

By the time the Suchocka Government took office in 1992 it was decided that the state would adopt a special military industrial policy. Discussions continued in a much smaller circle within the respective ministries about the nature of this policy. In May 1992 the Economic Committee of the Council of Ministers discussed two versions of the overall restructuring of the sector: a 'budgetary' and an 'optimal' version.

The first version suggested cutting back defence industry capacity to 12 per cent of its 1988 level and the dismissal of another 36 000 workers. The second version proposed cutting military production to 48 per cent of the 1988 capacity level and laying off 17 000 workers. Both versions called for financial support

---

[26] For example, tax avoidance was much more difficult for defence-related enterprises.

from the government in the form of securities and additional resources and used 1988 production capacity, rather than output, as the baseline for reductions.[27] By this time about 20–25 per cent of the defence industry's capacity was utilized and the programme therefore actually called for doubling the 1993 production levels. In May 1992 the government accepted the second, 'optimal', version. The government decision was apparently influenced by a series of strikes in the sector during 1992 and pressure from parliament—alarmed by the catastrophic forecasts of defence analysts. However, it took another year, until May 1993, to elaborate a concrete plan of action.[28]

The list of enterprises which would be defined as defence producers was itself the subject of negotiation. At different times different lists, including between 28 and 34 enterprises, were under discussion. The initial plan suggested that 28 of the 90 main arms producers would be preserved as the core of the Polish defence industry.[29] The 10 most important, including Lucznik (located in Radom), Mesko (Skarzysko-Kamienna) and PCO (Warsaw), would be converted to state treasury-owned single-holder stock companies. The remaining 18 enterprises, among them the 6 main aircraft producers and Bumar-Labedy (Gliwice), would be transformed to joint-stock companies with the majority of shares retained by the state. The 11 enterprises under direct Ministry of Defence supervision would remain fully state-owned. The rest of the enterprises (which produced transport, communications, anti-chemical defence, logistics and engineering equipment) would be privatized and left to carry out restructuring programmes on their own. However, they would maintain commercial links with the defence sector to ensure that national needs were met.

It was eventually agreed by the government that 31 enterprises would receive central support for restructuring and partial debt relief.[30] In the first stage the companies would be transformed into corporations and in the second they would be organized into four branch holdings—weapon producers; aircraft producers; radio location, electronic and optical instrument producers; and armoured vehicle producers. Thus, 31 enterprises with approximately 88 000 employees were to become the core of Polish military production—equalling the workforce employed directly in military production in 1988, the peak year.

The number of enterprises with special status diminished from 128 in 1989 to 90 in 1990 and 31 in 1993.[31] This brought a simultaneous decrease in production and a concentration of military-related activities. According to Deputy Minister of Industry Roman Czerwinski, the operations of the 51 firms that

[27] The document, quoted by Zukrowska (note 7), pp. 28–30, discusses 1988 production *capacity* and not actual output levels.

[28] Interview by the author with Dr Pawel Wieczorek, Military Department of the Central Planning Office, Warsaw, 29 Mar. 1994. For background discussions, see Perczynski, Wieczorek and Zukrowska (note 12); and Borzeda (note 4).

[29] Different publications offer different numbers for the companies selected, varying from 28 to 34.

[30] Gorczynski, E., 'Restructurization process of the Polish defence industry', Paper presented at Privatization Experiences and Policies in NACC Countries in the Field of Defence Industry, Taking into Account Privatization Experiences in Other Fields, NATO Economics Directorate, Colloquium 1994, Brussels, 29–30 June 1994.

[31] Interview with Pawel Wieczorek (note 28).

Table 6.2. The trend in production and employment in 31 core Polish defence enterprises, 1991–93

Index: 1990 = 100.

	1990	1991	1992	1993
Total sales	100	81.97	83.76	109.64
Defence sales	100	90.75	41.05	56.09
Total employment	100	79.51	66.51	59.24
Defence sector employment	100	69.49	51.64	46.75

Source: Gorczynski, E., 'Restructurization process of the Polish defence industry', Paper presented at Privatization Experiences and Policies in NACC Countries in the Field of Defence Industry, Taking into Account Privatization Experiences in Other Fields, NATO Economics Directorate, Colloquium 1994, Brussels, 29–30 June 1994.

would lose their special status in 1994 would be consolidated within the remaining 31 defence enterprises.[32] Recent research has suggested that a company needed at least a 60 per cent share of civilian production to be profitable.[33] As it was unlikely that the remaining defence producers would increase their civilian production to this extent, there were grounds to fear that they would produce losses that would have to be covered from central resources.

The restructuring plan was implemented rather slowly. By the spring of 1994 only four companies had been converted to state-owned joint-stock companies,[34] but there were no concrete guidelines for how these holdings were to be financed and managed. The only palpable idea was that, since defence enterprises that were to belong to the same holding were in different economic and financial circumstances, those that were better off should probably finance those that were worse off—an idea reminiscent of the traditional redistribution mechanisms among public enterprises under state socialism.

The new government, led by Waldemar Pawlak, confirmed the policy decided by the previous government. In January 1994 the new Minister of Trade and Industry, Marek Pol, declared that the state would intervene in favour of an interdependent group of strategic industries. Pol stated:

I am for state intervention, but not against reason and in accordance with rational commercial disciplines. These regulations concern both the state and the private sector, with a particular emphasis on the country's strategic sectors. I mean notably the arms industry, the fuel, energy, and heavy chemistry industry, since these branches are evidently closely related to each other. The existence of a well-developed but efficient

---

[32] *Jane's Defence Weekly,* 26 Feb. 1994.
[33] Quoted in *Warsaw Voice,* 26 June 1994.
[34] Interview by the author with Janusz Kostecki, Director, Military Department of the Central Planning Office, 25 Jan. 1994; and Interview with Pawel Wieczorek (note 28). By Oct. 1994, 6 companies had been converted, according to *Defense News*, vol. 9, no. 41 (17–23 Oct. 1994), p. 90.

and modern heavy industry can be to our advantage and creates the country's economic basis.[35]

Reading this quotation, one cannot tell whether it originates from the mid-1990s or the early 1950s. Research on emerging production and trade patterns confirmed that, despite spectacular changes on the surface, basic structures remained unchanged in the Polish economy.[36]

Although it was decided that state agencies would help defence enterprises it was an open question how, in the light of the state's diminished means. Preventing privatization was considered a protective measure because it ensured the survival of defence-related companies. Other forms of direct help were writing off debts, providing guarantees for bank credit or exempting defence firms from certain taxes. During the restructuring efforts of 1994, the debts of defence enterprises were to be reduced by 40–80 per cent and the rest was to be paid within three years.[37] Defence-related companies were exempted from value-added tax, tax on expenditures to develop new technology and import tax on products imported for them by the Ministry of Defence.[38]

The government assisted defence enterprises in indirect ways. Some of the major problems caused by the drastic decline of military-related production—such as unemployment and regional imbalances—were addressed. There were a number of government-backed programmes to help retrain and relocate redundant workers, partly financed by the European Union (EU) PHARE ('Pologne–Hongrie: action pour la reconversion économique', or Assistance for economic restructuring in the countries of Central and Eastern Europe) programme. The government encouraged and financially contributed to projects which tried to find solutions for regions and communities that were especially hard hit by the collapse of the traditional defence industry. From 1990 central budget allocations were available to promote regional development in these areas.

Wider, principally regional, projects that affected the future prospects of military enterprises included support for the creation of a tax-free zone on the territory of the Mielec aircraft factory, which was facing serious difficulties. The Mielec factory was based in the centre of the country on an enormous site where only about 30 per cent of the land and buildings were in use in April 1994. The project envisaged renting the existing establishments to make use of an airport with the second largest runway in Poland, access to a wide-rail track (linked to the former Soviet Union), a large number of well-trained available workers and a large pool of relatively sophisticated machinery at the plant. The project was discussed by the parliament and had strong government support.[39]

The most important form of indirect assistance to the defence industry was probably the decision to buy Polish products for the national armed forces

[35] Cited in Borzeda (note 4), p. 49.

[36] Brunner (note 4); and Socha and Sztanderska (note 4).

[37] *Polska Zbrojna*, no. 65 (31 Mar. 1994).

[38] Interview with Janusz Kostecki (note 34); and Interview with Pawel Wieczorek (note 28).

[39] Interview by the author with Wieslaw Pastula, Managing Director of the WSK PZL-Mielec transport equipment factory, 23 Mar. 1994.

rather than imports. At a meeting with workers from the Lucznik small arms factory in November 1992, the then Deputy Prime Minister, Henryk Goryszewski, declared that the Polish military would continue to buy Polish weapons, adding that the impact on the budget deficit was 'of little importance'.[40] Defence industry managers interpreted this speech as a sign that after years of chaos and hesitation the government had decided to support their sector. A year later Waldemar Pawlak, the new Prime Minister, confirmed that one of his priorities in restructuring the defence industry was to ensure that the armed forces would receive a level and standard of armaments and military equipment sufficient to match those of other countries.

Following these new policy directives, the 1994 budget committed the Ministry of Defence to purchase Polish products exclusively within the framework of its modernization programme. Although this measure initially seemed radical—and many commentators interpreted it as a step towards self-reliance—in reality all the major Polish development projects considered for armed forces modernization have significant Western inputs. The new version of Mielec's Iryda trainer and light attack aircraft was fitted with a weapon delivery and navigation system produced by the French company SAGEM; plans to modernize the Swidnik-produced Huzar helicopters include Western air-to-surface missile systems and chin-mounted cannon; the 100 Su-22 fighter in the Polish Air Force is planned to receive Western avionics; the PZL-130 Orlik trainer aircraft offered for export was to be fitted with a Pratt and Whitney engine and Bendix/King avionics and head-up display, while the major modernization plan for the Polish Navy—updating Kaszub Class light frigates—also counted on Western technology.[41]

By the end of 1994 the Polish Parliamentary Science Committee proposed central financing of the following programmes: the Huzar (an armed version of Swidnik's Sokol helicopter); the Gorilla main battle tank; improvements to anti-aircraft artillery; and further development of the PZL-130 trainer aircraft. Among these projects, the Huzar had the safest future since the Ministry of Defence was already buying 15 Sokol multi-purpose helicopters per year.[42]

Support for arms exports

Another form of indirect assistance was export promotion in the form of direct government support in negotiations and indirect support such as organizing arms trade exhibitions.[43] Official economic policy put great emphasis on export promotion, and weapons were considered as one of the few products of the Polish industry that had comparative advantages on international markets. As

---

[40] Quoted in Clarke (note 8), p. 41.

[41] *Jane's Defence Weekly*, 2 and 30 July 1994; 17 Sep. 1994; 22 Oct. 1994; and *Defense News*, 9–15 Jan. 1995.

[42] *Defense News*, 19–25 Dec. 1994.

[43] Regular arms exhibitions and conferences were held in the town of Kielce, which, according to ministry sources, was a completely local initiative. In 1994 a major military show was held in the town of Golynia. The largest exhibitor was Israel. *Defense News*, 10 Oct. 1994.

Jan Strauss, the Director of Cenzin, put it: 'We are too big a nation to make nothing more than melted cheese and wicker baskets. The arms industry is still a technological locomotive'.[44]

Finding new customers was an important goal of the new Polish foreign trade policy. While the country struggled to assert its independence from the WTO, the structure of its defence sector was still predominantly determined by it. This made Poland extremely vulnerable *vis-à-vis* the former Soviet Union and seriously limited its export potential. Seventy per cent of Polish arms (and 90 per cent of its artillery) were based on designs from the former Soviet Union. Although the country imported only 10 per cent of its military products from Russia, these included crucial spare parts.[45]

Between 1988 and 1990 new control mechanisms were introduced to regulate the arms trade. Thanks to the general trade liberalization implemented immediately after the political turnover, about 50 new arms trade companies emerged. As import–export regulations became tighter, the number of enterprises diminished: by 1994 about 20 enterprises were officially licensed to trade in arms but only about 10 of them played an important role. Apart from specialized trade agencies, some defence enterprises—for example, Bumar-Labedy (Gliwice)—were licensed to trade. Cenzin itself became a joint-stock company and intended to diversify its activities.

By 1993 the value of the export of Polish weapons had dropped to $50–60 million, or roughly 14 per cent of the 1991 level.[46] In an effort to boost exports, techniques such as barter trade were employed with both Eastern and Western partners—for example, Sokol helicopters were exchanged with Spain for transport aircraft.[47] The national armed forces of the newly created post-Soviet states were also targeted as potential markets. Military trade framework agreements and joint ventures were concluded with Ukraine and Lithuania.[48]

Each organization trading in weapons needed to have a special licence and each individual transaction had to be checked and approved by Cenzin. An end-user certificate was always required in the licensing process. The government maintained a 'negative list' specifying countries to which arms deliveries were totally prohibited. In 1993 this list included Afghanistan, El Salvador, Iraq, Libya, Mozambique, Myanmar (Burma), Somalia, Sudan, Taiwan and the former Yugoslavia. At that time a separate list named Iran, Israel, Syria and South Africa as destinations to which arms exports required an additional licence from the Ministry of Interior.[49]

In 1994 the negative list was revised and only those countries under UN embargo—Iraq, Libya, Somalia, Liberia, South Africa and the former Yugoslavia—were excluded from the circle of potential buyers of Polish

---

[44] *Warsaw Voice*, 26 June 1994.
[45] *Defense News*, 19–25 Dec. 1994.
[46] Perczynski, Wieczorek and Zukrowska (note 12), table 5, p. 10.
[47] *Defense News*, 19–25 Dec. 1994.
[48] *Defense News*, 17–23 Oct. 1994.
[49] Zukrowska (note 7), p. 33.

weaponry. As of June 1995, primary legislation on the arms trade was still in preparation.

Poland offered both Soviet-designed equipment (versions of the T-72 tank and various missile systems) and Polish-designed weapons (e.g., radio networks, trucks, electrical and optical equipment, and mines).[50] The most successful Polish export products were the W-3 Sokol helicopter, produced in various versions by PZL-Swidnik; firearms from Lucznik; ammunition from Pionki;[51] and a modernized T-72 tank (the PT-91 Twardy). The I-22 Iryda combat trainer aircraft from Mielec and the PZL-230F Skorpion combat aircraft under development in the Warszawa-Okecie plant were also offered for export.[52]

In the early 1990s several incidents underlined the difficulty of implementing export controls. For example, in 1992 a deal allegedly involving the provision of arms to Iraq and involving some high-level Polish politicians was uncovered in Germany. Later in 1992 Cenzin officials were alleged to have offered arms to a German journalist posing as an arms dealer for the former Yugoslavia.[53]

Cooperation with foreign partners

In the absence of significant government investment, both government and enterprise representatives saw foreign direct investment and cooperation with Western companies as the means with which to revive the sector. Foreign enterprises and investors were expected to bring capital, technology and markets. Joint ventures formed between Western companies and Polish enterprises were considered to be 'bridgeheads of capitalism', as Jerzy Kade of the Ministry of Industry and Trade put it.[54]

Although the relative levels of foreign direct investment in Poland were modest in the early 1990s (compared with those achieved by the much smaller states of Hungary and the Czech Republic), Polish defence enterprises cooperated with Western firms in military and civilian production. Poland signed a wide range of bilateral military agreements with Western countries which included cooperation in defence-related production. For example, the accord on defence industry cooperation with Sweden, signed in May 1994, included the testing of equipment produced by Bofors in Sweden for Poland's modernized T-72 tanks along with possible procurement of Identification Friend or Foe (IFF) and command and control systems.[55] A similar agreement, signed in February 1994 with the Netherlands, established contacts between the Polish Navy and the Dutch firm Hollandse Signaalapparaten (Signaal) for the possible upgrade of a modified Kashin Class destroyer.[56]

---

[50] *Jane's Defence Weekly*, 18 Jan. 1992.
[51] This enterprise did not feature on the official lists of military-related companies.
[52] *Warsaw Voice*, 26 June 1994.
[53] Clarke (note 8), p. 42.
[54] Quoted in *Warsaw Voice*, 26 June 1994.
[55] *Jane's Defence Weekly*, 28 May 1994.
[56] *International Defense Review*, vol. 27, no. 5 (May 1994), p. 6.

Other examples of cooperation with Western firms included a plan by the Warsaw automobile manufacturer Fabryka Samochodow (FSO) Warszawa to cooperate with an Israeli firm to produce military vehicles; cooperation between the Unimor electronics company (located in Gdansk) and the Swedish firm Ericsson to produce electronics; and an investigation by Huta Stalowa Wola (Stalowa Wola) and Mesko (Skarzysko-Kamienna) regarding cooperation with the Swedish company Bofors to produce Swedish-designed anti-tank guided missiles and artillery. Bofors was also working with Bumar-Labedy on upgrading the PT-91 Twardy tank in cooperation with the French agency SOFMA (Société Française de Matériels d'Armement). The French firm Thomson-CSF signed a deal with Radwar (Warsaw) to provide IFF systems for the Polish armed forces. The German firm Daimler Benz bought shares in the Wojskowe Zaklady Motorizacijne (WZM) Glowno automobile factory, which repairs military trucks and armoured personnel carriers, but this joint venture was intended to produce a minibus to be used by civilian security forces, for example, for delivery of money to banks.[57]

After the defence sector succeeded in re-establishing government backing for its projects, its expansion was principally limited by the country's general economic situation and civilian control. The level of support required for the defence industry in 1994 has been estimated at 7–8 billion zlotys for orders of military equipment and 5–6 billion zlotys for conversion. However, in the Ministry of Defence budget only 3.5 billion zlotys was allocated for procurement, and direct expenditure for conversion was minimal (although some military projects were financed from funds available for technology development or regional development).[58]

Since 1990 the Polish Parliament has to a greater degree become involved in discussions of defence industrial policy. Clashes have concerned information on defence spending that parliamentary committees requested and Ministry of Defence officials were reluctant to provide. Some concrete military development projects were also heatedly contested. For example, some parliamentarians have questioned the need to develop a new tank, the Gorilla, which has been funded at a low level since 1991 and is financed by the Polish Government's Central Committee for Scientific Research. The original plan was to incorporate components and sub-systems from NATO countries, but later it was decided that the tank would be developed locally. Foreign cooperation was to be sought through joint ventures to supply communications systems and software.[59] According to *Defense News*, funding for the prototype appeared to be secure in 1994 and development costs would take about 2 per cent of the $2.1 billion defence budget for 1994.

---

[57] *Zolnierz Wolnosci*, no. 5 (1993); Clarke (note 8); and Zukrowska (note 7), p. 37.

[58] *Polska Zbrojna*, 17 Feb. 1994.

[59] A model presented to the press in Oct. 1994 was fitted with a French sight-and-aiming system. The plans envisaged a prototype built principally of Polish elements, used in conjunction with Israeli systems. The new engine was tested at PZL-Wola (Warsaw).

Janusz Onyszkiewicz, former Minister of Defence and deputy chairman of the Parliamentary Defence Committee, insisted that the project would be too expensive and therefore futile. He confirmed his opposition to the programme in December 1994 with the statement: 'They will get the Gorilla over my dead body'. 'They'—the representatives of the Ministry of Defence and Ministry of Industry and Trade—had declared that the project was indispensable for the country's future defence. Kade argued that the new model should be developed and produced indigenously, since Poland could not afford to import tanks to modernize its aging arsenal. At the same time he acknowledged that the costs of the project would be high and should therefore be split between the government and the participating enterprises. In another interview he mentioned that in 1991 the government had created a special holding company to oversee the production of new Gorilla tanks but that progress was halted because of the precarious economic situation.[60] The fact that the Gorilla project reappeared on the agenda underlined the regained confidence of military–industrial circles by 1993–94.

Defence enterprises: between crisis and restructuring

According to Kade, head of the Military Department of the Ministry of Industry and Trade, the worst year of the crisis was 1992—when, because of the UN embargoes on Iraq and the former Yugoslavia, the industry lost contracts worth hundreds of millions of dollars and the Polish Ministry of Defence did not give any new orders to the companies (since it was still paying for previous deliveries). The procurement budget of the Ministry of Defence was 13.8 trillion zlotys in 1990 but had dimished to 3.4 trillion zlotys by 1993 (in constant prices).

In July 1993 the total debts of the 32 largest defence-related enterprises were three times larger than the aggregate value of outstanding claims and activities. Only one-third of the 32 companies had a net credit.[61]

In 1993–94, when encouraging signs of national economic recovery were appearing, most of the Polish defence enterprises were still in a crisis and struggling for survival. Enterprise managers claimed that the anticipated benefits from recovery—growth in the domestic market, easier credit opportunities and growing state (military) spending in the form of new army orders—were not being felt yet. A few producers had new contracts—for example, the Warszawa-Okecie aircraft company increased the share of its military output—but the rest of the companies, and particularly the subcontractors, were still in a precarious state.[62]

---

[60] *Defense News*, 10–17 Oct. and 19–25 Dec. 1994. The 1995 defence budget was expected to be $2.5 billion, which meant a decline in real terms taking into account the 27% annual inflation rate. *Defense News*, 10 Oct. 1994.

[61] *Polska Zbrojna*, 10 Jan. 1994. Company indebtedness grew at a dizzying speed after 1992. In 1993 total debts reached 12 billion zlotys; by June 1994 they exceeded 15 billion zlotys because of the high interest rates and the accumulating financial difficulties of the firms. *Polska Zbrojna*, 10 Jan. 1991; and *Warsaw Voice*, 26 June 1994.

[62] In Mar. 1994, in a meeting with defence industry managers, in response to the question 'Which was the worst year of the crisis and why?', one Polish manager answered half jokingly: 'That year is still to come'.

The sector seemed to have reached its lowest level in 1993, and in 1994 a slight increase in enterprise incomes and output was registered, probably because of the general economic recovery and growth in civilian output.[63] By July 1994, 14 of the then 31 core defence enterprises regained creditworthiness and achieved a profit. By the end of the year the Polish defence industry was expected to be out of the red.[64]

III. Examples of defence industry development

The relatively large size, variety and geographical distribution of the Polish defence industry created unique problems for enterprises. Plants in different branches had specific characteristics that were of special importance for problem-solving at both the enterprise and the government level. In October 1991 four of the major aircraft-producing companies decided to cooperate in R&D and marketing. Such cooperation was generally considered positive in the entire defence sector, even if it did not solve the fundamental problems enterprises faced. Managers in other sectors, in particular the subcontractors, often complained about the breakdown in communication and wasteful duplication of effort created by individual attempts to cope.

The concentration of old-style heavy industrial plants in certain parts of Poland created additional difficulties for restructuring. The future prospects of Bumar-Labedy or Huta Stalowa Wola, for example, were overshadowed by the fact that they were situated in the former central industrial region—a region with high unemployment, pollution and a legion of medium- and large-scale firms in deep structural crisis. Factories situated near the German border or near major cities like Warsaw and Krakow could benefit from the high rate of local economic activity.

The development of the Polish defence industry can be demonstrated through sectoral and enterprise examples.

Huta Stalowa Wola

Huta Stalowa Wola was the largest military-related enterprise in Poland. It was created in 1937 to supply the Polish armed forces in preparation for the threat of war. During World War II it was taken over by the German forces and produced weapons for the Reichswehr. The enterprise was reconstructed and expanded after the war. In 1989, 30 per cent of the production consisted of military end-items, 30 per cent metallurgy and 40 per cent civilian machinery. The sudden collapse of WTO-based cooperation was a major blow to the factory.

Output dropped from 2.8 billion zlotys in 1989 to 1.7 billion zlotys in 1991, and then rose to approximately 2.7 billion zlotys in 1993.[65] Huta Stalowa Wola

---

[63] Gorczynski (note 30).

[64] *Warsaw Voice*, 26 June 1994.

[65] These figures were provided in current prices. Taking into account the high inflation, the drop was actually significantly larger.

reacted by increasing the share of its civilian output and decreasing the size, overhead costs and scope of activity. In 1989 it employed 22 000 people, but employment fell to 14 500 by 1993. The enterprise introduced radical measures to decrease energy costs and sold or rented all social services and related establishments. It increased production of construction machinery, launched in the 1970s on the basis of licences from the US Harvester company. Many machines and most of the workforce formerly employed in military-related activities could switch to the new civilian profile relatively easily. Organizational changes were also made: the enterprise was divided into 14 functionally and financially independent divisions. Huta Stalowa Wola had to cope with a typical 'one town–one factory' situation. Of the 75 000 inhabitants of Stalowa Wola, 40 500 worked in or for the enterprise.

Huta Stalowa Wola seemed to have a rather efficient marketing department. About half of its construction machinery production was sold through US and Japanese cooperation partners on the Western markets. Some trade contacts with the newly independent countries of the former Soviet Union were restored and partners in Russia and Kazakhstan paid in advance and in cash. Other important trade partners were Germany, Hungary and Iran, and ties were set up with African countries. Huta Stalowa Wola had several permanent service facilities in its major trade partner countries to provide after-sales service.[66] It hoped to benefit from planned road construction to unite Poland's northern ports and its eastern borders with the West.

The company was still state-owned. It was scheduled to go through the commercialization process, but because of its strategic importance 51 per cent of the enterprise shares were to be reserved for the state. The General Director, Ryszard Grochowski, believed that Poland needed its own defence industry for security and economic reasons, but on a reduced scale: smaller size might eventually mean productivity and cost-efficiency improvements in the sector. By 1993 the share of military-related production in total production had fallen to 5 per cent. The director expected that this share would grow to 20–25 per cent in the near future, which he considered to be the optimal ratio.[67]

Huta Stalowa Wola's military production had two major profiles: armoured vehicles and artillery. The vehicles were based on the same technology used to produce bulldozers. Until 1991 they were produced under a Russian licence and about 90 per cent of production was exported. Production reached about 300 vehicles and 50 howitzers per year. An additional 20–25 per cent of 'special production' consisted of spare parts. When military orders stopped overnight, the company's storage facilities were filled with finished products. Despite their limited budget, the armed forces bought the majority of this equipment. From 1992 the company continued to be active in military R&D—partly in the R&D centre in Stalowa Wola (formerly an enterprise division, now an independent

---

[66] This was the case in both civilian and military sales. For example, the company sold its howitzers with complete repair kits.

[67] Interview by the author with Ryszard Grochowski, General Director of Huta Stalowa Wola, 23 Mar. 1994.

institute) and partly together with the armed forces. The company was also involved in military-related development with the Swedish company Bofors.[68]

PZL-Warszawa II

PZL-Warszawa II was a typical cooperative factory. It was a subcontractor for 10 other enterprises, producing a range of products from aviation to armoured vehicles and rocket launchers. The factory produced about 300 different products, principally precision engineering, electronic and optical sub-systems.[69] According to Waldemar Soroczynski, this wide production range could be an advantage because it made it possible to balance the variation in demand for different products. However, it could also be a serious disadvantage since the company was very dependent on the end-producers and found it diffi-cult to raise its prices in line with them. The enterprise management predicted the collapse of the traditional defence industrial system and prepared a business plan. They realized that their most important 'product' was their know-how, and they sold production technologies to Iraq immediately before the 1991 Per-sian Gulf War. This deal with Iraq was expected to attract further orders for technical assistance, servicing and complementary products. Instead, the war and the UN embargo against Iraq abruptly ended the deal, leaving PZL-Warszawa II with the problem of how to collect debts owed by Iraq.

The crisis of the Polish defence industry affected the company deeply. The following years were characterized by typical crisis symptoms: lack of orders, insolvency, unused capacities, large-scale redundancies, and a significant fall in output, sales and income. Employment fell from 4500 at the end of the 1980s to about 800 by mid-1994 and output dropped by 60 per cent between 1990 and 1994.[70]

PZL-Warszawa II tried the usual passive restructuring methods: it sold its social facilities, sold or rented surplus production capacities and space, laid off workers and tried to reduce expenditures to the lowest possible level. It also sought orders widely in order to acquire income. Between 1990 and 1994 repre-sentatives of about 200 foreign firms visited the company to negotiate possible cooperation. No major deal was struck, however, and in some cases it incurred serious losses by producing a prototype for a would-be partner before securing a contract.

Originally, 40 per cent of output was military and 60 per cent civilian. Sev-eral spin-off companies were created from former company divisions, which increased the share of military-related production in the residual enterprise to nearly 80 per cent. However, since the management recognized the dis-advantages of dependence on military orders, they kept trying to establish new

---

[68] Interview by the author with Tadeusz Suski, Commercial Director, and Alina Niedzalek, Representa-tive of the Foreign Trade Office, of Huta Stalowa Wola, 29 Mar. 1994.

[69] The only other company that came near to this in the interview sample was the Hungarian Danuvia, with about 200 different products.

[70] Although 1990–91 were generally considered the worst years for the defence industry, in 1990 PZL-Warszawa II was filling a major contract for Iraq.

civilian profiles. New production lines were introduced to manufacture minia-
turized and ultra-light aviation instruments for gliders and light aircraft. These
products were partially developed in the enterprise. In 1994 PZL-Warszawa II
was still deeply in the red and its future was rather uncertain. It was unlikely
that it would close down but unclear how it could overcome its difficulties.

The aircraft sector

The aircraft industry was considered one of the most successful and promising
branches of the Polish defence industry. In 1994 it consisted of five major
enterprises: PZL-Mielec (aircraft), Swidnik (helicopters), Okecie (lightweight
aircraft), and PZL-Rzeszow and Kalisz (aircraft engines).[71] Two R&D institutes
specialized in aviation research were located in Warsaw: the Instytut Lotnictwa
and the Instytut Techniczny Wojsk Lotniczych.[72]

PZL-Mielec

The largest aircraft producer was PZL-Mielec, established in 1938 in the small
town of Mielec in central Poland. During the war the factory worked under and
for the German military. After Poland joined the WTO in 1955, it began to produce military and civilian aircraft under Soviet licence. To compensate for
uneven military production rates, a wide range of civilian products were also
introduced. In addition to indigenous electronic golf carts, diesel engines were
made under licence from the British company Leyland and fuel-injection pumps
under a US Friedman–Meier licence. In the 1970s civilian aircraft production
was also expanded, and a large number of agricultural and passenger aircraft
were produced. In 1989–90, following the collapse of the Soviet market, sales
of these products dropped by about 80 per cent and production by over 30 per
cent, and by 1994 employment had shrunk from 22 000 to 9500.

PZL-Mielec restructuring began with help from a Western consultancy company, partially financed by the government. The experience was negative. The
management of Mielec decided to engage another external consultant at its own
cost, but the results were not much better. As Managing Director Wieslaw
Pastula put it in 1994, Western consultancy firms were only able to give a diag-
nosis but no practical or viable proposals for remedies. They were finance-
oriented and had no idea about or interest in the production processes or the
local circumstances of the enterprise. In the end the new director and his team
decided to prepare reorganization projects by themselves. PZL-Mielec was
decentralized; it became a (still state-owned) holding in which diesel engine,
fuel-injection pump and golf-cart production and the power plant were made
independent enterprises. All its social services were sold.

---

[71] According to *Aerospace World,* June 1992, in 1992 the sector consisted of 16 state-owned enterprises
employing 40 000 people—5 end-producers, 2 engine makers, and the rest supplying equipment and parts.
[72] Roman Czervinski, Undersecretary of State in the Ministry of Industry and Trade and in charge of
military production, was formerly the managing director.

The parent company's profile was also modified. Originally divided into 60 per cent military and 40 per cent civilian aircraft production, the new structure envisaged 30 per cent military production, 30 per cent civilian production and 30 per cent foreign cooperation. In 1990 PZL-Mielec began to produce spare parts and undertook some assembly work for the French company Aérospatiale. In 1992 it started to produce doors for Boeing aircraft. Other, minor assignments were performed for the Italian company Alena and the German company Stema.

In parallel, a financial restructuring took place. According to Pastula, by 1994 PZL-Mielec had managed to overcome its deep financial crisis and was by and large in balance. All the new production projects were prepared with detailed cost analysis, a thorough market and feasibility study, and strict controls. Business plans were prepared both by projects and by enterprise divisions. Even in the worst years of the crisis, the enterprise managed to get some credits from local banks or from the Polish Industrial Development Agency and, adding some of their own resources, invested in new machinery.

Active market research was undertaken. The enterprise had had its own marketing company for 20 years, including offices abroad, for example, in the United States. The aim was to find new market niches and adapt production to their special requirements. For example, on the basis of existing production lines new ambulance and fire-engine models were prepared. The company already had a Boeing quality certificate and was about to get an ISO (International Standards Organization) certificate. This was principally thanks to the fact that they managed to preserve the high quality standards inherited from previous military production. The company had its own R&D centre that employed about 1800 people and had close contact with the Warsaw-based institutes.

Mielec could have become one of the most successful defence enterprises in the region. The manager was dynamic, creative and gave the impression of enjoying the challenge of recreating a company facing many difficulties. However, there were serious difficulties.

The Polish Air Force refused to buy the I-22 Iryda—an aircraft specially developed for it—claiming that it had serious technological problems. The decision was a major blow to the Mielec aircraft plant that had built up its restructuring plans around the project and the revenues expected to stem from it. In the end, some units were ordered for trials and in 1994 the Ministry of Defence was allocated 300 billion zlotys ($14 million) to buy more planes.[73]

In 1994 impressive management plans were still in the initial stage of implementation. The company had huge unused production capacities and serious financial and marketing problems. In addition, there were many external obstacles over which the Mielec management had very limited control. The most profitable division engaged in diesel-engine production and the least profitable in aviation. However, most of the productive assets were tied to military-

[73] *Warsaw Voice*, 26 June 1994.

related aircraft production. This production rested on huge fixed assets and the market depended on political decisions, independent of the enterprise. Similarly, a plan to create for the company a duty-free production zone depended on decisions by the government and the parliament. Mielec depends on an efficient political lobby as much as efficient management for its future.

PZL-Swidnik

PZL-Swidnik was considered the most successful aircraft producer in Poland. Since PZL-Mielec and PZL-Swidnik had fairly similar starting positions at the end of the cold war, it is worthwhile to compare them. They were approximately the same size and had the same one town–one enterprise situation. They also suffered a similar financial and structural crisis and tried to cope with it in a fairly similar way.

PZL-Swidnik's main product was the Sokol helicopter, built for both export and domestic use. After the collapse of the old system, company output fell by nearly 70 per cent and employment from 8500 in 1989 to 5000 by 1993. In 1991–92, Swidnik stopped paying taxes to the government and servicing its debts to the banks. It sold all its social establishments or handed them over to regional authorities, from the school to the fire brigade. Some production activity was also 'decentralized'; in 1993 the power plant and the divisions in charge of transportation, social services and agricultural helicopter production became autonomous enterprises under the parent company.

To cope with the crisis PZL-Swidnik introduced new civilian production lines for wheelchairs, medical equipment and agricultural machines. It also produced a glider developed jointly with the Warsaw School of Technology. Cooperation with major Western firms was sought. It became a subcontractor to Aérospatiale, supplying wing sub-assemblies. In cooperation with a French company, partially financed with a loan provided by a French bank, the company built a completely new technology line for a special chemical treatment.[74]

Swidnik developed a version of the Huzar combat helicopter to be offered for export that was available with either Western or Russian weapons.[75]

In 1994 Swidnik was renegotiating its debts and stabilizing its financial position. The enterprise was one of the few military-related companies already feeling the slight economic recovery which Poland experienced from 1993. Both its civilian and military markets had slightly improved and it was easier to secure credit for new projects. The company aim was to get ISO certification, establish further cooperation with Western partners and develop a new type of helicopter. The latter project was jointly financed by Polish banks, a government agency for industrial development and the enterprise. Despite these promising signs, company performance was still below the 1988 level. Output

---

[74] Of the costs, 50% were covered by a loan received after the Polish National Bank issued a special guarantee. The rest was paid by PZL-Swidnik.
[75] *Jane's Defence Weekly*, 23 July 1994.

reached only about 65–70 per cent of the 1988 level, and only about 50 per cent of the productive assets were being used.[76]

In 1994 both PZL-Swidnik and PZL-Mielec were still fully state-owned. The privatization plans envisaged 51 per cent maintained state ownership and the rest distributed among the main creditors, employees and management.

A comparison of the cases of these two enterprises demonstrates that, in the troublesome and uncertain times of economic transformation, good luck, accident or factors outside the sphere of economic management played a disproportionate role in determining a company's destiny. The two enterprises had similar strategies for crisis management although Mielec's process of seeking new solutions was wider in scope. However, in mid-1994 it seemed that Swidnik's future was more secure than Mielec's.

The Polish armed forces ordered Swidnik's helicopters and an export market for them was re-established. The hesitation in ordering Mielec's Iryda jet trainer aircraft not only damaged the company locally but also reduced its prospects for exports. Another factor that helped Swidnik was its more favourable geographical position. While both enterprises were the main (practically the only) employer in their respective towns, the factory in Swidnik was located near Lublin—a regional centre of growth—and when the Coca-Cola company decided to establish a plant in Swidnik this had a further positive indirect impact on the enterprise.

[76] Interview by the author with Mieczyslaw Majewski, General Director, and Marek Waryszak, Financial Director, of PZL-Swidnik, 24 Mar. 1994.

Part III

Defence enterprises in post-cold war East–Central Europe

7. The special features of defence enterprises

I. Introduction

It is difficult to grasp the true dimensions of the arms industry and related branches in the East–Central European (ECE) region because of the secrecy surrounding and the complexity of military-related activities in the former classic command economies of these states. Similarly, while this sector certainly contributed to the crises in the budget, in production and in employment, a precise measure of the macroeconomic impact of the crisis in the military-related sector is difficult to obtain. In rare instances the impact of the crisis in a given sector is clear, such as the collapse of the electronics industry in Hungary, or in a given region, such as the high rates of unemployment in the Slovak military triangle or the Polish central industrial region. However, the overall impact of the collapse was greatest and most manifest at the level of the enterprises or firms in the region.

Military-related enterprises were unexpectedly abandoned with the heritage of the cold war embodied in their physical assets, production structure and way of functioning. They were left to fend for themselves because the state protection which had been provided to them for decades had vanished with the dramatic political changes that took place in the region—at least so it seemed between 1990 and 1992, when the authorities were preoccupied with political and personnel changes and when new government policy guidelines were being defined for the defence industry. Enterprises were also given an unprecedented degree of freedom: for the first time in decades, they had various options when making decisions about new goals, partners, strategies and a new rationale for their activities.

After some time an administrative reorganization took place in each of the ECE countries. However, during this short period of 'vacuum', enterprises learned a great deal about managing themselves. Previously, external conditions—the Warsaw Treaty Organization (WTO) production system and its special socio-economic position in the respective countries—had created fairly similar patterns of behaviour throughout the region. Then a process of differentiation took place in which enterprises in the same country had strikingly different reactions to the same economic environment. Although each country chose a different path in restructuring its defence industry, the differences were less country-specific than enterprise- or management-specific, illustrating the increased importance of decisions and strategies at the enterprise level.

The relationship between companies and society changed during the transformation process. After the political changes, enterprises were relatively separate from the national economic agencies in the 'transition economies'. These national agencies were highly politicized, while enterprises tried to distance themselves from direct political involvement, being motivated primarily by survival. The links that had acted as vertical communication channels in a hierarchical command system were distorted, while new ones were not yet efficient.

Because of their highly political nature, military enterprises experienced the separation as a less radical change than it was for the wider economy. Defence enterprises had been at the core of the command economy, when it was taken for granted that society would pay for the specific requirements and expenses of the military sector. At the beginning of the transformation, it seemed natural that the new political élite should refuse to maintain the defence industry, and the state more or less radically withdrew its protection. In this complete reversal, individual enterprises had to deal with the practical problems stemming from the heritage of the cold war. Understandably, they were reluctant to do so and were often unable to cope.

The spontaneous collapse of the defence sector caused enormous losses at the enterprise level. Many companies went bankrupt or had to down-size their activities significantly. The costs of unused production capacities, unsold stock and material reserves, and redundancy were borne primarily by the enterprises. However, when protection of the defence sector was reinstated, it was again the wider society that had to foot the bill first for the costs of the collapse of the sector and later for its revival.

In order to understand the crisis and the difficulties faced by industry managers, it is useful to summarize the typical features of a traditional defence enterprise in East–Central Europe during the cold war period.

II. State protection and special social status

With the installation of state socialism, most defence enterprises were taken over and managed directly by a department within a ministry. In Czechoslovakia, in the 1980s a special department of the Ministry of Industry and Trade (after the breakup of Czechoslovakia this department was in the Ministry of the Economy in Slovakia) was principally in charge of defence-related firms. A small group of enterprises, mostly those specialized in repairing military equipment, were supervised directly by the Ministry of Defence. Some other ministries, principally the Ministry of Finance and the Ministry of Foreign Trade (in Hungary the Ministry of Foreign Economic Relations), also played a supervisory and support role.

The ministry represented the state as 'property owner'—that is, it took decisions about the establishment or liquidation of the enterprise and appointed the general management. While historically the ministry had intervened in the actual management of the enterprises, by the 1980s this had largely withered away with the gradual dismantling of the classic command economy. In the early 1990s, in non-privatized enterprises the ministries still exercised the rights of ownership on behalf of the state. They were consulted when fundamental decisions were taken—for example, when a major change in the production profile was considered.

Direct ministry supervision meant relatively strict control on the one hand and considerable protection on the other. Defence enterprises were unlikely to face a crisis or, after the introduction of elements of a market economy, to go bankrupt. This was because of their special financing. First, they received their share of the state budget in the form of direct and indirect subsidies allocated through the defence budget. They could also count on the budget for other types of financing—for example, construction or labour costs—under other budget headings. Defence-related projects also tended to enjoy priority access to additional resources made available from the central budget and dedicated to, for example, 'technological development' or research and development (R&D).

Defence enterprises functioned in a shortage economy, which meant that some 'typical' features were more exaggerated and privileges were more important. For example, special communication networks took on greater importance in a society where underdeveloped infrastructure was a major obstacle to economic growth.[1] Budget constraints for defence enterprises were softer than usual and they could count on preference over other companies in the desperate struggle for the investment and R&D sources that created the basic dynamic of the modified command economy system.[2] Additional capital resources were provided in the form of direct allocations or loans granted on favourable terms.

In these conditions, typical for shortage economies, it was rational to accumulate reserves in case the supply system should break down. Defence enterprises had the opportunity to create larger reserves because of their specific security needs and their preferential access to supply. Moreover, they were obliged to create a certain level of reserves by central regulations. If in the past this was a significant advantage *vis-à-vis* other companies, today it is a mixed blessing. Some enterprises are desperate to get rid of their reserves of raw materials and spare parts—of a magnitude adequate for three to five years of production—while others can still capitalize on these reserves. For example, in 1994 the Hungarian Nike-Fiocchi enterprise still used fuel and raw materials accumulated by former partner companies which had changed their production profile. These reserves provided crucial inputs relatively cheaply.[3]

A vast network of subcontractors was formerly obliged or 'highly motivated' to cater to defence enterprises—also extremely valuable in the conditions of a shortage economy. Because there was a generally loose work ethic and horizontal inter-enterprise cooperation was at a low level, most of the civilian companies had to struggle permanently for proper and timely supplies.

Defence enterprises not only were systematically rescued if their activities caused major losses but also could afford specific inputs that made their position even more privileged. They were able to select their workforce in a privileged manner, enabling them to produce on a higher technological level than

---

[1] The internal communication systems that connected enterprises with their ministry and cooperation partners still function and remain useful given the erratic public telephone network.

[2] Bauer, T., *Tervgazdasag, beruhazas, ciklusok* [Economy of planning, investment, cycles], (KJK: Budapest, 1981) (in Hungarian).

[3] Interview by the author with Peter Szabo, Managing Director of Nike-Fiocchi, Fuzfogyartelep, Hungary, 14 Apr. 1994.

the average firm. With generous infusions of capital or loans, they could regularly update their capital assets, often with equipment that was internationally competitive. From the 1970s managers and engineers were occasionally allowed to travel to the West to visit trade fairs or companies or to purchase equipment. This was another precious privilege in the years when travel in general was rather restricted and when purchases paid in hard currency were extremely rare and costly.

In principle, the WTO member countries were not supposed to use any Western spare parts or machinery in their military-related production, to avoid dependence on unpredictable outside sources. However, in the factories of all four countries visited by the author, some relatively new Western equipment was seen and experts found who had travelled extensively in the West long before 1989–90.[4] In some cases this privilege created a basis for successful restructuring, while in others it was simply wasted. At the Hungarian MIKI enterprise a fairly high-level laboratory with a highly skilled workforce and up-to-date equipment existed at the end of the 1980s, when the company began to slide into a major crisis. In the early 1990s, when the new management tried to reorganize what was left of the company, these assets were used to try to establish civilian product lines and develop foreign cooperation. At the same time the management of the Czech Zeveta Bojkovice enterprise set up an industrial museum showing products ranging from obsolete manual tools to the latest machine tools controlled by micro-processors—the purpose of which was primarily to underline the prestige of the management.

Another element that raised the general technological level of defence-related companies in East–Central Europe was the widespread imitation and modification of smuggled equipment (a fairly common practice throughout the region). Many machines and instruments on the Coordinating Committee on Multilateral Export Controls (COCOM) list entered the region via engineers who saw them at fairs or obtained single samples that they were able to reconstruct.

In addition to their relative financial and technological advantages, defence enterprises either had their own R&D department, working exclusively for the company, or had access to the results of R&D conducted by central or branch military research institutes. They were well equipped, their employees were well paid and, in contrast to research carried out in the civilian economy, their results were introduced into production relatively quickly. While genuinely high-technology military research was concentrated in the Soviet Union, significant research was carried out by the military research institutes in each country. This high R&D content made military production more costly because its results were rarely transferred to the civilian economy.

The state also generally ensured critical inputs for military production. A whole network of subcontractors providing energy, raw materials, equipment or labour or performing some special technical service was organized by branch ministries to ensure that military-related production continued smoothly. These

---

[4] In each country visited by the author it was said that this was a unique advantage not offered to any other ECE country.

'satellite' enterprises were either obliged or paid extra fees to meet defence enterprise needs as a first priority and produce for them when and what they required.[5] Many enterprises were also given resources to establish their own internal supplier and infrastructure system so that production would not fail under any circumstances. Enterprises also benefited from inter-ministerial cooperation, which was not available to other sectors; for example, in order to increase output in response to an unexpected rise in demand, the Ministry of Defence often provided conscripts as a free or extremely cheap extra workforce.

The extra resources that defence enterprises enjoyed enabled them to recruit a highly trained, versatile workforce. In addition to the financial rewards, quali-fied workers, engineers and researchers found that the prevailing conditions, equipment and requirements gave them an opportunity to perform innovative tasks, often in small, motivated teams. They belonged to the élite, distinguished by their remuneration, social advantages and quality of work. This created a deep attachment to defence industrial activity, which explains why, despite the blows the sector has suffered in recent years and the attractions of civilian pro-duction, many core workers remained faithful to defence enterprises.

This human capital was one major advantage. It was related to another advantage that can be called 'network capital'. Because of the closed, secretive nature of the sector and the need for tight inter-enterprise cooperation, defence industry employees (workers, managers and their supervising authorities) cre-ated an isolated 'ghetto' within society in which people knew each other, exchanged information, provided each other with assistance and shared a strong feeling of mutual dependence.

The state 'cushioned' defence enterprises at both ends of the production chain. Enterprises did not have to worry about selling their output. Interstate agreements guaranteed stable markets, with fixed prices and high profits built in. In each country a monopolist trade agency, specialized in the arms trade, executed agreements concluded by the authorities.

The advantageous position of defence enterprises distanced them from eco-nomic considerations such as cost calculations, efficiency criteria and market-ing. Production and sales were both conducted in isolation from normal mar-kets.[6] Military markets were more demanding regarding technical than economic requirements, and military production had to meet rather unique quality standards amid the general sloppiness of a typical command economy.

A strict and meticulous quality-control system was built into the military production process. In some cases the product was checked at virtually each modification step. Quality control was carried out partly by specialists in the

---

[5] The existence of these extensive support networks is one factor that complicates the estimate of the real size of military production.

[6] The sector did share some characteristics with military-related firms elsewhere. In some branches the purchase of key machinery or inputs from the West created links between producers which, in some cases, turned into more direct cooperation after the Berlin Wall came down. For example, the department of the Hungarian firm Nitrokemia, which produced small arms ammunition, had technical and commercial links with the Italian company Fiocchi after 1967. The Italian company was the main provider of specialist machine tools. In 1990 the ammunition division separated from the parent company and became Nike-Fiocchi, a joint venture.

enterprise and partly by military inspectors. Although this made production slower and more costly than for the average civilian product, it was compensated by the higher prices enterprises received for their military output. In civilian enterprises, on the other hand, in the rare cases where there was genuine quality control it usually came at the end of the production process with the rejection of damaged items; it was rarely an integral part of the production process.

During the industrial adjustment efforts after the end of the cold war, this knowledge of how to produce a product of higher quality was a special feature that military producers could capitalize on. However, during the protracted crisis some considered it too expensive to transfer these processes to civilian production. One of the chief engineers at the Hungarian DIGEP enterprise argued that introducing the same high quality standards as for military production would make civilian products too expensive to be competitive. In contrast, other managers—for example, at the Slovak Martin Diesel enterprise—regarded these quality-control procedures as a major asset.

Defence enterprises had greater potential than other companies and the sector was considered one of the most productive branches of the economy, even taking into consideration the distorted cost and price calculations. It displayed strict quality control and equipment and labour discipline that was better than the average. However, since the defence industry also benefited from special conditions and allowances and taking into consideration those costs absorbed by the whole society, the balance sheet is more difficult to draw up.

The position of defence enterprises was a twin-edged sword since close ties to supervising agencies and the military were a privilege but also carried with them restrictions. In any event their position was very different from the general conditions of enterprises operating outside the military sector. Insulation from the economic realities of the country was one reason why most enterprises failed to see or prepare for the unfolding crisis. Most became virtually paralysed. Instead of facing the changing situation, they tried to ignore it and hoped that their supervising authorities would bail them out.

III. Organizational features of defence enterprises

Defence enterprises in East–Central Europe tended to be giant enterprises located on huge sites. They engaged in highly material-, labour- and energy-intensive production.

There were essentially two types of military-related enterprise. One was designed to be completely self-reliant, with water and energy supplies, a transport system and the full production cycle. Special workshops completed nearly all the steps of the production process, from work in foundries to product testing. In the second type the entire facility was set up for serial production of one type of product from sub-assemblies provided by subcontractors. In both cases a large amount of the capacity was chronically underutilized. However, because of the distorted price system, losses never appeared on the enterprise balance sheet.

As noted above, subcontractors and suppliers were required to meet their obligations to military enterprises regarding time and quality to a degree not seen elsewhere in the economy.

Although the general level of technology was higher in defence-related enterprises, this was not the case during each stage of production. In most enterprises manual production, as in the times of the industrial revolution, coexisted with computer-controlled, automated production lines.

In military production both demand and financial injections into the sector were prone to sharp fluctuations. Unexpected armed conflicts—such as the wars in Korea and Viet Nam—could lead to an urgent need to expand production. Enterprises also often received 'windfall' allocations made available by reshuffling state budget headings or a financial surplus created in the armed forces. These funds had to be spent immediately.

All these discontinuities made enterprises prone to bottlenecks and waste at the best of times. Moreover, whereas civilian enterprises would resist maintaining capacities that were not contributing to revenue, this was not the case in military production.

Losses created by the normal production process were multiplied by the fact that the defence industry was designed to increase production rapidly in time of emergency or war. They were oversized and over-equipped for peacetime production and maintained special 'cold capacities' (known as M-capacities, for mobilization). These consisted of workshops, equipment and a workforce that was not used but could be mobilized at any time. It was very hard to assess the size of these cold capacities, but one can assume that their level was fairly high. In the Hungarian Mechlabor enterprise a minimum of 200 people out of the 2400 employed in 1988 were sustained in this way. In the Czech Adast enterprise huge sealed workshops and documentation were preserved and in the Slovak Liptovsky Hradok enterprise whole factory floors were closed, partly as cold capacities and partly to cut costs. Monitoring the preservation of these capacities was used to justify reserving a 1 per cent 'golden share' or one seat on the Board of Management for a representative of the Ministry of Defence even at factories that were supposedly fully converted, like the Czech Adast enterprise. This meant that the military point of view was always represented in enterprise decisions and on occasion seems to have carried an influence out of proportion to the size of its representation.

The maintenance of unused M-capacity was usually covered by special budget funds outside the defence budget. In Hungary this was allocated directly by the Ministry of Finance and in Poland through the Ministry of Defence. Enterprise managers were particularly unhappy if this allowance was not paid in full or on time, as it was an additional financial resource that could be used, for example, to pay salaries or cover running costs.

Another typical technological feature of defence enterprises was the high percentage of single-purpose machinery. Depending on the nature of production, this could be an item of equipment or a factory line, but often whole workshops were dedicated to producing one specific military product. In certain branches, principally heavy weaponry and ammunition, the factory was often located far from public transport networks and the infrastructure, buildings, storage sites and laboratories had special safety features (see below).

When an item was in use in all the WTO armed forces, the specific military standard required additional investment. In vehicle production, for example, the standards were set taking into consideration the extreme meteorological conditions of the former Soviet Union. Special raw materials and thermal treatment were used in military trucks that were ultimately to be used in East–Central Europe.

Within the defence industry highly intensive production existed side by side with small-scale, bench-top production. There was a strong internal differentiation depending on the nature of production, and the conditions of, for example, heavy weapon producers differed strikingly from optical instrument producers. This diversity was masked by the high level of integration within the sector and the economic and social conditions in which it had functioned in the past. However, it surfaced and caused fundamental differences within and between enterprises once the coherence of the sector was broken. Managerial differences among enterprises began to play an important role.

Nearly all types of military production had a high labour content because of the special skills and often significant amount of manual work required. This made conversion difficult since the civilian production profiles envisaged were often capital-intensive and did not require the skills used in defence-related production.

IV. Special safety features of defence enterprises

Defence enterprises and the special departments of civilian enterprises that worked for them were secretive. Those that were not located in remote places were physically segregated, separated from civilian life and production by high fences, barbed wire, barriers, guards, dogs and other security devices.[7]

Defence enterprises had to ensure that nothing left the factory without authorization and that only those who belonged there could enter the factory. Workers, documents, materials and products were under strict security control, which made production slower and more costly and prevented the wider sharing of ideas and technology. The mobility of the specialized workforce was restricted even outside the factory. Core workers could not travel to the West although their managers and some designers occasionally could.

Security determined their location as well. In the 1950s, before aerial reconnaissance was fully developed, many enterprises—mainly those engaged in pro-

---

[7] Even the ministry departments in charge of 'special production' were isolated from one another, presumably to prevent data from leaking. By the early 1990s this tradition was preserved only in such places as the Polish Central Office of Planning, the Slovak Ministry of Defence and the Czech Ministry of the Economy, where the offices of the military department were still literally behind bars.

ducing heavy weaponry, ammunition and aircraft—were hidden in valleys or on immense tracts of land so that no one would detect them and so that testing could be carried out without disturbance.

In the past it had never been made public which factories actually took part in military production and most enterprises originally started their civilian production to disguise their military-related activity as much as to compensate for fluctuations in military demand. Purely civilian companies were often established close to defence-related firms with the sole purpose of reducing suspicions about the activities of the military plant. The Hungarian Nitrokemia enterprise was built in 1953 for military ammunition production on the shore of Lake Balaton, a major tourist attraction. To disguise its activity, a fertilizer plant was launched as a parallel company activity and a large paper factory was built close to the enterprise.[8]

Civilian production in this context was of secondary importance and low quality. The extra profits from military production offset the losses from civilian production, so the enterprise managers accepted the economic waste. These decisions were expensive at the macroeconomic level. At the time they were made, most of these decisions were unknown and thus impossible to oppose. Today they further complicate the problem of dealing with the consequences of the collapse of the defence industry.

V. The international dimension of defence industry organization

ECE defence enterprises were shaped by the WTO production system in which they functioned. The main guideline for the defence industry throughout the region was the concept of bloc security. The Czech Republic, Hungary, Poland and Slovakia each developed a far larger defence sector than its national resources or military requirements could support.

Within the WTO the interests of the Soviet Union carried special weight and other members had a clearly subordinate position. To ensure that each member country performed in accordance with WTO requirements without challenging the authority of the Soviet Union, a special division of labour was set up. A relatively restricted group of final producers was supplied by a vast layer of subcontractors both within and outside their countries. Producers of end-items often also prepared significant stocks of spare parts for final assembly by enterprises in the Soviet Union. According to many enterprise managers and engineers in East–Central Europe, they often did not know the final purpose of some of the parts they produced.

While the final producers in individual countries were often in a monopolistic position, parallel capacities were established elsewhere in the WTO. This

---

[8] Interview by the author with Jozsef Baracskay, Technical Deputy, and Istvan Szajko, Head of Division, Nitrokemia, Fuzfogyartelep, Hungary, 14 Apr. 1994. While this security factor was important, the production of ammunition, fertilizers and paper also uses some common raw material inputs. Collocation could facilitate the logistics of production.

was partly because one country could not meet the needs of the entire WTO but was also motivated by the desire of the Soviet Union to avoid dependence on any single country. Parallel production rarely meant competition under the WTO system, but it does today.[9] In the production of jet trainer aircraft, tanks and armoured vehicles, for example, Czech, Slovak and Polish companies are in a tough struggle with each other to enter the shrinking international market.

The WTO production system was built on the theory that no product could contain imported Western parts. Research, development and production of the most advanced systems were concentrated in the USSR and almost all other products were manufactured under Soviet licences. These guidelines were expected to ensure maximum independence and autarky in the face of a hostile outside world and, simultaneously, reassert the predominance of the Soviet Union. In reality, some Western components and machinery were used and the member countries increasingly contributed local adaptation and innovation. Each country had its own central research institutes, as did individual enterprises. However, these local R&D centres functioned in close cooperation and under strict WTO supervision.

Major decisions about the size and structure of the defence industry of the member countries were made in Moscow. WTO requirements were given to the national military authorities in the form of unit–material indicators which were transmitted to local defence industry officials and company managers through a special coordinating committee. Enterprises then adjusted to these orders.[10]

Each WTO member country was assigned a certain area or product in which to specialize. These assignments were changed relatively often so that no other country could develop a significant comparative advantage over the Soviet Union. The results of local military R&D could be introduced only if they were authorized by the highest WTO leadership—which in practice meant the Soviet authorities—and shared with the Soviet Union.[11]

Non-Soviet WTO member countries developed a heavy dependence on imports of parts, sub-assemblies and other inputs. They also created enormous capacities and reserves which became surpluses with the demise of the WTO and which enterprises found difficult to convert or shed. This is one of the reasons why the end of the WTO relatively quickly provided the impetus for selling arms and for intense military reorganization throughout the region. Each country felt compelled to complement its lopsided industry and shed the capacities and stocks that were established to satisfy the enormous needs of the former WTO.

---

[9] However, there was limited competition for the supply of, e.g., wheeled and tracked armoured personnel carriers to some countries.

[10] Interview by the author with Dr Laszlo Molnar, manager of the special division of Mechanikai Muvek, Diosd, Hungary, 5 Oct. 1993.

[11] It was a common complaint in former WTO military circles that the national armies subsequently had to pay high licence fees for their own national products.

8. The nature of the crisis in the traditional defence industry

I. Introduction

Reviewing the country studies presented in Part II, four blows can be seen to have pushed the traditional defence enterprises of East–Central Europe into a sudden, deep crisis, namely: the collapse of military–economic cooperation in the Warsaw Treaty Organization (WTO); the withdrawal of state support to enterprises; the loss of markets outside the WTO; and the dramatic domestic social and economic transformation which each country of the region has been going through since the end of the cold war. Any one of these developments would have created adjustment problems for industry, but all of them occurred more or less simultaneously and over a relatively short period of time. The shock effect was dramatic.

There were four immediate manifestations of this at the defence enterprises: an identity crisis, a financial collapse, a loss of markets and a structural/ technological crisis. In sections II–V, each of these dimensions of the crisis are explored in more detail.

1. The first major blow to traditional defence enterprises in the East–Central European (ECE) region was the sudden collapse of WTO-based military– economic cooperation. From one year to the next (at the turn of 1990/91) the huge, stable and lucrative military market in the region ceased to exist. In 1989–90, payments were stopped for some equipment and spare parts that had already been delivered but at the same time there were still some, albeit fewer new orders. In 1991 even these stopped.

In the post-World War II period the ECE defence industry was designed to cater to the requirements of the whole WTO. When the WTO ceased to exist, all the major defence-related companies in the region were left with huge stockpiles of finished military equipment, unfinished items still in production, spare parts and raw materials. In addition, there was a considerable volume of unpaid bills. Having lost their major source of income, these companies quickly became insolvent.[1] Unsold stocks and reserves imposed an additional financial burden. Defence enterprises had accumulated huge reserves—sufficient for at least one year's and often for three to five years' production. This was partly because the previous system of five-year plans gave a clear picture of produc- tion obligations but mostly to compensate for the unpredictability of supply in the economy.

---

[1] In addition, although the client (in many cases the USSR) failed to pay for deliveries, companies often had to pay after-sales tax. This was the case, e.g., for the Polish Warszawa-Okecie enterprise.

The collapse of the WTO military market contributed to the collapse of the civilian markets organized in the Council for Mutual Economic Assistance (CMEA) system as well. Defence enterprises everywhere in the region were dual-purpose firms producing for both civilian and military customers. In addition to their military orders, they generally exported large quantities of civilian goods to the same markets. This facilitated the internal CMEA clearing system by which trade had to be balanced. Arms exports could be balanced by both military and civilian imports. In this way military-related trade became a crucial determining factor in the whole foreign trade system among the ECE countries.

Apart from the loss of income and markets, the disappearance of the WTO and the CMEA also brought the collapse of an extended supply system for military-related enterprises. Producers could no longer rely on large, cheap supplies of raw materials and energy from the Soviet Union and lost intra-regional subcontractors as well. This was another factor that pushed production costs up and caused practical problems in reorganizing economic activities.

2. The second blow to industry was the more or less sudden withdrawal of the state from maintaining, protecting, partially financing and, if necessary, rescuing defence enterprises. Varying from one country to the next, the state 'abandonment' of military production was either sudden or gradual. In Hungary this withdrawal was initiated in 1988 and predated the political turnover. In Czechoslovakia and Poland, the change in state behaviour was sudden and unanticipated.

Radical cuts in the defence budget and the apparent willingness of the state to end its direct involvement in economic life led to a drastic drop in state orders, and all or most of the privileges which defence enterprises formerly enjoyed were eliminated. The number of state orders, which had been falling in the years preceding the political changes, often dropped to zero. Apart from the loss of stable and familiar local markets, the strictly centralized state coordination and regulation system disappeared. The ties between the defence industry, the armed forces and state-sponsored, military-related research and development (R&D) establishments were loosened or cut. Not only did national armies stop ordering their products but military-related enterprises were also deprived of the support of the armed forces in facilitating exports.

Direct forms of state protection—subsidies, access to investment and credits, tax allowances, export and import assistance, and various specific forms of remuneration—also came to an end. As a consequence, the main features of the traditional 'special status' enjoyed by defence enterprises disappeared.

As shown in the country studies in Part II, over time each government adopted some form of new measure to save enterprises that were bankrupt or on the brink of bankruptcy. These measures were initially meant to provide temporary relief for companies and were justified by the strategic or economic importance of production. The measures consisted of writing off bad debts, providing special funds or guarantees for bank credits, exemption from certain taxes, assistance in finding export markets and other, more subtle forms of government support.

Although the state still seemed to be ready to rescue defence enterprises from bankruptcy, there was no clear commitment to the military sector at the beginning of the transformation process. Many enterprise managers stated that they were simply 'forgotten'. Although in fact state abandonment was never total, for those in the defence industry it certainly felt as though it was. The lack of clear guidelines concerning the role of the state in the sector and future plans created the feeling that they were being let down, neglected, even cheated.

3. The third dramatic blow to the ECE defence industry was the loss of traditional markets in the developing countries and, in particular, among the Arab countries of the Middle East. After the mid-1970s, the demand for WTO-produced military hardware became manifest in several Arab states and at the same time specialist government agencies responsible for foreign economic activities related to arms and military technical cooperation in East–Central Europe gained more flexibility in doing business outside the boundaries of the WTO. Although by the mid-1980s there were some warning signs that the capacity of clients to pay was waning, this could still be interpreted as a temporary difficulty that could be corrected in time. Neither the 1990 Iraqi invasion of Kuwait and the UN embargo on Iraq nor the subsequent UN embargo on Libya was anticipated.

The advantage of finding buyers outside the WTO was that they generally paid for goods in hard currency rather than transferable roubles. Military orders also opened the way to civilian markets.[2] Some clients preferred to buy from smaller ECE countries rather than from the Soviet Union, which tended to impose more rigid bureaucratic procedures, in addition to attaching political and strategic conditions to equipment transfers. The loss of these markets, which were the most profitable, contributed to the insecurity and multiplied the financial problems of enterprises.

4. The fourth blow, the transformation process that shook all the ECE countries, added new elements to the crisis while making it extremely difficult for enterprises to address it. Following the spectacular political changes of 1989–90, each country introduced radical measures to achieve macroeconomic stabilization and a rapid transition to a market economy. There is not space in this volume to examine the wider process of transformation in detail. However, these steps created a new economic environment in the ECE countries but not a true market economy. Rather, a strange mix emerged in which new principles, institutions and rules began to coexist and interact with the inheritance of the previous system.

Four aspects of the transformation process had the most significant and direct impact on military-related companies.

---

[2] Specialist government agencies responsible for foreign economic activities related to arms and military technical cooperation could earn enormous profits in trade outside the CMEA by making use of the distorted exchange rates within the WTO–CMEA system. Military hardware could be bought for transferable roubles and resold at world market prices paid in hard currency.

1. *Commercialization/privatization.* All the state-owned enterprises were initially expected to go through the process of privatization or, as a preparatory step, 'commercialization'. This was planned as a series of organizational and legal transformations that would lead to the formation of 'normal' companies. All the countries in the region were more or less successful in introducing this process for enterprises engaged in low- and medium-level production or service units. However, each country had major difficulties in transforming large state-owned enterprises.

The most efficient programme for large-scale privatization was that introduced by the Czechoslovak Government in 1991, which was continued fairly consistently by the Czech Government after the breakup of the Federation. In the other three countries of the region large-scale privatization fell prey to fierce political struggles either between factions within the government or between the government and the opposition. Numerous amendments, distortions and suspensions blocked the process in some sectors in Hungary and Poland and on a large scale in Slovakia after separation from the Czech lands.

The mounting difficulties surrounding large-scale privatization had a significant negative impact on enterprise performance. During the process of privatization many fundamental decisions were postponed since even the near-term conditions were unpredictable. In this atmosphere many of the assets of enterprises were depleted. Skilled workers left, investment in and often basic maintenance of facilities were postponed, and the general chaos along with legislative loopholes gave rise to multiple methods of asset-stripping.

Because of the political and strategic importance of these enterprises, privatization was rarely promoted while at the same time the state owners were unable to allocate the necessary financial means for restructuring. Many companies remained under the supervision of the same ministries and departments as during the state socialist period. Others were transferred to state management agencies or holding companies. Those that were commercialized as a first step towards privatization retained a link to their traditional state authorities, and state agencies were the majority shareholders in most of the commercialized companies. There were very few genuinely private companies in the sector.[3]

2. The *tight monetary policy* introduced to achieve macroeconomic stability had a multiple and somewhat contradictory impact on defence enterprises. Future economic recovery and more or less controlled inflation were certainly favourable prospects. At the same time high interest rates, restricted access to credit, and a drastic reduction in resources for investment and development had a negative impact. The general contraction of the economy, in particular the drastic decrease in local public and private demand, was extremely damaging in that it created unexpected difficulties for companies that tried to overcome the void in military sales by increasing the scope of their civilian production.

3. *Trade liberalization* was welcomed by most defence enterprises because they were no longer obliged to deal with specialist government agencies

---

[3] In the author's sample about 10% of the enterprises were genuinely private.

responsible for foreign economic activities related to arms and military technical cooperation. They could apply for their own trade licences or choose between state and private companies which were licensed to conduct foreign economic activities, including arms exports.

At the same time, the sudden and almost unconditional import liberalization had a devastating impact on local production and trade. Many enterprises that managed to survive the crisis and create new, civilian profiles could not avoid bankruptcy because foreign products crowded them out of local markets.

4. The *shortcomings of the transition economy* and the fact that many old institutions and relationships had broken down while most of the new ones were still defective caused special difficulties for the defence enterprises. For example, the entire financial system was being transformed, but as yet there was no banking system able to provide flexible forms of credit or stock exchange. Capital formation was impossible for defence enterprises just at a time when new investment would have been vital to launch major restructuring programmes or to straighten their balance sheets.

The combination of administrative and tax regulations also disadvantaged defence enterprises. In theory, the market was now free for everyone without exception, but state-owned enterprises were often still limited in their wage, tax and often in their marketing policies. In Slovakia companies were forbidden to sell property over a certain (relatively low) value even though this was one way to raise capital. In Poland state-owned enterprises found it more difficult to get access to credit than private ones that were promoted by the state. Moreover, in Poland some special taxes were only paid by state-owned firms, like the special *popiwek* tax levied on wage increases above officially defined levels. With the exception of the Czech Republic, high turnover taxes were levied on all companies regardless of their status. However, it was much easier to collect taxes from state-owned or corporatized, former state-owned enterprises than from private ones.

There were also serious deficiencies in the labour market and, closely connected, in the social security net; for example, there were very limited resources to pay unemployment benefits. At the same time, mechanisms for easing labour mobility—such as retraining schemes and employment information—were not developed. Not only did the moral and economic weight of making workers redundant mostly rest on the enterprises but mass redundancies at state-owned enterprises could carry political costs. The lack of a fluid real-estate market, the difficulties of finding accommodation close to new employment, and the deficiencies in infrastructure and transport also limited the flexibility of labour.

Military-related enterprises depended on a subcontractor system in which the state played a major role in connecting producers of different kinds. As state agencies withdrew from the active coordination of inter-enterprise activity, it was at the level of the subcontractor system where this was most acutely felt. In some cases, for example in Slovakia, the subcontractor network collapsed. In others it functioned with major difficulties. Military-related companies either took over the functions of former subcontractors or tried to reorganize the system on a contract basis. In both cases reorganization increased the costs of production.

Although these developments induced a sense of uncertainty and even panic, they did not prove to be a strong enough impulse to prompt companies to introduce radical changes. Apart from inertia and a lack of experience in reacting flexibly to changes in market conditions, most enterprise managers did not believe that their conditions were changed permanently. Moreover, behind the radical public declarations about stripping the military sector of all its privileges, managers received many informal messages from official circles that made them believe that not all was lost. Further ambiguity was created by the fact that, in contrast to their public statements regarding the defence sector of the newly elected ECE governments, only that of Czechoslovakia implemented specific measures to promote conversion or any alternative to military production.

The other reason for incredulity among the defence managers was institutional. As long as their companies were not transferred to some state asset holding company (because of the slow pace of large-scale privatization this rarely happened until 1992 at the earliest) they continued to be supervised by the same ministries, usually by the same people or their former deputies. The radical political changes brought major personnel changes in the first rank of state administration, but the second and following ranks were normally left intact unless there were specific reasons for dismissing staff. Government officials in charge of 'special production' often came from the military or from military-related firms and had held their positions for a long time. They had significant knowledge of the specific problems of the sector and a high degree of identification and empathy with it. They tried to find solutions for 'their' enterprises and, despite their commitment to the official government line, found it difficult to write off defence enterprises.

II. The identity crisis

The official declarations that defence enterprises, like any other company, had to 'sink or swim' under the new market conditions plunged them into a deep identity crisis. The rationale for their existence had changed and this psychological shock seems to have been one of the most difficult problems to overcome. Without central prescriptions and directives or in fact being completely exposed to the free market, they no longer knew what the real purpose of their existence was.

Many managers felt very bitter about being 'let down' by the state after decades of protection. From one day to the next they seemed to have been left with the burdens of military production that had been imposed on them by the state. As Stanislaw Kaniak, Managing Director of the PZL-Wola Mechanical

Works in Poland, put it, they felt 'in a way cheated' by their authorities.[4] They found it very debilitating that the goals and criteria for success had become the private affair of the enterprise instead of being explicitly formulated and promoted by a central state agency.

Since they were originally created or taken over by the state to perform specific functions that enjoyed unquestioned priority in government programmes, enterprises found it difficult to cope with the unclear and changing nature of government policy. Official expectations concerning the enterprises still existed but it was more difficult to determine what these expectations were. Frequent changes of government (or changes of policy by the same government) became the norm. Hungarian managers most often complained about the lack of a clear state policy concerning the defence sector. Managers in Slovakia principally felt bitter about being simultaneously kept under rather close state control while denied sufficient financial backing. In Poland, although they complained about state withdrawal, managers were more confident about receiving some kind of central guidance in time. Managers in the Czech Republic were the least worried about state policy: they had the twin advantages of a relatively stable economic background and the genuine determination of central authorities to withdraw from direct intervention in enterprise management.

Second to the lack of central policy guidelines, privatization was the factor that most put into question the former identity of the companies. The large-scale privatization campaigns launched throughout the ECE region had to affect military-related companies in some way. In the very first 'privatization fever', in the early 1990s, governments often declared that defence enterprises would be treated like any other company.

Defence enterprise managers had an ambivalent approach to privatization. One group saw it as the ultimate menace and the clearest evidence that the state had abandoned them. Another saw it as a salvation from state authorities, which no longer had the resources to intervene on their behalf, even where there was the will to do so. Most enterprise managers (and government officials) expected privatization to aid the buildup of cooperation with foreign companies, which would in turn ensure investment capital and new markets.

In the new conditions many managers were in complete confusion about the criteria against which to measure their performance. In the past everything had been clear: they had to meet (or exceed) their planned targets and if there were no major losses or defects they were considered successful. Now, when asked about the goals and success indicators of their firms, they often hesitated. In the end about 70 per cent of the sample answered with one word: 'survival'. However, survival had many interpretations. It meant not going bankrupt, being able to pay bills and workers' salaries, and being able to retain as much of the workforce as possible. Some managers strove to keep only their best qualified workers in the hope of a future recovery.

[4] Interview by the author with Stanislaw Kaniak, Managing Director, and Kazimierz Nobis, Economic and Financial Deputy Director, PZL-Wola, Warsaw, Poland, 28 Mar. 1994.

Many managers saw new military orders as an indicator of success since orders would show which enterprises were likely to be among the few to continue to receive state support. Often the fact that they managed to sell anything at all was cited as a success, no matter what the product, buyer or conditions of sale. Even if in some cases they sold their products at a loss, getting some income to help them through a difficult period was regarded as an achievement.

Relatively few managers named explicit economic indicators as their goals or signs of success. The few who did wanted their company to achieve financial balance, escape the danger of bankruptcy and get access to new credits to accomplish strategic goals. Others named becoming profitable or competitive, principally on international markets. Some even aspired to become the best in their field. This was the ambitious goal of Martin Diesel in Slovakia. Finding new markets or establishing cooperation with a foreign firm was also considered a measure of success, since it generally meant that the firm was able to perform to an internationally acknowledged standard.

As a legacy of the previous system, the indicators of success and targets often included social dimensions. In 1993, at a meeting of the managers of ZTS Martin, Slovakia, an engineer and member of the top management who was a rather typical representative of the old-style management regarded as a success the fact that the company 'was able to keep as much of the workforce as was possible'. A year later Jozef Hanzel, the official company spokesman, stated that the company's aim was 'to look into profitability'.[5] The first goal was typical of the inheritance of the previous economic system, under which work was a constitutional right and large, state-owned enterprises provided multiple social services in addition to their productive functions. Under the quasi-market conditions of economic transformation, maintaining the defence industry was often justified by goals such as diminishing unemployment, helping to balance the state budget or substituting imports with cheaper local production.

With conflicting objectives or no targets at all, managers found it difficult to design strategies for restructuring. Many of the companies that tried to continue as if nothing had changed were among the first to go bankrupt. However, since many of them were large-scale companies that employed several thousand people, the government usually intervened at the last minute to help them survive.

III. Financial collapse

The lack of new WTO orders and payments, coupled with the abrupt withdrawal of state financial support, pushed most defence enterprises into financial

---

[5] Round-table discussion with Peter Magvasi, Financial Director, Jan Fillo, Director of Strategic Management, Juraj Kovacik, Manager of the Engines Division, and other members of the management of the ZTS Martin company at the joint Helsinki Citizens' Assembly–Institute for EastWest Studies meeting on conversion within the framework of the Foundation for East–West Development Initiatives (FEWDI), Martin, Slovakia, 29–30 Mar. 1993; and Interview by the author with Jozef Hanzel, Communications Manager of ZTS Martin, Martin, Slovakia, 16 Feb. 1994.

collapse. However, they had enjoyed a privileged financial position for decades and it is interesting to ask why so many of them collapsed almost immediately. Why were they unable to compensate for the losses of revenue?

A lack of internal cost-efficiency measures made defence enterprises extremely wasteful. In addition, enterprises often required large revenues to support a range of activities that were not directly related to their core activity. Moreover, the logic of their circumstances—in which income was a function of administrative decision rather than sales—pushed them to use or redirect their revenues rather than build up large financial reserves. Part of the outstanding enterprise profit was regularly taken and reallocated to other, less successful enterprises or to social and cultural activities. If they did not spend their yearly income, the central authorities could determine that they did not really need it and they would receive less the following year. Reserves tended to become embodied in other assets, notably capital investment—new buildings, machinery or social and cultural establishments. The most prudent enterprise managers tried to create a technological reserve on which they could draw when they were compelled to compete.

The dramatic financial collapse was understandable in those enterprises where the proportion of military-related production was relatively high. The average share of military production in total output at the most important enterprises varied from country to country. It was highest in Slovakia, with a share of nearly 50 per cent, and lowest in Hungary, with a share of about 30 per cent.[6] The 'critical share' of military production—the level at which the collapse of the defence industry devastated the whole company—also varied. Often, even companies where dependence was lower than average were pushed into financial collapse by the sudden loss of the extra profits and financial advantages they had enjoyed in the past thanks to their marginal military-related activity. However, many enterprises with a relatively low share of military production declared themselves victims of the collapse of the defence industry in the hope of getting help for restructuring.

The financial crisis of 1990–92 had three dimensions: insolvency, a gradual intensification of indebtedness, and an acute lack of resources for restructuring and investment.

1. The first sign of collapse was sudden *insolvency*. Since the enterprises' main foreign and local buyers and cooperation partners stopped payments and since state organizations did not bail them out, income suddenly diminished drastically. These first losses of revenue quickly developed into a more or less permanent state of insolvency. The high overhead costs associated with defence enterprises increased as markets declined. As sales and payments fell, unsold products and unused reserves of materials and parts had to be stored and main-

---

[6] From the author's notes on: SEMA Division Conseil, in cooperation with the Technica group and Sofres, 'The situation of the Slovak defence industry', Unpublished manuscript, [1992]; and Csobay, J., 'A magyar hadiiparrol, penzugyi szemmel' [The Hungarian defence industry from a financial perspective], *Penzugyi Szemle* (Budapest), no. 1 (1990).

tained. According to a 1991 sector study,[7] between 1990 and 1991 a dramatic increase in stocks of materials and energy took place in Slovakia. The Western average at similar companies was 60 days worth of stock, while, in contrast, at ZVS Meopta there were 461 days worth of stock; at ZTS Dubnica, 453; and at PPS Detva, 306. Even the lower stock levels—ZTS Dubnica, 109; ZTS Martin, 86; and PS Povazska Bystrica, 74—were still far higher than those in the West.[8]

Production costs also increased dramatically owing to the high level of unused production capacities. In the sample an average of only 30 per cent of the fixed capital formerly used for military-related production was used. However, unused capacities were not shed. Some employees were temporarily reallocated to other production, but most of the factories reduced work to one shift while many were closed on Fridays or sent their workers on unpaid holidays.

2. Prolonged insolvency logically led to systemic *indebtedness*. New debts began to accumulate in addition to the old debts that companies were unable to service and which were no longer forgiven. Most defence enterprises carried multiple layers of debt. The debts of the oldest enterprises generally dated back to the beginning of the 1980s, when booming military production and exports led to large defence-related investment throughout the ECE region. These debts, although sizeable, would in theory be relatively easy to service since they were principally government-backed, low-interest credits.[9]

Newer debts, stemming from the difficulties of covering daily overhead costs, accumulated quickly in the late 1980s and early 1990s, when the first signs of the crisis appeared. Even in companies where performance was not bad, this period suddenly produced increased debts. To maintain production, many enterprises opted for a unilateral moratorium on their social 'obligations' and stopped paying taxes and bills and servicing earlier debts. Companies often did not have enough money to pay workers' wages and were forced to apply for short-term, high-interest loans. For example, the Polish Warel electronics factory stopped paying its heating, electricity and telephone bills in order to pay salaries and then reported a gross profit in 1993.[10]

Accumulating debts to clients, subcontractors, cooperation partners, tax authorities and public utilities seemed to be the easiest solution since most of the creditors were state-owned and since existing legislation did not provide any efficient sanctions for payment evasion.[11]

The newest debts were created in cases of absolute emergency, mostly through short-term, high-interest loans that were used to pay salaries, finance urgent repairs or run production in the hope of making a specific deal. In all the

[7] SEMA Division Conseil (note 6).
[8] SEMA Division Conseil (note 6).
[9] To make matters worse, in Hungary and Poland retrospective interest-rate increases were introduced, which multiplied the burden. In Slovakia enterprises had to pay penalties for unpaid debts.
[10] Interview by the author with Leszek Radwan, Managing Director of Warel, Zaklady Elektriczne, at the Ministry of Industry and Trade, Warsaw, Poland, 27 Jan. 1994.
[11] In Hungary, where the tax authority published a 'shame list' of companies that failed to pay their taxes, those mentioned did not seem particularly affected by this.

transition economies, as credit conditions were fairly unfavourable for most economic agents, borrowing was often the last resort. Owing to their financial condition, most defence enterprises were not creditworthy, so banks were reluctant to lend to them. If they did decide to grant loans, the conditions were harsh.

3. The third aspect of the financial crisis was the *lack of resources* to invest in simple maintenance or future conversion of military development projects. Even companies with a vision for the future were not in a position to realize it. Of 33 enterprises asked, only 5 answered that they were able to make significant investments between 1990 and 1994.

The acute shortage of resources led to a dramatic erosion of the firms' capital assets. This is why many defence enterprises lost their initial advantage of a higher level of technological development and quality production during the first years of the economic transformation. The technological gap that separated them from the leading global producers of similar products—already large after the isolation and gradual reduction of resources during the cold war—has been increasing further. This has seriously hindered their chances of integration with or even simple participation in the world economy.

IV. The loss of markets

After the collapse of the immense WTO market, defence-related firms had to rely on their respective domestic markets while looking for new markets worldwide. For defence enterprises the radical cuts in military budgets reversed the norm by which they usually had more orders than they could fill.

Defence enterprises not only lost reliable and lucrative markets but were also deprived of the references that national armies could provide after using their products, which were in turn indispensable for export success. The few companies that had internationally marketable products sought references elsewhere. While this was a costly, insecure and slow process, references from renowned foreign companies or international quality certification were more marketable. Firms such as Aero Vodochody and Vlarske Strojirny in the Czech Republic, Mielec and Stalowa Wola in Poland, Comasec-Respirator and TAKI in Hungary, and Martin Diesel in Slovakia succeeded in getting International Standards Organization (ISO) certificates. They introduced Western quality-control systems and used their cooperation with well-known Western enterprises as a reference when they attempted to enter new markets.

The loss of large WTO military markets was a major blow, since most enterprises were established to produce for them. Sales dropped enormously, even at companies that kept their ECE markets. In theory, this loss need not have been a disadvantage. Enterprise managers often complained that within the WTO division of labour they had played a subordinate role—receiving second- and third-generation technology and being prevented from carrying out independent

R&D or cooperation with Western partners. Technological development could be promoted freely after the dissolution of the WTO.

In the past, the number of commercial and production deals between non-Soviet WTO member states was relatively modest compared to deals with the Soviet Union, and they diminished further after the end of the cold war. The new governments in the region were eager to establish trade and cooperation with Western partners, even at the expense of cutting traditional ECE ties.

During the chaotic years of political transformation, defence enterprises were crowded out of most of their traditional markets in the developing countries. Unfortunately, Czech and Slovak resentment concerning Western firms that were busy selling arms while they were also down-sizing their defence industry was justified. Traditional trading partners such as Iraq or Libya fell under UN embargoes. In other cases the United States in particular tried to prevent arms transfers to Iran and Syria, with which all the ECE countries had good relations.[12] Getting access to alternative military markets—Western or non-embargoed developing countries—was difficult, and the successes were generally limited to a relatively small niche.

Most enterprises lost not only arms markets but also the civilian sales which had been linked to military contracts with WTO and developing countries. Many managers found it more difficult to adjust to the sudden loss of the civilian markets of the CMEA than to the loss of military markets. In many cases indeed this loss dealt the final blow to ailing defence enterprises.

The former Soviet market was characterized by political and institutional insecurity in the new states and an inability to pay for goods in cash. The few companies in East–Central Europe that operated with a longer-term time horizon did maintain their sales or service agreements in the former Soviet republics or tried to establish new contacts. However, most of the companies that maintained (or re-established) commercial ties in these countries had to resort to barter agreements. This often meant delayed payments since the raw materials, oil, cotton or similar goods received as payment for their products were resold by a third company that specialized in managing barter deals. The ECE firms, themselves struggling with liquidity problems, could not afford such delays.

The worldwide recession and political events such as the economic sanctions imposed on Iraq also restricted civilian markets. Managers at PZL-Warszawa II foresaw the decline of military orders and tried to increase their civilian output from the mid-1980s. Their promising market in Iraq disappeared from one day to the next. However, the 1991 Persian Gulf War opened opportunities for some companies. For example, the Hungarian Mechanikai Muvek ammunition factory won a tender to recondition unused hand-grenades left behind in Kuwait by Iraqi troops.[13]

[12] *New York Times International*, 13 Feb. 1994.
[13] Interview by the author with Dr Laszlo Molnar, manager of the special division of Mechanikai Muvek, Diosd, Hungary, 5 Oct. 1993.

Defence-related enterprises often experienced a decrease in sales of civilian products in their domestic markets. Some market losses were the result of the general trends affecting all the companies and some were a legacy of military production. The civilian goods produced were usually consumer durables or capital goods, from sewing-machines and household mixers to tractors and construction equipment. With a restrictive monetary policy and recession, the beginning of the transformation period in each ECE country was marked by a sharp drop in investment and effective demand. A significant decrease in private consumption was accompanied by the loss of institutional customers such as schools, hospitals, railways and public transport systems. The crisis in the capital goods market hit the hardest in exactly those branches of economic activity where former defence enterprises could have offered their new civilian products—in road building, construction, public transport and agriculture.

The traditional pattern of consumption in East–Central Europe was another element that kept demand relatively low. Consumers do not annually replace goods that still function properly. The rapid social differentiation across the region favoured consumption—mostly of imported Western products—among the newly rich and prompted the cancellation or postponement of consumption among the newly poor.

Instant and almost complete import liberalization led to fierce competition in the internal markets of the region. Many local producers were crowded out of the markets because they had inferior-quality products or because Western firms knew how to carry out aggressive and efficient marketing. There was also a preference for the formerly 'forbidden fruit' of Western and Asian producers. The Slovak Meopta Optical Works tried to diversify its production by introducing photocopier machines, but even though there was a significant, stable market they were wiped away by competitors from the Far East. The Hungarian Orion enterprise, one of the few defence enterprises that had converted to civilian production before the Berlin Wall fell, was also pushed to the verge of bankruptcy because its domestic electronics products were not competitive with the Western and Asian goods that flooded into the market.[14]

Defence enterprises also generally lost out in the civilian markets because their high operating costs tended to result in expensive goods. Moreover, since the civilian side of production in defence enterprises was of secondary importance, it was relatively less advanced than the military branches. They also suffered badly from their lack of marketing experience.

V. The structural and technological crisis

The term 'structural crisis' here means those problems that stemmed from the fact that the defence sector was declared unnecessary or harmful by the new political establishment. In the new context defence enterprises were regarded

---

[14] Interview by the author with Jan Chovanec, Managing Director, and Laurenc Svitok, Commercial Director, Meopta Bratislava, Bratislava, Slovakia, 2 Apr. 1993; and Kiss, M., *Orion: A Marketing Case Study* (Privatization Research Institute: Budapest, 1993).

simply as a problem: an obsolete, environmentally harmful, inefficient, over-grown branch of industry in need of urgent and radical restructuring. Their specific features—such as large size, special security measures, mixed and highly uneven levels of technology, single-purpose machinery, and enormous stocks and reserves—were now often a burden that made restructuring difficult and costly.

The crisis pushed enterprises into a vicious circle. They already had large unused capacities and output generally fell faster than employment. Sales usually dropped faster than production, so unsold stocks kept increasing. These factors made production more costly and in turn made the products harder to sell, which contributed to increases in overhead costs, and so on.

Enterprises found it very difficult to adjust their scale of production to the new conditions. Those who in the past specialized in customer-tailored, 'élite' military production of, for example, aircraft or optical instruments found that, even if they found potential buyers, their prices were too high for the civilan market. Those enterprises that were geared to military mass-production were surprised to find that civilian markets were unable to absorb a similar volume of goods, even if they found appropriate new products. Some enterprises used their equipment to fill small orders, which made production extremely expensive.

9. Strategies for crisis management and survival

I. Approaches to crisis management

In the transformation of the political and economic systems, defence enterprises suddenly and unexpectedly became subject to a double transition from protected to exposed and from state-owned to private or quasi-private enterprises. Their main problems—financial collapse, lack of markets and lack of a feasible strategy—were of an economic rather than a technical character. Technical problems surfaced as the consequence of the first three aspects of the crisis.

In the past, defence industry managers had not been required to address economic problems nor were they obliged to address problems outside their immediate micro-environment, since their interests were well represented at higher levels. In the crisis, however, they were forced to address these questions. Whatever specific method of adjustment they chose, coping inevitably involved two main elements: (*a*) getting acquainted with the basic elements of economic management; and (*b*) trying to influence the wider social and economic conditions in which they had to act.

In chapter 8, four manifestations of the crisis in the traditional defence industry were identified: an identity crisis, a financial crisis, a loss of markets and a structural/technological crisis. Before considering longer-term approaches to restructuring, the first problem for managers was how to respond to these immediate threats to the enterprises and their employees.

Coping with the identity crisis

Enterprises used four general approaches to deal with the major facets of the identity crisis. One was to try to develop a programme strictly at the enterprise level—the 'lonely rider' approach. The second was to revive old-style political lobbying and the third was to try to find new forms of political representation. The fourth approach—conversion—implied a complete change of identity with a radical change in production profile and management. Since conversion is more far-reaching than the other crisis-management mechanisms, it is addressed separately in section IV.

1. *The lonely rider approach.* The dramatic loss of identity and security led to almost complete isolation at many enterprises. This feeling of isolation was sometimes reinforced by increasing competition between former partners for the diminished allowances available from the state administration, restricted

military orders or access to civilian markets. In some cases there was a complete break, when even elemental communication among the firms stopped.[1]

The breakdown of communication between what had been close partners was counterproductive at the enterprise level. Several firms often took up the same diversification projects and incurred unnecessary costs by, for example, paying individual licence fees and competing with each other on a restricted market. In Slovakia, for example, ZTS Martin and ZTS Dubnica both launched new excavators and bulldozers, products already made by PPS Detva, while ZTS Topolcany, ZTS Prakovice, Vihorlat Snina and VSS Kosice all engaged in production of a similar type of hydraulic equipment.[2]

2. *Old-style political lobbying* entailed personalized bargaining behind the closed doors of the respective ministries. Enterprise representatives travelled to the capital, met their ministry superiors and tried to convince them to act on behalf of their enterprise.[3] Officials from the responsible departments in the Ministries of Industry, Foreign Trade and Defence continued to represent 'their' enterprises in the government and in negotiations with foreign partners. However, these ministries had less patronage to distribute. They could mediate on behalf of the enterprises in export deals or to have debts written off, to receive guarantees for a bank loan or to be represented in discussions of long-term military development projects. Officials could also try to influence parliamentary discussions about levels of military expenditure and its distribution.

Most enterprises were still engaged in such lobbying, which often grew naturally from the communication and coordination that took place between enterprises and ministries. However, some used it as their only strategy of survival while others saw it as a complementary activity.

3. Defence enterprises began a *new style of political representation* as part of their attempt to find a place in the market and represent their own interests in as many forums as possible. Enterprises began to create new types of representative organization, association or business chamber which also engaged in political lobbying, but less at the individual level and more at the corporate level. These organizations made use of the enormous accumulated 'network capital' of enterprise managers and used their connections to perform some completely new functions—for example, to provide marketing or technical information or to organize lectures on topics like the banking system, computing or marketing.

In the Czech Republic the Research, Development and Production (RDP) Group tried to unite and represent companies formerly or currently involved in military-related production or interested in it. In addition to RDP, other representative organizations were created in the military sector. In 1992 the Ministry

---

[1] This was an astonishing change since in the past one of the best sources of information about enterprises had been to ask managers about their partners.

[2] From the author's notes on: SEMA Division Conseil, in cooperation with the Technica group and Sofres, 'The situation of the Slovak defence industry', Unpublished manuscript [1992].

[3] In a small country like Hungary where, although there were some parallel productive capacities, there was no real competition between the enterprises, enterprises had to prove that their product was the most promising. In countries like Poland there was sometimes fierce competition between firms of the same type to produce, e.g., aircraft.

of Defence established the Federal Union of State Enterprises and Joint Stock Companies with 31 enterprises related to the ministry.[4] In mid-1994 a new Association of Armament and Ammunition Producers and Businessmen was created in Vlasim with the aim of representing the sector in economic and political forums.[5]

In Hungary Szeles Gabor, head of the Videoton Holding, launched an initiative to set up a chamber to unite and coordinate companies. Similar organizations had already been initiated by other military-related companies, loosely connected to some official forum—such as the Chamber of Commerce or the Defence Committee of the Parliament. In Slovakia the Union of Engineering Industry was set up, headed by Peter Magvasi, at that time financial manager of ZTS Martin.[6]

Only Poland lacked such an initiative at the enterprise level. According to Waldemar Soroczynski of PZL-Warszawa II, this was because enterprises enjoyed their recently acquired freedom too much. Any type of coordination or cooperation appeared restrictive. The enterprises may also have known that their supervising ministries would reorganize political representation for them. At the same time, the labour unions representing defence enterprises lobbied extremely actively for the revival of military production.

These industrial organizations are too new for it to be possible to reach any conclusion about their importance.

Coping with financial crisis

Enterprises took specific steps to cope with the financial crisis they faced.

1. Enterprises tried to *cut their overhead costs* by laying off workers and trying to sell machinery, spare parts, raw materials and other reserves. They also tried to sell or rent out their premises to cut costs and raise revenue. Some got rid of entire workshops that were impossible to maintain—those built for completely autarkic production—and tried to sell or rent out their extensive infrastructure.

Only a few enterprises retained their social infrastructure. Stadiums, crèches, schools, worker hostels, canteens and even fire-brigades were either handed over to the local municipal government, sold or closed.[7] The negative impact on

---

[4] *A Revue*, June 1992.

[5] *Hospodarske Noviny*, 1 June 1994.

[6] Magvasi, P., 'Approach of the Union of Engineering Industry to the process of conversion of armament production in Slovakia', eds Z. Kominkova and B. Schmognerova, *Conversion of Military Production: Comparative Approach*, Papers presented at a conference organized by the Slovak Academy of Sciences and the Friedrich Ebert Foundation (Slovak Office of the Friedrich Ebert Foundation and the Institute of Economics of the Slovak Academy of Sciences: Bratislava, 1993).

[7] A few enterprises used this social infrastructure to compete for labour or to compensate their employees for the loss in real wages. The Czech Sellier & Bellot, e.g., maintained its health-care institutions to provide its workers good and cheap services that were appreciated at a time when the state health service was rapidly deteriorating and private service was expensive. Warel used its stock of flats to attract young professionals. Interview by the author with Jiri Kuchar, Director of Development, Sellier & Bellot, Vlasim,

the workforce of shedding these functions was rarely compensated by higher material gains. In some cases the consequences extended far beyond the factory gates, in places where practically everything was provided by the main local employer, a military-related company. This was true of, for example, ZTS Martin and Povazska Bystrica, Slovakia; Huta Stalowa Wola, Poland; Adast Adamov, the Czech Republic; and Videoton, Hungary.

2. To reduce the high level of inter-enterprise indebtedness, military producers had to *renegotiate their debts* with subcontractors and partners. Different methods were used for this transaction in each country. In the Czechoslovak Federation, one of the first economic decisions taken after the political changes was to abolish the mutual indebtedness that was paralysing inter-enterprise cooperation. After disintegration of the Federation this project was carried out in the Czech Republic but halted in Slovakia. All the enterprises (not only the military-related ones) had to present their claims and debts to the Chamber of Industry and the National Property Fund. Through a computerized balance mechanism, mutual indebtedness was written off. Pending debts were transferred and managed through the Bank of Consolidation.[8]

In Poland enterprises went through individual debt-renegotiation processes with their creditors and, if they did not reach an agreement, settled the debt in court. Both procedures were long and expensive but, if successful, the companies could go ahead with restructuring programmes.[9]

Most of the enterprises in Slovakia and Hungary continued to multiply their debts. In Hungary the commercialization process of former state-owned enterprises offered an easy way of getting rid of debts. In one method of commercialization the former state-owned enterprise was first converted into a financial holding with divisions from which smaller independent business corporations (mostly limited companies) were established. The financial holding inherited the debts and the new companies began life with a clear balance sheet. Later, the holding was generally declared bankrupt and liquidated. In a unique case, the Dunai Repulogepgyar aircraft enterprise planned to buy its holding company.[10] In Slovakia debts were generally distributed proportionately among the spin-off companies.

3. While enterprises often reached agreement with partner companies, they hoped that *debts to state agencies and state-owned banks* would sooner or later be forgiven, and in some cases government agencies did write off significant

---

Czech Republic, 21 June 1993; and Interview by the author with Leszek Radwan, Managing Director of Warel, Zaklady Elektriczne, Meeting at the Ministry of Industry and Trade, Warsaw, Poland, 27 Jan. 1994.

[8] According to a number of the author's Czech interviewees, in military industrial circles some informal means were used to ease the burden of mutual indebtedness in addition to the official method. Companies used inter-enterprise 'vouchers' backed by a commercial bank which in theory functioned as drafts. Unfortunately, under the conditions of general crisis and eroding trust, some of the companies were badly cheated in these deals. Interview by the author with Petr Lajzner, Economic Deputy Director of Policske Strojirny, Policka, Czech Republic, 16 June 1993.

[9] As was the case in Hungary, the advantage of these lengthy procedures was that during the negotiations the companies did not service their debts.

[10] Interview by the author with Dr Geza Peter Kovacs, President and Director of Dunai Repulogepgyar, Csepel, Hungary, 15 Apr. 1994.

amounts. In Hungary some debts were written off on an individual basis. For example, the debts of HM Radar Rt—the successor to Finommechanikai Muvek, once one of the most significant military producers—were written off by an individual decision of parliament.[11] In Slovakia the government pledged 2 billion korunas in 1993 to relieve the financial burdens of the military-related companies.[12] In the Czech Republic the state wrote off the debt of 2 billion korunas of the Skoda Works—the financial holding to which Skoda-Plzen, the initiator of the RDP Group, belonged.[13] In Poland some outstanding debts to the state were forgiven.[14] The official justification for forgiving outstanding debts was usually the companies' macroeconomic importance or future development potential. Only in Slovakia and to some extent in Poland was it said openly that the state helped these companies because of their military status.

Debts could also be liquidated by converting them into shares. Debt-equity swaps with state-owned banks, foreign trade companies and government institutions such as the Ministry of Defence or former R&D funding institutions began to become popular. This was a way of institutionalizing what had been informal dependencies and loyalties. Bureaucratic supervision was converted into ownership, and state agencies could shape strategic decisions through their position on the Board of Managers or Council of Shareholders. Since they tended to be majority shareholders, this state influence was more marked than that of smaller shareholders who became proprietors through other methods of privatization.[15]

This intertwining of military-related producers, banks and state agencies might in the future become the basis for extremely influential new power groups. Through this concentration of economic and political power such groups might be able to influence the main policies and direction of the embryonic transforming economies.

4. Defence enterprises also began a *search for new capital*. As mentioned above, defence enterprises (like most other enterprises) found it difficult and expensive to acquire credit from commercial banks or the national bank. More often they sought access to special state funds allocated for R&D or regional development projects. Many companies participated in competitions for technology development or job creation. Conversion projects received no special priority and enterprises could apply for money for military-related projects. The Czech Sellier & Bellot enterprise covered one-third of the costs for development of new ammunition for its NATO-standard hand weapon, the Lada, from a

---

[11] Interview by the author with Istvan Hamar, Director, and Janos Medgyesy, Chief Adviser, Military Industrial Office, Hungarian Government, Budapest, 1 Dec. 1993.

[12] *Pravda*, 31 Jan. 1994.

[13] *EastWest*, 27 Apr. 1994.

[14] Interview by the author with Dr Pawel Wieczorek, Central Planning Office, Military Department, Warsaw, Poland, 29 Mar. 1994.

[15] Most privatized Czech companies had several tens of thousands of small shareholders. However, they rarely represented a significant voice in decision making. The management of Sellier & Bellot, Vlasim, had to rent a stadium to host its 10 000 shareholders. Ceska Zbrojovska, Uherski Brod, had 15 000 private coupon holders, but only about 100 attended the first shareholders' meeting. Interview by the author with Jiri Kuchar (note 7).

state subsidy for job creation. The Polish Mielec aircraft company participated in a competition announced by the Polish Industrial Development Agency to launch new civilian products but did not receive any special treatment.[16]

Access to capital could also be sought in the framework of programmes not related to military projects, financed by foreign governments—for example, for environmental protection or industrial cooperation. In these cases companies applied for assistance for a specific activity and, if they received it, the financial infusion could help them to survive. The Hungarian Currus military repair enterprise modernized its air-pressure equipment using favourable loans from the Coal Assistance Fund set up as a gesture of gratitude to the Hungarian Government for opening its borders to refugees from the German Democratic Republic in the summer of 1989. The company also sought assistance through a Finnish cooperation programme.[17]

Occasionally, companies applied for credit from local branches of foreign banks. Only the best companies could apply but, if successful, they could draw multiple benefits from it. They could carry out transactions in foreign currency, without exchange costs, keep a foreign currency account and benefit from advantageous interest rates. Only a few companies in the Czech Republic and Hungary used this method. In Hungary only Videoton-Rendszertechnika (the military-related branch of the large private holding) was able to apply for loans exclusively in foreign currency.[18]

In rare cases enterprises applied for credit from a foreign bank. This required a well-prepared project, foreign cooperation partners and, even in cases where these were present, a loan guarantee from the national bank. The Warszawa-Okecie aircraft company received credit from a US bank after it had acquired a special guarantee from the Polish National Bank.[19] Swidnik in Poland received loans from a French bank under similar conditions.[20] The Czech Zbrojovka Vsetin company received a significant loan from Russian banks.

It is important to note that no form of capital provision was specially targeted for conversion. Only in the former Czechoslovakia did the national R&D agency announce a special competition for conversion projects. Assistance for conversion from Western governments or international agencies was very limited. Western companies did find some avenues for cooperation with East–Central European (ECE) enterprises. However, since conversion is a time- and resource-consuming activity, it is not surprising that most cooperation took place in the military field or in already established civilian projects.

---

[16] Interview by the author with Jiri Kuchar (note 7); and Interview by the author with Wieslaw Pastula, Managing Director of the WSK PZL Mielec transport equipment factory, Mielec, Poland, 23 Mar. 1994.

[17] Interview by the author with Janos Acs, General Director, and Gyozo Czene, Economic Deputy to the General Director, Currus Ministry of Defence Combat Vehicle Technique Company, Godollo, Hungary, 6 Apr. 1994.

[18] Interview by the author with Megyeri Sandor, Managing Director of Videoton System-Technics, Szekesfehervar, Hungary, 8 Apr. 1994.

[19] This was a rather special case because the company could hardly cover its overhead costs and had no access to capital on the Polish financial market because of its low credit rating.

[20] Interview by the author with Wojciech Wyciechowski, Sales Manager of PZL Warszawa-Okecie, at the Ministry of Industry and Trade, Warsaw, Poland, 27 Jan. 1994.

Searching for markets

The search for markets took several forms.

1. *Waiting for new state orders*. When the political transformation began, most defence producers in East–Central Europe had pending orders from their respective armed forces that either were never filled or were filled but never paid for. There were a few companies that could afford to wait for new orders because they had other, civilian projects running. Nevertheless, many believed that orders from their national armies could save them and they lobbied for them desperately. For others, such orders could have offered temporary relief in the difficult period of transformation. This was the case in the Mielec aircraft factory, whose director had many projects but needed the resources to implement them. When a promised deal was suspended by the armed forces in early 1994 Mielec found itself in difficulty.

The often expressed desire of ECE states to join NATO made many companies optimistic about their future prospects. They assumed that the armed forces would need to be modernized and that they would not be able to depend on imported equipment. Companies in the Czech Republic seemed to be the most prepared for this stage. Some, like Sellier & Bellot, Ceska Zbrojovka and Tesla Praha, were ready to launch mass-production as soon as the armed forces gave them the signal.

2. A common attitude among defence enterprises was what Waldemar Soroczynski, Technical Deputy Director of the Polish communications equipment company PZL-Warszawa II, called *'looking hysterically for markets'*. This meant trying to sell anything at any price on any market, which often had negative consequences. Some factories got involved in secret affairs with embargoed countries or criminals and some of these deals became public. Others, eager to enter new markets, sold their products for less than the production cost. The Slovak Meopta optical instruments factory dumped its civilian products—photocopiers and overhead projectors—to obtain Western orders.[21]

Another common negative aspect was that companies diversified production to an economically and technologically unsustainable degree in order to meet any order, however small. They often created such a wide product range that production costs became high and quality dubious. Some enterprises became involved in assembly work; for example, Tesla Pardubice, the Czech producer that developed the sophisticated Tamara surveillance system, received a considerable proportion of its income from assembling toasters and coffee-makers for a German firm for sale in third markets. A significant number of highly skilled workers were engaged in engraving 'Made in Germany' on these items.[22]

3. All the defence enterprises in the ECE region established or enlarged their *marketing* departments in response to the loss of traditional clients. Personnel

[21] Interview by the author with Jan Chovanec, Managing Director, and Laurenc Svitok, Commercial Director of Meopta Bratislava, Bratislava, Slovakia, 2 Apr. 1993.
[22] Interview by the author with Josef Opocensky, Chief Executive Officer of Tesla Pardubice, Pardubice, Czech Republic, 16 June 1993.

were sent on marketing courses organized locally or abroad and some courses were financed from international sources such as the European Union PHARE ('Pologne–Hongrie: action pour la reconversion économique', or Assistance for economic restructuring in the countries of Central and Eastern Europe) programme. International agencies financed some foreign consultancy firms to prepare marketing studies for enterprises, and other approaches were also adopted. The newly established marketing department of the Hungarian scientific and technical instrument firm MIKI was provided with in-house, customer-tailored, practical instruction by Canadian experts, financed by a Canadian Government assistance programme.[23]

Companies also revised the nature of their contacts with the foreign trade agencies that had managed trade in their products. Producers were now able to decide whether or not to continue employing these agencies to supervise cooperation. These agencies had the special experience, contacts and know-how required in this sector but, with the liberalization of foreign trade, many new private or semi-private agencies acquired a licence to trade in weapons. These firms were often set up by former officials in the state administration, the armed forces or the defence industry—rarely by adventurous newcomers. The new companies were more flexible, often targeted special market niches, and were more disposed to use non-standard commercial methods such as leasing and barter. Military producers now had the opportunity to choose the most suitable company for their specific needs.

The most dynamic and adventurous companies tried to find lucrative civilian or military market niches and some were quite successful. For example, the Polish Swidnik aircraft company developed and produced a glider that won prizes in international competitions. However, only in rare cases did this type of production occupy the bulk of the capacity of the company. In most cases producing for a lucrative market niche was a colourful but marginal activity. At Mielec, the ingenious general director set up a small workshop to produce replicas of vintage cars for sale in the Nordic countries. However, this was not enough either to pull Mielec out of the crisis or to convince the company that civilian production had a real potential.

Many enterprises tried to build up foreign cooperation and some, like Aero Vodochody in the Czech Republic and Comasec-Respirator in Hungary, succeeded in building up cooperation with stable, long-term future prospects for securing either domestic markets or opportunities to enter third markets. Establishing a joint venture was often the best way to open markets. Some ECE traders were able to engage partners in the former Soviet Union to pay for deliveries, and the Russian partners of the Polish Stalowa Wola enterprise even paid in advance. Szeles Gabor, who in addition to his position as the head of Videoton was also the head of the Hungarian Alliance of Entrepreneurs, declared that markets in the former Soviet Union could be exploited with the proper trading partner—most often outside the state bureaucracy.

[23] Interview by the author with Dr Geza Tothszollossy, Director General, MIKI Engineering, Budapest, Hungary, 7 Apr. 1994.

Despite these efforts only a handful of the market and cooperation contacts in the sample of companies resulted from systematic market research. Most were based on previous personal ties or accidental encounters. The most successful external links were those in which foreign partners located an ECE enterprise and established the initial contact. In connection with privatization plans for ECE airlines, for example, Boeing screened regional aircraft producers and found the highest-quality subcontractors—Aero Vodochody in the Czech Republic and Mielec in Poland. Tesla Praha contacted IBM accidentally and performed short-term subcontract work for them. After that, IBM connected Tesla Praha with AT&T, which became a joint venture partner.

Former trade and cooperation partners often became new markets or business partners without any effort on the part of enterprises to find alternatives or revise the basis of the relationship. This might have been due to the inexperience of military-related producers and their relative urgency. From the perspective of a radical change in production profile, these relationships could as easily conserve former patterns of production and trade and/or lead to total dependence on a single partner. A typical case is that of the Hungarian Danuvia Engineering Works, which set up a joint venture with its former major partner, the German company Rexrott. Danuvia was one of the very few companies that had converted to civilian production at the beginning of the crisis in Hungary. However, since Danuvia was on the brink of bankruptcy, it accepted the conditions set by the German company, one of which was to cancel a rather promising civilian product that was taken over by the new joint venture. After a few years of joint production, the two companies separated: Rexrott took the best workers and left Danuvia to supply spare parts. Danuvia felt obliged to accept this move since it saw no alternative.[24]

Retooling and reorganization

Defence industry managers were compelled to restructure their enterprises as part of their struggle to cope with the structural crisis in which they found themselves. The strategic choice that enterprise management made concerning future development of the industry determined how their specific technical problems were treated. Conversion to civilian production meant shedding the special technical features required for military production and reorganizing the workforce and management. In this case they faced the severe financial, technical and market-related problems associated with conversion[25] but at the same time they became free to develop in a new direction.

If the enterprise remained in military-related production, special equipment and other arrangements were not an obstacle but capital-intensive qualitative changes were still needed. The basic dilemma was how to finance this transformation. If the state covered the costs, dependence on state authorities and

---

[24] Interview by the author with Laszlo Sebestyen, Director of Danuvia Engineering, Budapest, Hungary, 16 Feb. 1994.
[25] See section IV in this chapter.

limited restructuring were to be expected. This was the case in many Slovak enterprises. If a foreign partner covered most of the costs, then the enterprise became part of a larger production and sales network, which became the major factor in enterprise decisions.

II. Survival strategies

The methods of coping with the different aspects of the crisis presented in chapter 8 always formed part of a wider enterprise policy. Enterprise strategies are rarely fully consistent and often have improvised elements. There are also hardly any archetypal models among the enterprises examined as the basis for this study. However, on the basis of declared goals and the methods of addressing major crisis areas and creating projects for the future, one can distinguish three different types of survival strategy. They range from almost complete inertia to dynamic restructuring.

1. The main feature of the first strategy, *passive survival*, is to diminish running costs without changing the production system; for example, employees are made redundant on the basis of formal criteria rather than future development considerations. If they are close to retirement age, they are given early retirement; if they commute to work, the enterprise no longer covers their travel costs and they are forced to leave.

The production profile in this case is essentially left unchanged, even if the enterprise produces losses or creates products that are hard to sell. The minor changes that are occasionally made are made because of erratic market demands. Production is financed by reallocating financial resources—for example, suspending payment obligations or seeking short-term credit. Additional income might be generated by selling or renting premises and machinery, even below the market value or at the risk of destroying productive assets. A desperate but unstructured and unsystematic search for new markets might also be attempted.

This type of enterprise would need to be found by a potential business partner or a buyer who could dictate the conditions of the deal, including the right to make structural changes. Managers are usually keen to revive old-style political lobbying and actively participate in new political representative organizations in the hope that this will solve their problems.

2. In the second model, enterprises introduce *semi-active strategies* intended to generate new income with new products and/or services. Managers make some organizational changes to create 'islands' of development within the company where new products are developed or production is reorganized. This often happens when foreign cooperation affects a relatively small segment of the enterprise's activities.

A slightly longer-term perspective is employed and some strategic decisions are made or at least prepared. Enterprise behaviour is less motivated by immediate panic but, in common with the passive strategy, this is principally a reactive strategy.

3. Some enterprises undertake *active strategies* involving radical internal restructuring of the enterprise and its activities. In these cases cost reduction is seen as a means of enhancing efficiency. The reduction of personnel is made considering the medium- and long-term development projects, and a long-term perspective is employed in internal reorganization and in building up external relations. A major emphasis is put on active and innovative marketing and on employing research and development (R&D) results, either internal or acquired. Foreign cooperation is not only a source of income but also a means to implement positive backward linkages, new know-how, technology, methods of organizing production and/or establishing systematic market contacts with longer-term prospects.

The examples in this section illustrate typical patterns in enterprise survival strategies.

An example of the *passive survival strategy* was the Czech Zeveta Bojkovice enterprise, once one of the major ammunition producers of the Czechoslovak Federation. The sudden stop of military orders pushed them into an unexpected crisis. The value of production fell from 400 million korunas to 260 million korunas in 1992 and was expected to shrink further in 1993. By 1993, 800 of the 1800 workers employed in 1989 had left the enterprise. Production required a relatively small group of skilled workers and a large number of unskilled ones. Faced with the insecure future of the company, the best trained workers, engineers and some of the managers left, leaving behind a large pool of unskilled workers. The remaining staff was employed in poorly organized, fundamentally unchanged production lines. One-third of the workforce was kept for a potential revival of military production.

The management tried to set up foreign cooperation with a German, an Italian and a US–Dutch company, but all the negotiations fell through. Simultaneously, it was decided that the enterprise would introduce a radical conversion to civilian production, using revenue from the last large sale of ammunition and some of its government subsidy. Zeveta Bojkovice purchased new high-technology equipment but failed to conduct preliminary studies on technological compatibility and market opportunities. These investments did not produce the expected yield and most of the expensive machinery was of no practical use. The company owned a mix of machinery ranging from obsolete hand tools to the latest laser and plasma cutting tools. It was a visual illustration of the extraordinary simultaneous opportunities and irresponsibility of military-related enterprises.

Since Zeveta Bojkovice's management did not check its negotiating partners' liability and reliability, many informally arranged deals fell through. For example, an investment of 3.5 million korunas in machinery to produce ignition switches for washing-machines was based on an offer to buy 260 000 switches per year. When the production line had already been set up, it transpired that the client would buy only one-third of the output. The laser cutting machine bought to produce measuring equipment for export to Latin American and Scandinavian countries was used only one-third of the time since Zeveta Bojkovice could sell only 60 000 of the 200 000 units it was able to produce at full capacity.

When these poorly prepared efforts failed, managers decided to leave or gave up. In June 1993 many workshops were shut down, the bulk of the machinery was unused and workers were sent home on unpaid holiday. The company was privatized in the first wave of coupon privatization. Forty-eight per cent of the shares were owned by investment funds and 22 per cent by a single Czech–Austrian firm. The managers hoped that at the first shareholders' meeting this firm or the Ministry of Defence would intervene and take control.[26]

Companies that followed a similar pattern were the Polish PZL-Wola, the Hungarian Danuvia, the Slovak ZTS Martin and the Czech Avia enterprises. Success or failure was often strongly branch-dependent, and ammunition producers faced difficult problems in general. However, there were examples of enterprises in the sample where a different type of management improved the outlook even in this branch: for example, the Hungarian Nitrokemia and Nike-Fiocchi enterprises were both in a relatively stable position and had relatively promising future prospects.

The *semi-active survival strategy* was the most common choice found in the sample. The Bumar Labedy engineering factory in Gliwice, Poland, provides one example. The enterprise was one of the major arms producers in the cold war era, with nearly a 90 per cent share of military production before 1989. It made a wide range of tanks, tractors and heavy transport equipment, principally for the WTO and Soviet markets. The Soviet 'disaster', as Henryk Pfeifer, the President and General Director, put it, brought the collapse of these markets.[27] The simultaneous loss of domestic orders was also a major blow to the company. By 1991 output had dropped to 30 per cent of the 1988 peak production level and by mid-1994 it had risen to only about 40–45 per cent of this level. The workforce had diminished by one-half. According to the company managers, in 1993 the share of military production was negligible and only a couple of tanks and some spare parts were sold to the Polish armed forces to fill previous orders.[28] The management hoped that a 50 per cent share of military production could be re-established.

In response to the crisis, Bumar-Labedy broadened its existing civilian production lines, principally to act as a subcontractor for foreign companies. The company provided frames for the whole range of cranes produced by the Krupp Works of Germany and spare parts for Volvo-Michigan and had smaller con-

---

[26] Interview by the author with Vaclav Sust, Production Manager of Zeveta Bojkovice, Bojkovice, Czech Republic, 17 June 1993.

[27] Interview by the author with Henryk Pfeifer, President and General Director, and Piotr Oleksy, Marketing Manager, Bumar Labedy Zaklady Mechaniczne, Gliwice, Poland, 25 Mar. 1994.

[28] Although managers at Bumar Labedy implied that military production was dying out, they were also developing a new product: a modernized version of the T-72 tank, the Twardy, which was considered as a potential export success and candidate for large-scale production. *Warsaw Voice*, 26 June 1994.

tracts with Dutch, German and Italian firms. To find new markets, they advertised their products and productive capacities in the Polish press and abroad. In order to improve their financial situation they sold most of their social establishments and tried to generate new income by renting out premises and searching for new sources of assembly work.

Bumar Labedy also went through a major decentralization. Several of its former internal divisions, for example, transmission and spare-parts production, some civilian assembly and some social services such as catering, became independent 'profit centres'. The rest of the civilian assembly and military-related production stayed within the parent company. In July 1993 the enterprise became a treasury-owned joint stock company, one of the first commercialized companies in a group of 31 select enterprises that the government decided to keep in order to maintain military production.

Formally, the management did everything it could to restructure the company. At the same time it clung to the idea that the government was responsible for helping the enterprise. Piotr Oleksy, the marketing manager, stated that all large-scale, state-owned enterprises and the entire military sector needed active government support and promotion to survive.[29] Despite the fact that they had a well-functioning civilian profile, they seemed more interested in developing military-related production, partly because the conditions for it existed and partly because of the promise of government backing.

The internal restructuring carried out at Bumar-Labedy was important, but aside from inevitable formal changes such as the creation of independent subsidiary companies from former divisions it did not substantially alter the internal organization or production methods. In the spring of 1994 only 30–35 per cent of the productive assets were used and according to the firm's managers the staff of 4600 remaining at the parent company was still excessively large for meeting production requirements. The company carried out an advertising campaign to promote its products but failed to research potential new markets actively or to offer new types of activity.

The case of Bumar Labedy was fairly typical of the situation of the whole heavy-weapon production sector. However, there were examples of enterprises with a similar profile that applied different strategies. Martin Diesel, a spin-off enterprise from ZTS Martin, the Slovak counterpart of Bumar-Labedy, was a rare example of an enterprise with a dynamic strategy.

The Hungarian TAKI Research Institute for Telecommunications exemplified an *active strategy*. Its main profile was to develop and produce small series of defence-related electronics and civilian microwave technology. At its peak in the mid-1980s, the company employed almost 1300 people but by 1992 it was on the brink of complete bankruptcy, had no new orders and was heavily in debt. Its workforce decreased to 550 and the best experts left—principally to go to the private sector or recently established joint ventures with a similar profile. The Managing Director, Istvan Erdei, was appointed as a crisis manager by the

[29] Interview by the author with Henryk Pfeifer and Piotr Oleksy (note 27).

state-owned holding company in charge of restructuring and eventually privatizing state-owned enterprises. His aim was to keep the institute together, preserve the special, high-level work culture and demonstrate that the enterprise could run profitably.

Erdei and his team elaborated a three-month, a one-year and a medium-term crisis-management programme. The first programme aimed at avoiding immediate bankruptcy by selling some property (the enterprise was established on very valuable real estate) to service the most urgent debts. The one-year programme included a thorough economic, financial and marketing analysis of all company activities, by department and project, and the medium-term programme was set up on the basis of the results.

TAKI's profile was concentrated on new civilian production lines. An inventory of the training, skills and ambitions of the workforce was carried out and matched with the medium-term enterprise strategy. On this basis some employees were made redundant, new people were hired and the whole staff was reorganized in new, project-based teams. Each team had independent financial management, which helped them to become accountable.

In November 1993 TAKI won a contract to produce digital telephones in a tough competition. This was considered a turning-point, from both the economic and the psychological point of view. In late 1994 about 25 per cent of TAKI's activities were military-related and it was planned to increase this share to 50 per cent. The management also envisaged major investments over the following three years, since TAKI would be unable to compete on new civilian and military markets without a fundamental technological revamp.

Other companies that accomplished dynamic and genuine restructuring were the Czech Aero Vodochody and Sellier & Bellot firms; the Hungarian Comasec-Respirator Rt, Videoton-Rendszertechnika and Dunai Repulogepgyar; and the Slovak Martin Diesel. Certain elements of this strategy were also present in the reorganization of the Polish Mielec and Huta Stalowa Wola, Slovak PS Povazska Bystrica and Czech Adast enterprises.

III. Results

Approximately 70 per cent of the enterprises in the sample followed semi-active survival strategies. In each country a small group, 5–10 per cent of the sample, successfully took up active strategies and seemed likely to progress further. The remaining 20–25 per cent seemed to be in hopeless circumstances and likely to go bankrupt without a government rescue package.

As noted above, at the beginning of the transformation process defence-related enterprises enjoyed certain advantages over their civilian counterparts, and the most competent managers used them to rescue their companies. However, many advantages eroded rapidly and most of the military-related companies found themselves embroiled in problems similar to any large, state-owned civilian company, sometimes made worse by the specificity of military production.

The successful companies were those which were able to build on the positive elements of their military heritage and shed the negative elements. They were able to mobilize their network and information capital and keep and renew their higher than average technology base and workforce, while eliminating wasteful, inefficient and irrational product lines. Most companies reformed some elements of their enterprise while keeping others unchanged. However, because of the overall political and economic changes and their increased freedom of manoeuvre, they could now pursue a far larger range of policies in their struggle for survival.

It was very rare for a company management to opt consciously for a long-term strategy and adjust all other decisions to it. Managers usually found a partial solution to one structural problem and, depending on the outcome of that measure, moved on to other questions. Most often, whether or not a reliable market could be found was the decisive factor in success or failure, but this most often implied that they operated on a 'political' market—that is, state orders achieved through lobbying. If the company had a promising market, other dimensions of the crisis became less pressing. However, sometimes even securing a market was insufficient to offset rigid financial constraints. The Adast enterprise in Adamov, the Czech Republic, was a conversion success story. It managed to introduce a completely civilian production profile consisting of printing machines and oil pumps, and most of its output was exported. However, in the United States, where the company had its own sales office, customers preferred to pay in instalments, a luxury that German and Japanese competitors could afford but Adast could not.[30] Technical problems that required new investment were always addressed last and largely depended on solving other aspects of the crisis.

The first fundamental decision concerned the overall survival strategy. The question of conversion versus remaining in military production (or more often the relative emphasis between the two) was decided afterwards. Where there was a political preference for conversion, therefore, the decision should not be left completely to the enterprise level. In these cases macroeconomic incentives would be required to make conversion attractive to the enterprises.

There seemed to be no correlation between the survival strategy chosen and the decision to remain in military-related production. Active companies did not necessarily choose to convert and some passive ones shed their military production. There were companies that opted for conversion (or were pushed into it) and accomplished a costly and painful change in product profile but, since the attitude of management did not change, they were still basically motivated by panic and inertia and extended the period of their crisis. Others accomplished an active restructuring that could include conversion but also took up offers for military-related production that seemed attractive from the business point of view.

The question of adopting a military or civilian identity was often directly linked to the director's personality. There were very few enterprise managers who did not feel a nostalgia for the 'golden years' of military production and in particular for the special social conditions they had enjoyed. Over 90 per cent of the managers employed in the sector after the political changes had advanced from technical posts or lower-level management positions. They were still insiders in the sector but usually had a more dynamic view of its possibilities. For the few who were new to the military sector, the main issue was enterprise survival. They did not value military-related production unless it offered special advantages. Imre Spronz, Managing Director of Hungarian Comasec-Respirator, noted that 'military orders were just the icing on the cake'.[31]

Based on the sample of evidence there was no direct correlation between the success of the host country in terms of macroeconomic performance and defence industry restructuring and the chances for self-sustaining development for an enterprise. While the most successful country in macroeconomic terms has been the Czech Republic, there were examples of Czech companies that had sunk into inertia and were facing serious problems. Slovakia or Hungary did not manage to solve the principal problems of their macroeconomic or defence industrial restructuring, but in both countries there were successful companies that managed to accomplish genuine transformation.

The correlation between the survival strategy adopted by individual enterprises and the specific defence industrial restructuring policy followed by individual countries was important but not exclusive. The latter created a stimulating or suppressing environment for enterprise decisions but was no longer the principal or single determinant of company strategies.

Similarly, whether the enterprise was state-owned, commercialized or private did not seem to determine its survival strategy. Most of the firms were in some stage of commercialization, a few were genuinely private, and the smallest number were traditional state-owned enterprises. The author met private owners who seemed as nonchalant about the economic aspects of their firm's performance as their ministry-appointed predecessors had been. On the other hand, there were managers of fully state-owned companies with a genuine entrepreneurial spirit.

No link was found between political participation, the survival strategy adopted and its success. Most enterprises were active in political lobbying regardless of their strategic choices. As Jaroslav Mikolasek, Director of the microwave division of the Czech Tesla Praha enterprise, observed, if for no other reason 'it is necessary to lobby to prevent others from lobbying'.[32]

---

[31] Interview by the author with Dr Imre Spronz, Managing Director, Comasec-Respirator, Budapest, Hungary, 16 Feb. 1994.

[32] Interview by the author with Jaroslav Mikolasek, Director of the Microwave Division of Tesla Praha, Prague, Czech Republic, 22 June 1993.

The major determinants of survival strategy were the stamina of the managing director and his team, the product sector and level of technology of the enterprise, the nature of its external relationships and often simply luck. The style and the personality of the management became decisive because, thanks to the general liberalization of the economy, the end of isolation and strict central control over the military sector, companies had greater autonomy. Moreover, the often chaotic and inefficient macroeconomic regulations during at least the first period of transformation together with the immature new market economy gave enterprise decisions and accidental factors greater importance.

Five years after the fall of the Berlin Wall, most ECE defence enterprises were still producing military-related products, albeit on a considerably smaller scale. Their raison d'être and their environment changed dramatically, but most of them survived. From the perspective of the enterprises, this could undoubtedly be considered a success. It illustrated their managers' stubbornness, inherited from the previous system, and impressive survival skills, learned quickly during the tough years of economic transformation. They were able to find some market opportunities, mobilize some financial resources and acquire some military orders.

The most important Western support for conversion came in the form of technical expertise and advice. International agencies assisting the transformation processes rarely put special emphasis on the question. The European Bank for Reconstruction and Development (EBRD) does not have any military conversion programme as such for countries of the region. It supports restructuring and privatization of enterprises, some of which happen to produce military products as well.[33] NATO runs a defence industry conversion pilot project with the aim of acting as a clearing-house and promoting an extensive dialogue on conversion problems, but it has not participated directly in implementing (or financing) projects at enterprises located in the ECE countries.[34]

The most active international organization in this field has been the European Union through its PHARE ('Pologne–Hongrie: action pour la reconversion économique', or Assistance for economic restructuring in the countries of Central and Eastern Europe) programme. PHARE finances technical assistance at both the government and company level. Typical assistance at the company level might include elaboration of global strategy studies, business plans, privatization plans, marketing studies aimed at finding civilian markets for modified ex-military products, partner searches and the like. PHARE has concentrated its efforts in Poland and Slovakia, where the arms sectors were specially developed. In Slovakia 550 000 ECU have been disbursed and 450 000 ECU committed to defence industry conversion. In 1991 PHARE financed a sector

---

[33] The EBRD prefers the term diversification to the term conversion and believes that the most practical approach for defence manufacturers is to expand civilian production without necessarily reducing their military activities. Author's correspondence with Sven O. Hegstad, EBRD, 12 Dec. 1994. See also EBRD, 'The policy of the EBRD towards conversion', Paper presented at the NACC Symposium on Harmonizing Conversion Strategies, Budapest, 15–17 Nov. 1995.

[34] Author's correspondence with Gerard Malet, NATO, 20 June 1994.

study[35] and in November 1993 it financed a conference in Brussels aimed at establishing contacts between Slovak and Western companies. Technical assistance was given to Povazske Strojarne (in Povazska Bystrica), Vychodo Slovenske Zelezarny (VSS, the Slovak Steel Works, in Kosice) and Vihorlat (Snina). In Poland, PZL-Wola received special technical assistance.[36]

Most enterprises managed to survive with minor reforms but without fundamental restructuring or good future prospects. Very often enterprise managers were caught in a 'survival trap'. When asked in interviews if they planned to introduce major changes in their enterprises in the future, they said that this was no longer necessary. If their company survived the difficult years of political and economic transformation, this was proof that their strategy was successful and there was no need for a fundamental change.

However skilful the manager, at some stage most defence-related companies needed some kind of help from government agencies. The new forms of state assistance were more subtle and less intrusive, but they were often essential for helping the company to survive. Such assistance was acquired in the form of securing special conditions such as a bank guarantee, for example, or a ministry-backed export. Sometimes it consisted of channelling extra resources from the state budget to defence-related firms.

These elements cast doubt on whether enterprises that have survived so far really have found viable long-term strategies. It is more likely that many of these companies will continue to report economic losses and remain a burden to the economy. Fundamental change will require further negative or positive incentives and special encouragement if restructuring is to involve conversion.

IV. Conversion experiences

The experience and the specific problems of conversion are addressed in detail as a separate survival strategy for two reasons. One is that the scope of changes required by thorough conversion extends far beyond the enterprise level. Conversion in a strict sense means a radical change of production profile and the employment of the workforce and capital assets formerly tied to military-related production in the civilian sphere. However, military considerations and methods inherited from a command system were deeply embedded not only in the enterprises directly related to the military sector, but in the whole economy and the way it was run. Therefore, the scope and depth of changes need to go far beyond the factory gates. They imply a radical change of attitudes and structures and the introduction of a completely different rationale in management, organization and economic decision making from the shop floor right up to the level of the government.

The second reason is that the post-cold war period offered a unique opportunity for large-scale conversion not only within individual enterprises but

---

[35] SEMA Division Conseil (note 2).

[36] Author's correspondence with Ignacio Iruarrizaga, EU PHARE, 12 Dec. 1994. Interestingly, in interviews carried out at these companies, EU assistance was not mentioned.

throughout the ECE region. In all the countries of the region there was a great deal of 'conversion rhetoric' in statements on political, economic and social change. It is worth studying why, in the end, large-scale conversion failed.

The path of conversion first in the Czechoslovak Federation and then in the Czech and Slovak Republics is presented in detail in chapters 2–4 in Part II. In Poland and Hungary, promoting conversion was never developed into a government policy. In Poland, conversion was proclaimed an objective in 1988 but no policy was designed or introduced to promote it. Enterprises were asked to prepare and implement conversion projects on their own. In the early 1990s the Polish authorities suggested to Western countries a programme in which Polish military-related firms would convert to production of agricultural and food-processing machinery which would be bought by the Soviet Union with Western aid and/or credit. According to Jerzy Kade, head of the military department of the Polish Ministry of Industry and Trade, the project would have contributed to conversion in Poland and benefited the Soviet Union. Unfortunately, the apparent lack of Western interest ended the project.[37]

In Hungary, too, conversion was not officially promoted. A small budget allocation was made for conversion, although companies applied for only a portion of the amount. Government assistance in Hungary and Poland consisted mostly of measures to ease the financial difficulties of enterprises, as discussed above. Since state backing was customary, enterprises did not interpret this as special assistance for conversion. For managers, conversion became associated with their general abandonment and, not surprisingly, they developed a rather antagonistic attitude towards it.

When it was not seen as a negative development, conversion was interpreted to mean diversification—usually the introduction of new civilian profiles alongside military production. It could also mean gradual substitution of military products by civilian ones. Other interpretations gave the word conversion completely new meanings; for example, Hungarian officials interpreted it as conversion from offensive to defensive weaponry, conversion from Eastern- to Western-designed weapons, and rationalization of defence production.[38] In the ECE tradition of interpreting history in terms of conspiracies, it was often claimed that conversion was a plot to destroy the defence industry by an idealistic but harmful government (an interpretation found in the former Czechoslovakia), by the Czechs (found in Slovakia) or by Western competitors (found everywhere).

Despite shortcomings at the macroeconomic level, there were interesting cases worthy of attention. Many companies realized that they needed to convert or at least diversify their activities for the sake of long-term survival. In the

---

[37] Interviews by the author with Jerzy Kade, Director of the Military Department of the Ministry of Industry and Trade, and other representatives of the ministry and the defence industry, Warsaw, Poland, 27 Jan. 1994.

[38] Kovacs, S., at a round-table discussion among defence industry producers and customers, Budapest, Hungary, 25 Nov. 1993; Interview by the author with Gyorgy Buda, Deputy Director, Ministry of International Economic Relations, Budapest, Hungary, 29 Nov. 1993; and Interview with Istvan Hamar, Director, and Janos Medgyesy, Chief Adviser, Military Industrial Office, Budapest, Hungary, 1 Dec. 1993.

most successful cases, managers foresaw the collapse of the ECE defence industry and enterprises such as Bakony Muvek (Hungary), Adast (Czech Republic) and Meopta (Slovakia) began to convert their production facilities before the crisis unfolded.

Other companies tried to survive but failed because of the unfavourable external conditions. MIKI and Orion (Hungary), PZL-Warszawa II (Poland) and Tesla Liptovsky Hradok (Slovakia) probably could have survived the crisis in the defence sector without major disruptions if the collapse of civilian markets had not pushed them to the verge of bankruptcy. Even such enormous conglomerates as ZTS Dubnica (Slovakia) could have been transformed much more successfully if the former Soviet market for gas pumps had not collapsed, pushing the enterprise into further losses and indebtedness. Some companies, like Aero Vodochody (Czech Republic), which foresaw the crisis in the military sector and moved in the other direction—developing military production and introducing NATO standards at the beginning of their transformation—proved to be the most successful survivors. However, Aero Vodochody was one of only a few companies that predicted the saturation of its military market and planned for a gradual increase in civilian output.

There were many creative conversion projects that aimed to use existing technology, professional experience and workers for non-military purposes. Unfortunately, many did not get beyond a first prototype or a short production series. The engineers of Mechlabor (Hungary) produced an electronic wheelchair that was able to perform much better and cost about one-third the price of similar models on the Western market, but the Hungarian social service system did not have the resources to buy them and the company's marketing department could not find any other buyers. Swidnik (Poland) produced a similar wheelchair as a diversification product which was ordered by the Polish social services. Probably the most successful Hungarian conversion products were the fire engines assembled on tank chassis which were used to fight fires in the Kuwaiti oilfields during the 1991 Persian Gulf War.

The Czech Prototypa Research Institute that had concentrated on military-related research and development (R&D) created a number of new products. Before the division of the Federation they produced equipment to monitor pollution with their Slovak partner Konstructa using the same containers that were used for the Tamara surveillance system. Technology used to produce hand weapons was adapted to production of a nail-gun that could shoot nails into concrete. Instruments and technologies for ammunition production were converted to production of oil-drilling equipment and fire extinguishers. A mine plough called 'the Bolshevik' was adapted to clear territories formerly used by the military.[39]

One of the most successful cases of conversion in Slovakia was the Vihorlat Snina enterprise, which became a European leader in producing die-casting machines, hydraulic jacks for trucks, and agricultural and forestry equipment.

---

[39] Interview by the author with Jiri Nepovim, Manager of the Design and Development Department, Prototypa, Brno, Czech Republic, 18 June 1993.

The research institute attached to PS Povazska Bystrica (Slovakia) developed a special non-chemical technology to harden materials. The company hoped to finance further development of the project and find new uses for it.

The case of Vlarske Strojirny (Czech Republic) illustrated how even partial conversion could have a positive impact on an entire company. The enterprise began to produce mountings for diesel engines for Bosch (Germany). The sub-contract provided employment for 50 of the 1350-strong workforce that were still with the company in 1993 (in 1989 Vlarske Strojirny employed 2300). However, even though the Bosch assignment was marginal from the perspective of value added or employment, it had a positive impact on the entire company. As a precondition for cooperation, Bosch carried out an audit of company assets and a thorough analysis of company performance. The management learned a great deal about their own enterprise from this study and intended to implement changes. They also tried to use the organizational and accounting methods established in the framework of the subcontract for other activities. The Bosch assessment was used as a reference when searching for other foreign contacts and helped them to find a Swiss partner. Vlarske Strojirny also had other conversion projects: it expanded its existing textile machinery production and produced rubber pipes, ventilators for gas-pumps and photocopiers. In addition, it assembled small-sized, narrow tractors from components produced at Zetor in Brno.[40]

Despite these promising beginnings both in conversion and general restructuring, the company unfortunately went bankrupt. Vlarske Strojirny was one of the rare cases in which genuine privatization took place. A young Moravian businessman, Ivo Exel, bought the enterprise in 1993. According to some of the previous managers, he won the bid because he was the only one who claimed to be able to pay in cash—he paid a purchasing price of 300 million korunas and assumed 400 million korunas in debts. He promised to keep the company intact and not reduce employment. It later turned out that he had a secret agreement with five other partners, including experts from the former Antonin Zapotocky Military Academy. For some reason the partnership did not hold and Exel was the only investor left in the project. In the end he mortgaged the company's real estate for further credit. By the end of 1994 the company had incurred a loss estimated at 150 million korunas, 80 per cent of its employees were on compulsory holiday, and the National Property Fund started a lawsuit against Exel.[41]

Company management often did not properly assess what conversion would imply at the level of their enterprise. In only a few cases in the sample was a systematic inventory of the premises, machinery, stocks and labour made and assessed in the light of alternative production. Only in the cases of the Hungarian TAKI and Czech Adast enterprises did the senior manager mention that a thorough analysis of the workforce had been made and matched with long-term company strategy. Some kind of sectoral-level coordination—for example, sur-

[40] Interview by the author with Jiri Smotek, Chief Engineer at Vlarske Strojirny, Slavicin, Czech Republic, 17 June 1993.
[41] *Lidove Noviny*, 16 Dec. 1994.

veying idle production capacities and facilitating new civilian cooperation—could have been taken up by central supervising authorities. In an interview carried out in the presence of Military Industrial Office representatives, the manager of the Hungarian Nike-Fiocchi enterprise suggested that an inventory be made of the civilian profiles and capacities of the military-related enterprises and that the authorities should attempt to coordinate and promote them. There was no reaction and none of the enterprises bothered to carry out this relatively simple task themselves.

From the beginning a number of conversion stereotypes were established and many factories were unable to see beyond them. It seemed obvious to tank producers that they should switch production to tractors, bulldozers and construction machinery. Many companies developed the same new products and became competitors on already limited markets. The fact that Vlarske Strojirny built tractors of a smaller and narrower type intended for individual farmers working on small plots or vineyards seemed quite revolutionary.

Conversion of what had been dual-purpose enterprises often meant that the divisions engaged in civilian production increased their output and, during the internal reorganization or decentralization process, became independent civilian enterprises. At the parent company, military production became more concentrated.

There were cases of 'fake' conversion such as when the Czech Adast enterprise stopped producing rocket launchers and transferred this activity to ZTS Dubnica in Slovakia. What appeared to be conversion at the enterprise level was actually a geographic reallocation of military activities at the macro-level. After Czechoslovakia broke up, Adast agreed to re-establish its military production. The Polish proposal to regroup military-related production in select core enterprises was also a concentration of activity rather than conversion.

Most enterprises accomplished partial conversion of existing production or introduced new civilian lines alongside their military-related activities. These diversification projects did not bring major changes in the way the enterprise functioned. The principal function was to help the enterprises survive, often until military demand was revived.

In these cases the same poor and rigid planning, inflexibility and inefficiency that in general characterized military production were also characteristic of conversion projects. New products were manufactured without market research or much attention to design or cost efficiency. However, the civilian market no longer behaved as it had in times of shortage, when it absorbed even poor-quality products. The Lombardini project of ZTS Martin discussed in chapter 4 was a classic case of such poor planning. Many entrepreneurs admitted that their civilian production was expensive and not of the highest quality. Instead of looking into the production process and seeking to improve it, conversion often became a scapegoat for the failures.

One reason why enterprises found conversion such a difficult undertaking was that they had to struggle on their own with its far-reaching negative side-effects. In many cases a successful transformation required major cuts in levels of production and in workforces. Unemployment stemming from internal reorganizations and planned conversion imposed a major economic and moral burden on companies since new labour legislation, which was introduced in all four countries, obliged enterprises to pay compensation to workers who were made redundant. According to company calculations, it was often cheaper to keep low-wage workers than to pay compensation from the drastically diminished enterprise budget.

The absence of feasible regional development projects that could have addressed these problems held back enterprise managers who might otherwise have committed themselves to conversion. In 1992–93 the directors of the Slovak ZTS Martin enterprise were very reluctant to undertake elemental reorganization projects because they feared having to deal with redundancies. Increased unemployment would have caused major social tensions in a town that was totally dependent on the firm. This was typical for many one town–one enterprise cases. The Slovak Meopta enterprise had an easier situation because of its location outside Bratislava, which could offer alternative employment opportunities.

Attitudes towards military versus civilian production varied from company to company. Many managers found the idea that their companies could be reoriented to civilian production both absurd and impossible. The long tradition of military-related production, the strong coherence of the sector and the specific skills it required were more important than anything civilian production could offer. As Jiri Nepovim of the Czech Prototypa Research and Development Institute put it, 'conversion was an obligatory exercise, while military-related development was a genuine challenge of creative work'.[42]

Other companies welcomed conversion despite its obvious difficulties, preferring to expand their civilian profiles as military production became unpredictable and less profitable under the drastically changed conditions. The directors of Currus (Hungary) or Warszawa-Okecie (Poland), for example, confirmed (to some extent in spite of their subjective preference for military-related activity) that under the new conditions they were obliged to rely increasingly on civilian production. Others enjoyed the increased independence and broader perspectives of civilian production. According to Jan Dosek, General Manager of the Czech Adast enterprise, both management and the workforce preferred civilian production because it had a more future-oriented perspective and because the work tasks it required were more versatile. In other cases there were divergent views within an enterprise. In PS Policka (Czech Republic), the general director saw conversion as a major blow to the company, while his deputy found civilian production more interesting and challenging than military production.

[42] Interview by the author with Jiri Nepovim (note 39).

Reasons for failure

There were several reasons why conversion did not succeed in East–Central Europe despite what seemed to be favourable conditions after the cold war. These can be described at three levels: the enterprise (micro) level, the national economic (macro) level and the international level.

The enterprise level

At the enterprise level the primary explanations for the failure of conversion were: (*a*) a lack of commitment to or belief in the idea itself; and (*b*) a lack of specific know-how.

The *lack of commitment to conversion* was a reflection of the fact that the typical features of military-related enterprises did not prepare enterprises to cope with a dramatic challenge. Defence enterprises were reluctant to change, in particular if the required changes meant giving up an identity that had provided so many privileges for them in the past. When they were asked to change on a voluntary basis, most managers simply could not envisage such a move.

Authorities suggested conversion in a transitional period when the centralized command economy was clearly falling apart. Enterprises used their newly found freedom to resist a state policy which seemed to be in conflict with their own short-term interests. Even if conversion might have positive long-term effects, in the hectic and uncertain period of social and economic transformation most enterprises had a short time horizon: they concentrated on immediate survival.

A significant amount of money that had been targeted for conversion was used for other purposes. Additional credits were used to ease the immediate burdens of the crisis-stricken military producers and permitted them to postpone radical changes. Conversion subsidies and credits for conversion could be used to maintain ailing military or civilian production, but many firms did not make use of the conversion funds if doing so required genuine restructuring. Only 10 of the 36 Slovak military-related companies took the opportunity offered by the state to write off single-purpose machinery.[43] In 1992 the Czechoslovak Federal budget provided 116 million korunas to contribute to the costs of retraining the workforce, but enterprises applied for only 8.5 million korunas and actually spent only 6.5 million korunas.[44]

The lack of a genuine commitment to conversion in industry was mirrored by a lack of consistency at the government level. Even in the Czechoslovak Federation the official attitude had a 'stop–go' character, with the importance of con-

---

[43] Mikusova, K., 'Fiscal and credit policy of the government: impact on the conversion of military production', eds Z. Kominkova and B. Schmognerova, *Conversion of Military Production: Comparative Approach*, Papers presented at a conference organized by the Slovak Academy of Sciences and the Friedrich Ebert Foundation (Slovak Office of the Friedrich Ebert Foundation and the Institute of Economics of the Slovak Academy of Sciences: Bratislava, 1993).
[44] *Telegraf*, 19 Aug. 1992.

version often declared but rarely efficiently promoted. The government further confused the signal by turning a blind eye to military production for export.

There was also a *lack of know-how* in spite of the fact that many conversion projects were technically impressive. Workers and engineers developed specific forms of creativity to survive under the permanent shortages and malfunctioning of the command economy. However, innovation took place within the existing organizational structures and forms of management, and little attention was paid to economic feasibility.

Financial, cost or marketing considerations were ignored in most projects, and neglect (or ignorance) of the true market for a product was a common problem. New civilian products were designed without assessing the actual needs and opportunities of the domestic or foreign markets. In the PS Policka ammunition factory in the Czech Republic, the management examined nearly 100 conversion proposals and selected 10 plans. Some products, such as spare parts for hydraulic brakes, sold relatively well but markets could not be found for most of the new products. There was a depressed demand for durable consumer goods like vacuum cleaners or household food mixers, while more sophisticated products—such as pneumatic equipment—quickly had to face competition with well-established Western firms.[45]

As described in chapter 7, defence enterprises were even less suited to adjust to changing external conditions than their civilian counterparts. Environmental damage and the presence of hazardous materials became another obstacle to conversion since they reduced the likelihood that alternative economic activities would relocate to the area. The Slovak 'military triangle' was established in a stunningly beautiful natural setting that became seriously damaged by pollution and disposal of a huge amount of waste material. This endangered the region's potential for tourism and recreation activities. Possibly the worst case of this kind was the Polish central industrial region around Katowice. At the time of the collapse of the old command economy system, this district had become a huge industrial wasteland with extreme health risks, large factories, unemployment and pollution.

The national, macroeconomic level

At the national level, conversion was unsuccessful for four main reasons: (*a*) the social forces pushing for conversion were weak; (*b*) the authorities were fully engaged with the needs of the wider transformation underway in the economy and in society; (*c*) there was a lack of resources for investment in change; and (*d*) there was a lack of markets for alternative products.

1. The *social forces pushing for conversion* at the national level were weak. Even in Czechoslovakia, where conversion at least temporarily ranked among the high-priority government projects, there was no real constituency of offi-

[45] Interview by the author with Bohumir Pospisil, General Director of Policske Strojirny, Policka, Czechoslovakia, 15 Apr. 1992.

cials who promoted and coordinated it. In addition, the programme was launched in a period when the state was expected to withdraw completely from economic intervention. No government agency was officially responsible for conversion. The ministries nominally in charge refused to address the multiple and complex requirements and complications that emanated from the process—such as unemployment, lack of financial resources and regional tensions. These problems were passed around between government agencies: the Ministry of Industry assigned them to the competence of the Ministry of Labour, which sent them to the Ministry of Defence, and so on, and federal agencies referred them to local authorities and vice versa. In the end they remained the responsibility of the enterprises.

As conversion lacked an official advocate, no important social forces or groups pushed for it either. Most projects were designed by the enterprise management in cooperation with their white-collar personnel or outside experts but were rarely discussed with worker representatives. Except in rare cases, worker and union participation was missing from the planning and implementation of conversion projects. This could explain why workers were not on the whole very supportive of conversion. They were the immediate losers in the contraction of the defence industry and the difficulties related to conversion. At the same time they were not involved in the process of finding solutions and often were not even informed about projects. Instead of a long-term, viable alternative to an obsolete and wasteful industrial system, they experienced conversion as a direct threat to their jobs or habitual work tasks.

Apart from a few exceptions, neither enterprise management teams nor government officials dealing directly with the defence sector were genuinely committed either. Most often the same people and departments that had dealt with military production were appointed to deal with conversion. Their perspective was typically enterprise- or sector-oriented, not long-term or macroeconomic. They primarily wanted 'their' enterprises to survive the crisis.

While no social forces lobbied for conversion, the groups that lobbied against it were rather strong. To some extent the traditional military–industrial lobby—which seemed to have collapsed with the political system that created and protected it—began to re-emerge and reconstruct itself in all the ECE countries after 1991. Based on the élite of the armed forces and the interest groups attached to the reformed defence industry, this group became one of the few coherent pressure groups in what were disunited societies. It could build alliances across a broad spectrum that included former communists and liberal market supporters. It could unite the management of military factories, those who had become prosperous thanks to new business opportunities, and a bitter and insecure workforce which was not offered any alternative to an escape into the past.

2. A second major problem for conversion was the implementation of the programme in a period when the transformation of the region was causing eco-

nomic and social dislocations and difficulties.[46] This *problem of historic transition* to a fully fledged market economy was made even more difficult by the deep crisis that had become acute and visible from the late 1980s. Even without conversion, the economic crisis produced unemployment, a drastic drop in living standards, social tensions, growing inequalities while moving enterprises into a state of sectoral and regional disequilibrium, and virtual bankruptcy. Conversion, at least in the short term, aggravated these problems. Since the two processes unfolded simultaneously and their consequences were interwoven, it was easy to confuse the issues—mainly to serve short-sighted political interests. Conversion became a scapegoat for major economic and political problems.

The strict neo-liberal stabilization measures introduced to establish the new economic model created additional difficulties for conversion. Because of the restrictive monetary policy, credit was in short supply and public expenditures were radically curtailed. The sudden withdrawal of most state subsidies and the simultaneous increase in the tax burden contributed to the financial collapse of most military enterprises. Under these circumstances, the conversion subsidies eventually provided by governments were often used for purposes other than conversion. The idea of 'seed-money' was difficult to establish in an economy where most companies were insolvent, where there was a general lack of capital and where old practices—such as false accounting, inter-enterprise indebtedness and mobilization of informal personal networks to get access to scarce resources—were still largely unchanged. In addition, the lack of liquid resources created a complicated system of mutual indebtedness among enterprises. On the basis of former ties, many defence enterprises created informal, non-cash systems of exchange. These barter-based systems fostered the conservation of existing structures both within and among enterprises, instead of stimulating the radical restructuring envisaged in conversion programmes.

Properly functioning market institutions, flexible factor markets and a well-developed, versatile banking system could have eased some of the pains of conversion. Enterprises could have applied for medium- and long-term credit to make the difficult transition from military to civilian production. Unfortunately, decentralized regional banks, banks oriented to specific sectors and small to medium-sized banks were either absent or undercapitalized in the crucial two- to three-year period in which enterprises were considering the relative merits of conversion and military production. The credit policy of the central bank and the main commercial banks was short-term because of the volatile economic situation and also because they enjoyed a monopoly. Other macroeconomic factors—such as the rigidity of the labour market, the shortcomings of the social safety nets, the persisting shortage of housing and the underdevelopment of infrastructure—also had a negative impact on conversion.

The high tax and interest rates that were levied indiscriminately on private enterprises did not favour new firms that could be set up using the premises and

---

[46] The problems for defence enterprises posed by the transformation process are described in chapter 8 in this volume.

assets of former military enterprises and employing workers who were made redundant. At the same time, the restrictive monetary policy led to a drastic fall in private and public consumption which limited the market for new civilian products.

3. The problem of *lack of markets* owing to the fall in private and public local demand severely affected conversion products. The internal market of most of the transition economies shrank in the first years of transformation at the same time as import competition became more fierce. Increasingly, 'prestige consumption' crowded out many local producers since those with disposable incomes preferred foreign goods. The prospects for export were not very promising either, and the difficulties of penetrating potential markets were reinforced by a lack of marketing experience at defence-related companies.

The marketing problems were a clear manifestation of the division that existed between military and general social development. During the period of the classic command economy, all social needs were adjusted to a production system defined by military logic. In the strict hierarchy of needs, the military came first and public and private consumption followed. For this reason infrastructure, light industry, housing and agricultural production were neglected and individual material needs had to be fulfilled from the remaining resources. The primacy of military interests contributed to shortages which in turn created a seller's market. Even poor-quality civilian products could be sold without great difficulty.

In most cases after the political changes—but in two cases (Hungary and the former Yugoslavia) preceding and paving the way for political change—private consumption radically detached itself from the logic of the previous economic system. The 'liberated' private demand led almost immediately to a Western-type pattern of consumption. The discrepancy between what a military command economy could offer and society's real needs was then fully revealed.[47]

In addition, potential foreign markets were also limited because of both the lack of demand and government protection. Although the enormous markets of the former Soviet Union could absorb durable consumer goods and other typical conversion products—such as agricultural and construction machinery—they were in an even deeper crisis and chaos than their ECE counterparts.

4. *Financing conversion* was one key requisite. Military-related enterprises themselves were hardly able to finance projects on their own, since they were in a deep financial crisis. Because they lacked budgeting experience and because of the traditional practice of over-calculating production figures in the framework of a central plan, the cost calculations presented to government by

[47] The 'liberated' private consumption almost immediately became subject to patterns of Western consumer societies which, at least at first sight, are not determined at all by military rationale. However, the defence industrial sector in Western economic–social systems is strikingly similar to that in a typical command economy. Both are characterized by extreme protectionism, captive markets, lack of genuine efficiency criteria, and deep personal and political interrelationships. In one sense the defence industry can be interpreted as the ultimate expression of a consumer society in that production is for destruction, which gives rise to additional production. At the same time, it has features of a classic command economy in that politics dominate the economy and society. The linkages between the 2 systems that opposed each other during the cold war era were in fact more numerous and deeper than was apparent.

military-related enterprises for conversion projects were fairly high. In addition, projects promised a long-term yield and many of their benefits were not immediately evident at the macroeconomic level. Taking the estimated losses of the defence industry owing to the loss of markets together with the total costs of conversion (on the basis of the original plans presented), the proposed sum would have exhausted most of the available state resources.

The calculations seemed even more discouraging when compared with the immediate gains stemming from arms exports and the lower cost to enterprises of modernizing military production in the hope of a future increase in domestic military expenditure. These calculations reflected a short-term and strictly enterprise-centred perspective. In the longer term and in the wider societal perspective, investing in developing the defence industry requires a huge investment. However, these costs are spread over the whole of society and not covered directly by the enterprises.

There were very few economic agents, special banks or investment funds that were able or ready to invest large sums to promote conversion within the respective countries or outside them. The largest resource was the state budget. However, the ECE economies already had overstretched budgets owing to their structural crisis and the costs of the wider transformation process.

To have succeeded, conversion would have had to be made a high-priority political target and in this way benefit from the fairly limited state resources. This was done in 1989–90 in Czechoslovakia—the only country of the region where considerable economic resources were allocated to conversion—but the resources proved insufficient in regard to the real requirements of the process and the reluctance or economic incompetence of enterprises involved. Because of the political shifts taking place in the Czechoslovak Federal Government, the active promotion of conversion silently withered away and conversion became an 'enterprise affair'. The other countries provided even less official financial assistance, reflecting the fact that government motivation was even weaker there.

It is important to note that even the limited economic resources, coupled with the apparent commitment to convert and privatize defence enterprises, had a huge impact on Czechoslovak firms in 1989–92. In these decisive first years, just after the dramatic collapse of the sector, they were pushed (or felt pushed) to take long-term decisions concerning enterprise strategy. This jolted many enterprise managers out of their complacency and prompted them to act. Although the policy guidelines later changed, Czechoslovak (principally Czech) companies were the first and most efficient in coping with the crisis and overcoming it. It is a sad irony that their dynamism later was again focused on military-related production. The momentum of Slovak companies was lost in the political muddle that preceded and followed the disintegration of the Czechoslovak Federation.

The international level

At the international level, the favourable external conditions that facilitated the end of the cold war and the collapse of the political regimes in East–Central Europe became unfavourable in the years following the spectacular political changes. These dramatic changes were due to the heritage of the previous authoritarian system on the one hand and to the crisis of the traditional political systems in the entire developed Western world on the other. The previous state socialist system did not teach its people the methods of democratic, peaceful problem-solving and, instead of resolving deep-rooted ethnic and social conflicts, tried to suppress them. When the heavy repression loosened up, all these unresolved problems surfaced with a shocking violence. The traditional political parties and political institutions of the West at the same time were unable to use their prestige and influence to prevent or assist the solution of the escalating problems of the East and often, as for example in the Yugoslav crisis, their inability to act consistently just made things worse.

Instead of enjoying peaceful cooperation and regained freedom, East–Central Europe became a new centre of crisis, with wars in the former Soviet Union and Yugoslavia and serious ethnic, political and social conflict in all the newly independent countries—even the most prosperous ones like the Visegrad states. The long, deep economic crisis produced thousands of economic refugees (in addition to thousands of political ones) and sharp social diversification. Illegal economic activities flared up, including the growth of a shadow economy and more sinister smuggling of weapons, drugs, people and nuclear materials, carried out under the control of internationalized criminal networks. All these elements made East–Central Europe an extremely volatile and fragile region. In this new situation, the ideas of demilitarization and conversion seemed slightly absurd.

The deep, worldwide recession meant that conversion (and, in reality, the whole restructuring process) had to take place with much less foreign help than was promised or hoped for. Representatives of the defence industry often complained that they were given many promises of help and although they took part in numerous seminars and conferences on the topic they received little effective assistance in the form of aid, investment, enterprise networking, know-how exchange or market research.

The military imprint on society

Even taking into account the obstacles to conversion listed above, it might seem strange that the ECE defence industry, which represented a relatively small segment of the economy, without great international importance, could not adjust or even be fully converted to civilian production without major complications. However, the defence industry was considerably larger than was apparent from official data since statistics usually only took into account the end-producers of weapons and (in some cases) their major subcontractors.

Many subcontractors and enterprises that provided the basic raw materials, energy, transport services, and so on were never classified in the statistics as military-related.

Various unofficial attempts to quantify the sector produced estimates that were higher than the official data. For example, according to Hungarian economist Andras Brody, the costs of military-related activity in Hungary were five times higher than shown in the published data, even using a narrow definition.[48] Aleksander Muller of the Warsaw School of Economy estimated that about 40 per cent of the Polish economy was in some way related to the military sector.[49] The fact that the structure of the military sector was like an iceberg, with much of it out of direct view, made it extremely difficult to assess its genuine impact on the whole economy. This also meant that conversion was a larger and more complicated task than was initially assumed.

In fact, the difficulties encountered by the ECE countries in making fundamental changes also lie much deeper. Military production and the connected system of economic management left a very deep historical imprint at the personal, enterprise and macroeconomic levels in these countries. Not even the important economic and political changes or the announcement of a conversion policy were able to overwrite this.

The armed forces and the local defence industry played a special role in the history of these countries throughout the 19th century. In the Czech lands and Hungary, the military tradition of the Austro-Hungarian Monarchy left the first deep impact, in the form of an authoritarian tradition of social management. This pattern extended, for example, into the schools. In Poland, the rationale for a strong national army and local arms production was justified by a centuries-long armed struggle for independence.

The development of national defence industries was intensified in the interwar period. In Hungary this first took place with the active help and cooperation of fascist Italy and later adjusted to the expansionist policy of another ally, Nazi Germany. The Programme of Gyor set very high targets for military production. It envisaged and partly accomplished the militarization of a large segment of the Hungarian economy, including raw materials, energy, heavy machinery and transport equipment production. Enterprises involved in the project were put under military control.[50] In Czechoslovakia and Poland, defence industries were also developed in a time of an emerging threat of war. When war broke out, both countries were occupied and local defence industries were used by the occupying forces.

After World War II, reconstructing local defence industries became part of the forced industrialization programmes implemented by the new, communist governments. Strategic considerations prompted decisions about the location

---

[48] Brody, A., 'A hon vedelmerol' [About defending home], *Valosag*, no. 6 (1990); and Interview with Andras Brody in *Figyelo*, 20 Dec. 1990.

[49] Interview by the author with Dr Aleksandr Muller, Warsaw School of Economics, Warsaw, 28 Jan. 1994.

[50] Lengyel, G., *From Controlled Economy to War Economy: The Hungarian Economy Between the Two World Wars* (Brooklyn College Press: New York, N.Y., 1993).

and type of industry and the scale of investment in different industrial branches. The predominance of heavy industry and raw material production over agriculture, infrastructure and other industrial branches was ultimately justified by the need to fulfil military requirements. Military considerations also distorted the implementation of many apparently civilian projects. According to the research carried out by Andras Brody, the Budapest underground system was built deeper than was technologically necessary and the country's western highway network, heavy metallurgy and certain branches of chemical industry (such as fertilizer production) were all developed with possible military mobilization in mind.[51] While other countries also take strategic factors into account in planning their infrastructure, they have rarely done so to the same extent as in the state socialist countries.

The establishment and crystallization of the WTO reinforced these tendencies. The structure and size of local defence industries were determined by the needs of the entire WTO system. Certain production branches had to be developed and, since all the ECE countries were rather poor at the beginning of their state socialist period, they had no resources left to develop other areas that would have better corresponded to their natural endowments and traditions.

Military considerations became frozen into the structure of the economy. Branches of industry that were connected with the military sector were formed so that they could perform optimally in case of an emergency. Their production capacities were designed to be larger than peacetime demands required and their reserves, capital assets and workforce had to be maintained by regulation or decree. As a legacy of the permanent state of emergency during the early 1950s, economic 'campaigns' remained a major instrument for increasing output. The strict vertical hierarchy of economic organizations was another feature carried over from the past.[52]

This imprint is very difficult to erase and, even after the disappearance of the classic state socialist systems and the WTO, it still haunts all the former East-bloc countries. The structural deformation of the economies, unusable production capacities and ecological damage will overshadow development for some time to come. The lopsided structure and import dependence of the defence industries and the outstanding debts of the former Soviet Union reinforced the military imprint on the ECE countries.

The trade system that was built on military exchange created a systematic drain of resources from the ECE countries in that the former Soviet Union ran permanent, high-volume trade deficits. After the collapse of the WTO and the Council for Mutual Economic Assistance (CMEA), each country in the region faced the problem of dealing with the huge accumulated debts that were subsequently taken over by Russia. The original Soviet intention was to offset debts

---

[51] *Figyelo*, 20 Dec. 1990.

[52] See more about the nature of the system in Bauer, T., *Tervgazdasag, beruhazas, ciklusok* [Economy of planning, investment, cycles], (KJK: Budapest, 1981); Kornai, J., *A hiany* [The shortage], (KJK: Budapest 1985); and Peto, I. and Szakacs, S., *A hazai gazdasag negy evtizedenek tortenete, 1945–1985* [The history of four decades of the national economy], (KJK: Budapest, 1985), (all in Hungarian).

against establishments left behind as Soviet troops withdrew. President Boris Yeltsin subsequently suggested servicing the debt in kind, with military hardware and spare parts. This proposal was accepted by Hungary and Slovakia, creating the potential for a future armament rivalry between the two countries, but the Czech Republic and Poland initially rejected the offer. Russian representatives also suggested converting the debt into shares in Russian enterprises that were scheduled to be privatized. This suggestion was well received by all these countries, notwithstanding their concerns about the insecurity of the Russian transformation process and more detailed questions about the selection of enterprises, implementation procedures and legal conditions. The need to import spare parts, contract repair work and convert former Soviet debts into new military inputs or into property holdings in Russian enterprises all helped to revive former military-based connections and maintain a special role for the defence sector in the transforming economies.

Genuine conversion of industry to civilian production implies a radical change in the way the economy is managed. At the macroeconomic level the patterns of investment, enterprise and resource allocation in a military command economy are completely different from those in a civilian market economy. In a command economy, the starting-point is military security and, for East–Central Europe in the context of the cold war, bloc security. In a civilian economy these decisions are determined by natural and social resources and the exploitation of comparative advantages. In a command economy there is a strong central and vertical system for both decision making and dependence in which economic units are primarily connected to each other through the centre. There is also a tendency towards strong monopoly. In a civilian economy, multiple and diverse economic agents interact with each other through a flexible network of both horizontal and vertical contacts.

The differences are fundamental at the enterprise level, too. Beyond the special features of the social situation and management system, the basic rationale for production units is fundamentally different. At defence enterprises production is geared to accomplish a 'military–technological optimum', while at civilian companies the aim is to reach 'market-value maximum'. At the former, efforts are made to raise the special utility value of the product, that is, the capacity to destroy or to avoid being destroyed. Every other aspect of the process is subordinate to this main principle. Civilian companies, on the contrary, try to raise the exchange value and, ultimately, their levels of profit. Other dimensions are subordinate to these goals.

The insensitivity to exchange value gives military production an uncontainable character in that no internal economic 'brakes' control or restrict production and production costs. Therefore, limitations should be imposed externally—by introducing strict socio-economic controls over defence enterprises and connected sectors. This requirement is extremely difficult to meet when military-related production enjoys a special status in society. Since the military sector is tightly interwoven with the political (and often economic) élite, there is always a possibility to soften budget constraints. In addition, the main centre of demand for the products of the defence industry, that is, the armed forces, themselves have an extremely loose and inefficient system for managing the economic aspects of their activities.[53]

Altering these structural features and mechanisms, which are typical for a command economy deeply inspired by military considerations, is a central task for the current transformation process throughout the ECE region.

The military imprint is of crucial importance at the enterprise and even at the personal level. The arms industry preserved its long-standing traditions and 'guild mentality' under the umbrella of special social protection. The military heritage became embodied in the enterprises' physical assets, machinery, work methods and workforce. Unskilled workers were attracted to military-related production mainly by the special economic benefits it offered. However, many employees at a senior level or in skilled trades, particularly in R&D departments and design bureaus, had a deep, personal attachment to the defence industry. The fact that most of the military enterprises survived was only partly due to lax economic legislation and renewed state protection; it also owed much to the efforts of the managers, workers, engineers and designers.

[53] After the political changes in the countries of the region, there were some promises to change the armed forces' internal economic system and introduce stricter and more efficient economic management. Minor reforms were introduced in Hungary and Poland. The only country that until the end of 1994 succeeded in implementing fundamental changes was the Czech Republic. See, e.g., Bautzova, L., *Ekonom*, no. 8 (18 Feb. 1993).

10. New features of the defence industry in East–Central Europe

I. Introduction

The recent macroeconomic and political changes and the significant modifications of enterprises have meant that East–Central European (ECE) defence-related companies have distinctively different features compared with the enterprises of the cold war period. The following section presents the most important of their new characteristics.

II. Internal changes at the enterprises

Because of the sharp fall in demand from the late 1980s and the end of the cold war, military-related enterprises have generally become smaller in terms of both their size and sales. Many of their multiple social functions and civilian service activities have been eliminated and they have been slowly converting into enterprises that concentrate on production, often of a relatively limited product range.

All the military-related enterprises went through significant reorganizations. Changes were made in their administrative structures and large reductions were made in their workforces. They all set up new marketing departments and some created strategic development divisions. Since the conditions under which they functioned were much more demanding than those in the past, they were also supposed to function more efficiently—and some undoubtedly did. At the time of writing, in late 1994, however, it was still too early to judge whether or not the measures that were introduced had led to the desired efficiency gains.

Most of the enterprises intended to increase the share of civilian production in their output to compensate for the unpredictable demand for and profitability of military production. The most successful companies intended to combine their military and civilian production in such a way that success in one sphere would advance the other. This was easiest to do in the case of electronics and telecommunications equipment producers or hand-gun and small arms makers, where shifts between civilian and military-related production did not require major technological shifts.

While maintaining a mixed profile was a rational strategy for most enterprises, in a small group the share of military-related production increased significantly—to 80 or even 100 per cent. This was principally a result of the legal and structural reorganizations where, through decentralization, commercialization or privatization, either military-related divisions became independent or their share of civilian production became a negligible part of their output.

Military-related activity usually remained concentrated in the parent companies. In Poland and particularly so in Hungary, the state supervising authorities intentionally created purely or predominantly military enterprises.

Two types of military enterprise seemed to have the best chance of survival and prosperity. The first was the small to medium-sized, flexible and completely or predominantly military-related company. Examples of this type were the Hungarian FEG, Polish Swidnik and Czech CZ enterprises. These companies' relatively small size and specialization in one product type provided them with a niche that had good prospects for profitability. The second type of enterprise was a division within a huge private or partly state-owned holding with a varied production profile. The holding had access to large amounts of capital and could establish and manage a wide range of contacts that could benefit the military division. The military-related division at the same time generated profits, some of which were reinvested in other projects of the holding. Examples of this type were the Czech Skoda-Plzen and the Hungarian Videoton-Rendszertechnica enterprises.

From the technological point of view, companies with the most promising prospects were involved in high-technology, dual-purpose production, in most cases cooperating with leading Western corporations. They managed to reassert their position partly because they accomplished a technological change and partly because of their external ties. Examples were found mostly in the electronics, telecommunications and aircraft industries, such as Videoton and TAKI in Hungary, Aero Vodochody in the Czech Republic and Swidnik in Poland.

Another type of enterprise that may have a stable future is that with a small military division with a stable demand around which a civilian profile could be built. The Czech Sellier & Bellot enterprise, for example, complemented ammunition production with packaging and production of packaging machines. Both activities became rather profitable. In the Hungarian Comasec enterprise, production of equipment for safety in the workplace prospered, to which military-related production was added.

When civilian and military profiles had nothing to do with each other, companies had difficulties to maintain independent production lines. Ideally, production was combined in a way that helped to diminish production costs. Military and civilian production became more interrelated and interdependent, both within individual enterprises and at the macro-level.

The most crucial change that took place at military-related enterprises was a radical renewal at the level of management. In the majority of companies the top managers were appointed after 1990. Many of the previous managers left the sector on their own, choosing early retirement or other occupations. Some were dismissed immediately after the political change and some were replaced by representatives of the new political élite. Since the talent, attitude and ambition of management became crucial factors in enterprise survival, the almost complete renewal of top management was one of the most important changes that took place at the enterprise level, including a change in generation, profession and attitude.

Most managers under the previous system were close to retirement, since these posts had often been assigned for the entire active lifetime of the individual provided no serious mistakes were committed or other, mostly politically motivated, changes did not necessitate their dismissal. The managers were generally engineers or former soldiers, and political reliability was considered more important than managerial skills.[1] In contrast, the new managers were generally between 40 and 50 years of age and had a university degree or some kind of training, often in economics or business studies. They were more dynamic and entrepreneurial than their predecessors, partly because they were less restricted and partly because they were engaged in a fierce struggle for survival created by the new conditions.[2]

Many of the new managers considered that the existing managerial group at their enterprise was a major bottleneck that impeded progress. Some insisted on changing or retraining most of the old managers or bringing in a completely new team, leaving the former managers with only formal functions. As Ryszard Grochowski, Manager of the Polish Stalowa Wola enterprise, put it, 'most managers needed to be brainwashed'.[3] The combination of insecurity and dynamism in the military sector led to new managers being appointed at an unprecedented rate. This had the potential to create some positive mobility, but it also contributed to insecurity and introduced a short-sightedness that was detrimental for long-term projects.

Although these changes in management were important, it is also noteworthy that most of the new directors came from the same fairly restricted circle and their background was in defence-related production, administration or research and development (R&D). Most of the new managers had occupied managerial positions in the second or third rank of the previous hierarchy. Although the military sector became more open, its nature was not completely changed. The emerging private or semi-private military-related sector offered an unprecedented opportunity to many former defence industry managers, professional soldiers and administrators who capitalized on their experience and contacts. For example, Jeno Laszlo, former head of the Hungarian Military Industrial Office (MIO), created his own defence production and trade company after being dismissed from his position; Josef Fucik, former head of the military department of the Czechoslovak Ministry of Economy, was employed by a private company; and the Czech Tesla Pardubice enterprise was bought by a consortium founded by General Oldrich Barak, former Head of Procurement of the Czechoslovak Army.

---

[1] This does not mean that managers were in the past not talented or efficient but that their talents were manifested in other ways than in the economic efficiency of the enterprise.

[2] The fundamental change of managerial attitudes can be illustrated by an anecdote. At the end of an interview conducted by the author with the manager of the Polish PZL Wola company, he was asked what he would ask for if a good fairy could fulfil 3 wishes. After a short and heart-rending briefing about the desperate state of the enterprise, he replied: 'This is the desperate situation where we were pushed. What can you do for us?' In stark contrast Miroslav Macko, commercial manager of the Slovak ZTS Dubnica, replied: 'Thank you, we do not need any fairies here. We would just like to be let alone to work'.

[3] Interview by the author with Ryszard Grochowski, General Director of Huta Stalowa Wola, Stalowa Wola, Poland, 23 Mar. 1994.

III. New social and economic status

Defence enterprises ceased to be an isolated circle of privileged and protected firms. Despite the fact that in each country state agencies made a new selection of military-related enterprises and ensured some privileges for them, the circle was much smaller and their status less advantageous.[4] In addition, although the firms that were declared 'strategically crucial' could count on certain official protection and promotion, the basic principle was that they had to cope under conditions similar to their civilian counterparts.

The selection of protected or specially supervised enterprises became more open and transparent. Military-related enterprises were no longer isolated from the realities in their own countries and they were encouraged to establish contacts both in the local economy and abroad. Even though certain ties with state supervising agencies were maintained, enterprise managers had considerably more freedom to take decisions at the strategic and daily level. In the past they had formed isolated, secretive and informal cliques, while now they were openly and formally united under a state or private agency. They spontaneously created their own professional or political representative organizations.

Instead of the previous, hierarchical, ministry-centred organizational structure, most of the companies are now organized under private or state-owned holdings. The Hungarian Videoton and Czech RDP Group are examples of functioning private holdings. In Slovakia and Poland the process of establishing such holdings is still under way and the holdings are likely to remain under state control. Even when the holdings are state-owned, this new inter-enterprise organizational structure is a more business-oriented association, rather than a bureaucratic system for political control. However, the importance of political factors is not disappearing entirely. Examples of the Czech RDP Group and the Hungarian Videoton Holding illustrate the fact that political and inter-enterprise lobbying is still a very important part of defence industrial activity. Videoton confirmed its position when it beame an exclusive supplier of the Hungarian armed forces, while the attraction of RDP began to falter when it became clear that it was unable to ensure the requested official backing for its activity. Taken to excess, however, political lobbying can alienate potential business partners. Both RDP and Videoton lobby so aggressively that other companies try to avoid cooperation with them or attempt to group themselves into competing teams.

At the beginning of the transformation process it seemed that the main factor that would determine the future status of military-related companies was privatization. Because of the complications of privatization in general and specific issues raised in the defence sector, enterprises in Hungary, Poland and Slovakia were doomed to a protracted process of decision. Even in the Czech Republic, where privatization policy was the most clear-cut and efficient, there were

---

[4] The exception was Hungary, where the MIO operated with 'inflating' lists. However, even there the circle of effectively protected companies was much smaller than it had been previously.

many administrative and organizational shortcomings. The prolonged existential insecurity was certainly one crucial cause of the deterioration in enterprise performance.

However, when an enterprise was privatized or commercialized, the ownership change did not necessarily induce other fundamental changes. It was a generally positive measure in that the enterprise was able to free itself from the restrictions of state ownership (stricter administrative control) and could gain access to some of the advantages that private companies enjoyed (such as certain types of credit). In some cases privatization was a precondition for foreign direct investment, while in other cases state ownership was seen as a guarantee of survival and possible future state orders, and foreign partners therefore insisted on it. In the case of the Slovak Martin Diesel and Hungarian Dunai Repulogepgyar enterprises, for example, the creation of a promising joint venture was suspended because the privatization process was blocked. In the case of the Czech Aero Vodochody and Hungarian Matrafem enterprises, potential foreign investors wanted them to preserve some shares in state property.

Throughout the region, cases of privatization in which a private person or company actually bought an enterprise were rare. Most of these purchases were made with foreign capital through the establishment of a joint venture by a division or an entire enterprise. There were only a few cases where local entrepreneurs bought military-related companies. Moreover, in most cases these deals turned out to be dubious—as in the cases of the Hungarian DIGEP–Army-Coop and Czech Vlarske Strojirny enterprises. Privatization of the Hungarian Videoton and the Czech Skoda companies were special cases in that private entrepreneurs were massively backed by state-owned banks and given other political guarantees.

Most often the smaller units within a formerly state-owned enterprise became independent private or commercialized companies. The new enterprises generally concentrated on one or two main activities. While they were smaller and had a new structure, they rarely had an infusion of new capital and were generally led by the former division management. In most cases the state retained a majority shareholding in which the state was represented by different privatization agencies, state-owned banks or other institutions (such as those in charge of regional development or technological innovation that had previously contributed to financing military-related projects).[5] In carrying out this process, debts were often exchanged for a share of ownership, after which state financing agencies (usually nationalized banks) became the major shareholders.

In most cases in the sample for this study, these new owners did not act as genuine proprietors and were passive. At the Hungarian Videoton enterprise the main new owner, MHB (the Hungarian Credit Bank), which was the principal financing agent of privatization, left the company alone and made no effort to

---

[5] As Adam Stranak put it, 'privatization was the state's last desperate manoeuvre to save defence industry firms'. Interview by the author with Adam Stranak, Engineering Deputy President of Aero Vodochody, Odolena Voda, Czech Republic, 21 Apr. 1994.

introduce any particular efficiency or profit criteria.[6] In other cases, for example, at the Czech PS Policska or the Aero Holding, the banks aimed at short-term gains that were detrimental for the long-term restructuring strategy of the enterprise. In the case of the Polish Stalowa Wola company, the bank that received a large percentage of its shares in exchange for bad debts sold the company's products at lower prices than those of the company itself, hoping to accrue immediate revenue but at the cost of the long-term interests of the company.[7]

Whether a company was state-owned, corporatized or private did not seem to make a difference in terms of the scope of restructuring military or civilian production profiles. The decisive factors were the enterprise management and the general economic environment.

As a consequence of the complex and somewhat chaotic transformation process, the borderline between private and state economic activity was no longer clear-cut. Private and state-owned companies cooperated or competed to secure state allocations in the same ways they had in the past, when they were all state-owned and -managed.

Even at the personal level, the borderlines between state activities and private activities were often blurred. In Hungary and Poland in particular, several managers in state-owned defence industry or state officials dealing with the sector also had their own private companies, for example, for import–export, consultancy or research. In some cases the private activities had nothing to do with the military activity.[8] In others they complemented the main activity.[9] The complicated networks of cross-ownership, the strong personal links between the protagonists of the sector and the connecting activity of their enterprises created significant overlaps between the private and public spheres.

IV. The new role of the state

Decisions that have a direct impact on defence enterprises—for example, on security policy, military doctrine, military reform, application for NATO membership, the size and structure of the budget, privatization and export licensing—are inevitably taken at the state level. In addition, the defence sector is affected by economic policy choices regarding taxes, wages and labour regulations. However, as a result of recent macro- and micro-economic changes in the defence-related sector, the state has much less control over and much less benefit from the defence enterprises in East–Central Europe.

At the same time, from the perspective of the state, the income-generating capacity of the defence industry has seriously diminished. Shrinking arms

[6] In late 1994 a State Audit Office survey called the bank an inefficient owner and questioned the transparency of the whole privatization deal. *Nepszabadsag*, 9 Mar. 1995.

[7] Interview by the author with Tadeusz Suski, Commercial Director, and Alina Niedzalek, Representative of the Foreign Trade Office, of the Huta, Stalowa Wola, Warsaw, 29 Mar. 1994.

[8] E.g., one manager had a small furniture company.

[9] E.g., one manager ran a translation and interpretation agency specialized in professional military–technical texts.

exports have meant shrinking hard-currency revenue as well as a drop in tax revenue because of reduced income at the enterprises and tax evasion. Privatization rarely generated large amounts of capital, since it mostly occurred through a debt-equity swap or against credit. In the rare cases when some cash was generated, it was generally used to support other crisis-stricken divisions in the former company or other state-owned enterprises. In the case of the sale of DIGEP, for example, revenue was transferred to the state-owned parent company from which the division was separated and was used to pay bills and salaries. By the time revenues from defence-related activity went to the state treasury, they had been diminished through multiple diversions.

A mutual alienation of the state and enterprises occurred as they benefited less from their contacts. In comparison with other economic sectors, the defence industry could still be fairly lucrative—especially if exports were realized. In the Czech Republic, Poland and Slovakia, where arms exports were most successful or seemed to be most promising, the state returned to supporting firms directly or indirectly. In Hungary, where defence-related activity did not promise to be lucrative, official backing of the sector remained half-hearted.

After the first years of the transformation, the new political establishment redefined its role in the military sector and reasserted a role in influencing basic decisions, whether the enterprises were private, commercialized or fully state-owned. State regulation and protection were more indirect and included open competition for R&D funds or targeted credit. Those enterprises that succeeded in establishing a relative independence from the state enjoyed a new, more partner-like position during the new administrative–political reorganization. Other enterprises were left to close down or were rescued and brought under state protection. They returned to an administrative dependency that resembled the old one but was more transparent.

In each country there was a delay in introducing new laws to clarify the relationship between the state and the defence industry. Under these conditions the relationship tended to be defined by regulations that could be changed by the government more easily than primary legislation, which required the consent of parliament. The introduction of new regulations which were not consistent with each other or with public statements by politicians about the future directions of policy introduced confusion among industrialists about what they could and could not do.

In public statements, export control was sometimes said to be the only form of regulation needed. In Hungary and the Czech Republic it was assumed that strict control over arms exports would in practice regulate arms production as well. However, export regulations were often difficult to implement. If no other limits were imposed on the weapon production process, the urge to sell the existing stock was a strong incentive to evade regulations.

The fact that governments were unable to prepare and introduce new laws on defence or arms trade in the period 1989–91 can be interpreted as inefficiency or as a deliberate preference for *laissez faire* at a time when enthusiasm for free-market ideas was greatest. Several Slovak experts claimed that the efficiency of Czechoslovak conversion policy was limited because the government did not prevent the continuation of arms production and sales.[10] The state also faced the problem that deals which were not officially sanctioned were difficult to prevent, detect or punish.

The new state involvement in the defence industry was more limited, more indirect and more business-like. Interference in management became fairly rare, and central coordination of inter-enterprise activities disappeared. There were no direct production orders, prescriptions or plan targets. The informal bargaining process between managers and state officials did not disappear. It remained the major instrument for influencing crucial decisions such as writing off enterprise debts, providing subsidies or promoting exports. Some external limitations—such as the budget process or other public controls—now had to be taken into consideration.

In addition to informal ties, state influence took new, formal forms as well, such as export control mechanisms, state representation in the enterprise management boards or through the supervising holding.

Under the new conditions institutional ties between military-related enterprises and state agencies had to be contract-based and follow economic efficiency criteria. Ministries or representatives of the armed forces negotiated and signed contracts for state orders, maintaining capacities to be available in case of a sudden decision to mobilize additional production or facilitating credit.

In the past the cooperation and harmony of interests functioned reasonably well among the three major participants in the defence sector: the state, represented by the Ministry of Defence or the Ministry of Industry and Trade; the defence enterprises; and the armed forces. Military-related R&D, along with financial and material transfers for production, sales and the purchase of inputs such as raw materials and energy supplies, was principally coordinated by central state agencies. However, after the political turnover there was no longer an official agency to play this role. The different agents of military-related activity—the armed forces, enterprises, research institutes and state agencies—had to begin to redefine their relationships after the previous planning mechanisms were dissolved. Defence enterprises lobbied the national armed forces to place even minor orders for their products. Most R&D activity was abandoned because of the lack of resources, and there was a fierce struggle to acquire funding for projects at the military-related research centres.

To make things more complicated, not only did the previous meticulous state coordination disappear but the state itself became more difficult to identify. The more or less monolithic, centralized state hierarchy was replaced with a more shapeless, less defined entity in which different state agencies participated, often each with its own agenda. Ministries and state property-managing

    [10] Stanek, P., 'Problems of employment related to the conversion' and Outrata, P., 'Conversion and industrial policy in the Slovak Republic', eds Z. Kominkova and B. Schmognerova, *Conversion of Military Production: Comparative Approach*, Papers presented at a conference organized by the Slovak Academy of Sciences and the Friedrich Ebert Foundation (Slovak Office of the Friedrich Ebert Foundation and the Institute of Economics of the Slovak Academy of Sciences: Bratislava, 1993).

agencies, banks or the armed forces had different interests and required different forms of interaction with enterprises.

There were tensions and sometimes clashes between the arms producers, representatives of the armed forces, research establishments, and ministry and other state officials. Contradictions surfaced in connection with updating and financing cold capacities and the army procurement and modernization policies—which often did not take into consideration the capacities and needs of the defence industry. Some enterprises tried to find individual solutions to this problem and to conclude agreements that provided a special supplier status for them—for example, the Hungarian Videoton-Rendszertechnica, Czech Aero Vodochody or Polish Swidnik enterprises. In Slovakia research, development and military production remained tightly coordinated by central state agencies.

In each country one argument presented for rescuing the defence-related enterprises was the need to modernize the equipment of the armed forces. This was said to be required to provide security guarantees to the new ECE democracies, to reach a high technological level prior to NATO membership and as part of a wider military reform stressing professional armed forces. However, the armed forces did not necessarily connect their modernization strategy with a revamping of the local defence sector. They were busy reasserting themselves as non-political national institutions and tried to avoid any appearance of lobbying for the military–industrial élite that could damage their democratic credentials. At the same time they tried to adjust themselves to a new objective: the desire for NATO membership. The armed forces were not immune to the demonstration effect from which society as a whole suffered. In the absence of administrative and political obstacles, they were keen to purchase Western technology instead of more modest local products. The only serious restraint was the severely trimmed defence budget.

Western security concerns were an unexpected brake on the development of the armed forces of the region. Countries in the West were eager to establish new regional balances and did not welcome developments in which any country created armed forces that seemed to overpower those of another.

To summarize, the new forms of relationship between the state and defence enterprises became more open, controlled and market-like. The new conditions of cooperation, however, created more blurred borderlines between the military and non-military sectors of the economy. Where enterprise and market-type relations were the most developed, for example, in Hungary or the Czech Republic, civilian enterprises could enter military production on a contract basis if the opportunity seemed attractive. At the same time, unlike in the past, when they usually neglected civilian production, military-related enterprises now were eager to find stable civilian orders.

As state and private ownership and military and civilian activities were no longer clearly separated, defence enterprises became involved in a complicated network of cross-ownership and cooperation. The defence industry became more integrated with the rest of the economy, more diffuse and more organically embedded in the new, still fairly chaotic economic and political system.

This meant that its activities became much more difficult to identify, account for and eventually convert.

V. New external links

Although the declared official aim was to rebuild *national* defence industries, the ECE defence enterprises increasingly cooperated with foreign firms. The forms of cooperation ranged from simple assembly to the establishment of joint ventures. The new external links were motivated primarily by a desperate urge to sell anything, to anyone and at any price. Four patterns of external partnership are discernible.

1. *Contacts with Western industry* were possible after the cold war. The desire to join NATO and the need to export created an enormous eagerness on the part of ECE military producers to establish trade and cooperation contacts with Western companies. Foreign direct investment was seen as the salvation for ailing local industries and, at the same time, as a dynamizing force that would accelerate *rapprochement* with the West. Western investors were supposed to bring capital, high technology, know-how and new markets that would benefit the whole economy. At the same time ECE defence enterprises did not have to accept the risk that their civilian counterparts often faced— absorption into a Western company—because, owing to security considerations, the state rarely allowed a foreign takeover.

This coincided with the interests of Western defence enterprises, which, facing a simultaneous crisis in the Western defence sector, needed to increase their competitiveness and find new markets. East–Central Europe offered unprecedented new opportunities since Western companies could significantly diminish their production costs by moving production to countries where factor costs (especially labour) were significantly cheaper. In addition, Western partners could profit from the synthesis of the formerly separate Eastern and Western equipment and from several advantages provided for foreign direct investment throughout the region.

Despite these advantages, in the first years after the end of the cold war the scope of cooperation in military production was modest, in both quantitative and qualitative terms. Although each ECE country had at least a dozen cases of existing cooperation, usually simple assembly work or production of spare parts, Western partners tended to limit themselves to a partial usage of existing facilities. They seemed to operate with a short time horizon, targeting the cheapest and least risky forms of cooperation without significant new investments or restructuring. Major restructuring would have required considerable financial resources, given the decrepit state of most defence enterprises in the region. Long-term product development or research projects were even more rare.

Very few foreign partner companies were ready to share the costs of eventual research or establish the conditions necessary for cooperation with ECE firms.

In general they entered into joint projects if they were supported by their own state—for example, in the form of interstate economic cooperation. The exceptions were large transnational corporations and some US firms, where cooperation was usually initiated and partially financed by the enterprise. Western cooperating companies were often helpful brokers to find credit opportunities in their respective countries for ECE partners.

By 1993–94, when the new political establishment of the ECE countries came to reassess the importance of domestic arms production and urged the national armed forces to purchase local products, Western companies understood that in order to sell they needed to cooperate with local enterprises. This new awareness led to more intensive contact building, this time on both sides. As the results of ongoing projects such as the modernization of T-72 tanks or aircraft of Soviet design have shown, intense cooperation with Western countries may become significant in certain select programmes. Western cooperation partners see an enormous business potential in these contacts. Pierre Pellegrin, marketing manager of the Belgian company SABCA, noted: 'One can expect big changes in the defense market in the next 10 years, and new products resulting from the mix of two military cultures will be available at unbeatable prices'.[11]

2. *New ties with the developing countries* also became possible, the most obvious being those with a former socialist orientation and some non-aligned countries that already had huge stocks of ex-WTO military hardware. India, Viet Nam, some African countries and to some extent China were seen as the main partners. China was both a potential customer and a powerful competitor for the ECE defence industry. The most agile defence enterprises intended to establish new links with Asian and Latin American countries—particularly those that were actively promoting their defence industries, such as South Korea, Malaysia and Thailand.

Unlike the past, when military-related trade with the developing countries was arranged and promoted at the state level, new relationships could now be initiated and established through contacts between enterprise representatives and potential customers. At a later stage, in particular in the case of large-scale deals, state agencies—usually the former arms-trade monopolist company, the National Bank and the Ministry of Defence—provided special expertise in negotiations and obtaining references or bank guarantees.

3. *New forms of East European contacts* also emerged after the cold war. One declared goal of the Visegrad arrangement was to create a regional cooperation system that would include the military sector. The countries could have made use of their partly parallel, partly complementary defence production potentials and their tradition of close cooperation. There were some declarations in high-level military circles in each country that even preparing for NATO membership could take place as a joint effort.

---

[11] *International Herald Tribune*, 8 June 1994. SABCA participates in the modernization of T-72 tanks along with Slovak partners.

Later, emerging nationalism and increasing competition on world markets became a stronger impulse than cooperation. This led each country to develop and if possible complete the production cycles in its own defence industry to establish a new type of national self-reliance. Most of the previous cooperation links were broken and (especially in the Czech Republic and Slovakia) production capacities were re-established. This led to a huge waste of resources at the regional level. Unused production capacities were rapidly amortized and if a decision were taken to develop new systems (for example, a new air-defence system in each country) it would be extremely expensive to implement. By competing with each other, East European countries on occasion crowd each other out from international markets.[12]

New or surviving contacts between ECE firms were rather limited and either enterprise-based or dependent on the personal relationships between managers. Most were maintained on the basis of previous cooperation by individual enterprise managements since the official policy, especially in the first few years of the transformation, did not encourage contacts. New cooperation contacts were aimed at market niches or at substituting for discontinuities in production. The consequences of the disintegration of Czechoslovakia, for example, opened opportunities for Hungarian and Polish enterprises to sell equipment, spare parts or other products previously provided by the other part of the Federation. Similarly, new contacts emerged with Russian and Ukrainian partners that had lost Soviet subcontractors in the political turmoil.

At the very beginning foreign direct investment by the East (mostly Russia) was not even considered as an opportunity. Later, all the ECE countries realized that significant capital and eventually orders might come from the East. Trading with the new states of the former USSR posed many practical problems— including time delays and a need to barter—which discouraged the formation of many potential partnerships. However, companies with a long-term development strategy realized the importance of maintaining links with the new post-Soviet states. The most ambitious ones maintained their established trade and service networks or tried to build up such networks, even if there was no serious business for the time being. They tried to facilitate barter trade, for example, by using foreign agencies that were specialized in such deals. Many set up joint ventures and pressured their governments to take up the Russian offer to exchange debts for shares in Russian companies that were scheduled to be privatized.

4. The involvement of the ECE countries in the *black market* is very difficult to quantify but has probably increased compared with the past. Before 1989–90 strict administrative control, a high use of capacity (many companies had more orders than they could meet) and the fact that they could earn high profits legally meant that there were very few incentives to risk illegal transactions. Black market connections were mainly related to an extremely lucrative indi-

---

[12] E.g., Poland, Slovakia and Ukraine have competed with each other for the sale of T-72 tanks to Pakistan.

vidual deal or the activity of Soviet soldiers stationed in ECE countries who used arms sales as a source of personal income.

After the end of the cold war, the situation changed completely and the attraction of black market deals became quite evident. In addition, with the escalation of wars and conflicts in the region, there were changes on the demand side: customers were now at the doorstep of crisis-stricken factories. There was no need to transport weapons to other continents or to deal with a large number of middlemen. Apart from the politically motivated customers, there was also an enormous increase in armed criminality in all these countries and, according to media reports, arms were often bought locally or in neighbouring countries.[13]

At the same time, even with this probable increase in suspicious deals, it is unlikely that the black market demand could save the companies facing bankruptcy. In an 'optimal' case this activity might provide just enough revenue to bridge a short period before a more significant state or enterprise decision was taken.

[13] In Poland, *The Independent*, 20 Apr. 1991, p. 12; in the Czech Republic, *Balkan News* and *East European Review*, 1–7 Oct. 1995, p. 16 and *OMRI Daily Digest*, no. 184, part II, 21 Sep. 1995; and in Hungary, *The Independent*, 21 Jan. 1992, p. 8.

Part IV
Conclusions

11. Conclusions

I. Introduction

In 1988–90 the ending of the cold war, the general crisis of the defence industry and the radical system changes in East–Central Europe created extraordinarily favourable conditions for demilitarization and conversion in the countries of the region. By the end of 1994, however, intensive defence industry restructuring was under way. There were several reasons for this turn of events.

The external conditions had changed considerably: the countries of Western Europe had been trapped in a long economic recession that led to economic and political protectionism. Internally, the countries in East–Central Europe were going through a deep crisis of the traditional political structures. Internationally, the all-European institutions that were envisaged as new vehicles of common development and integration faced major difficulties.

The regional cooperation and solidarity that was anticipated in East–Central Europe in fact diminished as the countries became engaged in competition with each other and felt threatened by the escalating, bloody conflicts close to their borders in the former Yugoslavia and the former Soviet Union. At the same time the quick transition they were attempting to make to a Western-type consumer and welfare society became instead a difficult and protracted socio-economic transformation. The changes in the political system were followed by economic crisis. This political and economic context forced the military sector out of its traditional position of privilege. At the same time, the hardships and complications of the transformation undermined the entire undertaking to convert industry from military to civilian production.

All the governments in the region envisaged an export-led development that would both help them overcome their difficulties and integrate them with Western Europe. In their overall export-promotion policy, arms exports represented a relatively developed industrial sector that was able to find international markets. Weapons were seen as products that could be traded without moral or ideological barriers to sales. It was also envisaged that in the macroeconomic transformation the state would withdraw from economic management and that central authorities would deal with trade on a business-like basis.

Conversion was largely left to the market forces and the efforts of individual enterprises. However, the quasi-market economy that developed in the period of transition was not particularly suitable for nurturing civilian production by defence-related enterprises, nor were other economic conditions such as taxes, interest rates and access to preferential credit. At the level of the enterprises, the chaos of transformation often induced inertia. Survival proved to be a stronger impulse than restructuring, and the technological, economic and psychological bonds with military production were very strong.

Alongside the economic transformation, the changes in political conditions also had an impact. Both 'soft' authoritarian and technocratic liberal governments advanced economic and political arguments to justify support for a modernized defence industry and reformed national armed forces. The East–Central European (ECE) countries embraced a new nationalist ideology in which the army and the local defence industry found a new role to play. In the milder versions of this ideology that emerged in the Czech Republic and Poland, reformed armed forces featured as a guarantee of their regained political independence. In Slovakia, the image of strong armed forces and a revived defence industry was used as a symbol of national unity. For all the countries of the region, a revamped defence industry was presented as a significant national achievement and an instrument that could assist them in their desired integration with the Western world.

Another important internal policy factor that acted against conversion was the fear of possible social tension which a radical down-sizing of the defence industry could cause. Political risks attended, challenging a military–industrial lobby that was regaining importance as well. During the spectacular political transformations of 1989–90 corporate representatives of the old *nomenklatura* became fairly dispersed. The formerly dominant élites from the old party structures disappeared—albeit temporarily as most of them subsequently reappeared in different political or economic incarnations. Most of those in large-scale state-owned enterprise management either retired, became redundant or changed their activity. The trade unions dissolved into factions, even in Poland. The army, however, managed to survive the change—albeit with necessary reforms. Its survival meant that local defence industries could survive as well.

As a result of these fundamental changes, which took place in the five years after the systemic political changes, radical demilitarization and conversion disappeared from the agenda of governments. On a smaller scale, and with many significant modifications compared with the previous period, national armed forces and defence industries re-established their position in the new systems that were in the making in the region.

II. Defence industry restructuring: alternative approaches

After the partial withdrawal from protecting defence enterprises and hesitation about the future of the sector, by 1993 all the Visegrad countries opted to promote military-related production—albeit on a reduced scale. In all of them (although to the least extent in Hungary) the defence industry was presented as a crucial, dynamic branch of the economy, both technologically and from the point of view of export potential. The effort to modernize the armed forces and the hope of a rapid integration into NATO also contributed to this decision.

The different approaches to restructuring the defence industry in East–Central Europe were determined by the general state of the transformation process in the country as well as by the specific state policy towards the sector. The Czech and the Slovak approaches represented opposite ends of the spectrum.

Czech restructuring took place in the framework of a rather thorough macro-economic transformation to a market economy, with a theoretically non-interventionist state policy. The majority of the defence enterprises were corporatized and/or privatized and subject to market regulation. They were organized under a private holding and a ministry—two clearly defined power centres between which there seemed to be good cooperation. There was selective state intervention to promote certain branches of the defence industry and arms exports were justified by new, liberal market arguments.

Slovakia, in contrast, embodied a modified version of the old-style, centrally regulated model in which promotion of a partly reformed defence industry was seen as one possible way to ensure political and economic survival. In Slovakia the macro-transformation took place slowly and with strict limitations. The defence sector was controlled by a politically strong but economically weak administrative centre. Some privatization took place, but most of the military-related firms were to be reunited and coordinated under a state holding. The need for a defence industry as a whole was justified by a perceived threat to the national security and the need to earn hard currency in order to restructure the economy and ease the social tensions unleashed by the global transformation process.

The Hungarian and Polish cases combined certain elements of these two approaches. In Hungary and Poland the backdrop to change in the military-related sector was the relatively developed market relations and multiple, often conflicting state power centres. In both countries the defence industry was promoted in the hope that it would attract major foreign direct investment, contribute to economic prosperity and reinforce security.

In Hungary defence enterprises received mostly moral support from different government agencies which could provide only limited resources for maintenance or restructuring. Most of the enterprises were commercialized or privatized and they were by and large subject to market regulation. The leading branch of the sector was reorganized by a private holding.

In Poland most of the defence enterprises were still state-owned or commercialized firms in which the state retained a majority stake. They were expected to cope with market economy conditions, but at the same time they were promised some state protection and promotion. The core defence enterprises will remain under the control of a state holding company or under the direct control of government ministries.

After the breakup of Czechoslovakia the defence industry was stabilized relatively quickly in the Czech Republic. The sector was partially modernized and several enterprises decided to return to military-related production.

The relative success of the restructuring of the Czech defence industry can be attributed to several factors. The long-standing traditions of the industry, as well as the relative stability and prosperity of the country, played an important role. After the Velvet Revolution, Czech defence enterprises faced radical restructuring in a fairly stable macroeconomic environment shaped by a fairly consistent macroeconomic policy. Economic liberalization, privatization and the introduction of elements of a market economy took place systematically, even if unevenly and sometimes with serious shortcomings. In 1989–92, a crucial period of radical change, Czech companies were simultaneously pushed to convert to civilian production and to become entrepreneurial. It was in fact a 'sink or swim' situation, and most enterprises realized this.

It was very telling that, although according to official estimates the worst year of the defence industry crisis was 1993, most enterprise managers claimed that the worst year for them was 1991—the year of the first, unexpected shock and the first serious enterprise collapses. After 1991 managers realized how serious the challenge was and tried to act according to the new economic and political rules. While most defence enterprises elsewhere in the region were still floating in official and entrepreneurial insecurity in 1994, most Czech companies had made strategic decisions and were carrying them out by 1992. Some of these decisions may have been proved wrong, or were later changed, but it was undoubtedly an advantage that they were made. Companies did not waste time waiting for favourable signs from the authorities.

Another crucial factor in the success was the subtle but definite and efficient state backing of the defence industry. Official representatives of the Czech Republic were busy promoting arms sales in the hope that a renewed, modernized arms industry would contribute to the country's economic prosperity and positive trade balance. It was also expected to help modernize the new national armed forces that aspired to rapid integration into NATO. The Velvet Divorce boosted the revival of the defence industry in the Czech Republic. The urge to substitute for lost military production and the renewed support from the government gave wings to defence industry managers.

The starting position of Slovakia was markedly worse than that of the Czech Republic, both in general terms and in respect of the defence industry. The Slovak economy was poorer and less developed to begin with and after separation in 1993 it suffered a dramatic decline for the next two years. Resources for development of any kind were restricted.

In Slovakia there was much less erosion of the old-style bureaucratic coordination system than in any other ECE country. The power structure remained much more monolithic, partly as a result of Prime Minister Vladimir Meciar's effort to build a personality-based, centralized system of patronage. Despite several fractions and serious tensions, rather close cooperation between the defence industry, army and state agencies did continue. The fact that Slovakia continued to invest in developing new systems, such as modernized T-72 tanks and Zuzana self-propelled guns, required a concentrated effort to mobilize resources, under intensive state coordination.

The methods used to revamp ailing military production were different in Slovakia and the Czech Republic. The Czech authorities provided indirect support and rarely offered substantial financial contributions. The state's economic interference was much more explicit and direct in Slovakia. State subsidies were given directly to military-related companies, both to help them confront difficulties stemming from the immediate crisis and for conversion projects. At the same time, conversion projects gradually became diversification projects and full-scale conversion was postponed indefinitely. Civilian production was to complement military production, providing additional income and, importantly, making it possible to avoid further job losses. State agencies provided direct support to finance the development of new military products and in some cases to launch production.

Direct state intervention turned out to be expensive at the macroeconomic level in Slovakia. It did not force enterprises to change their way of management and increase efficiency. Allocating the limited state resources on military-related projects also meant depriving other sectors of vital financial contributions.

This practice had been followed for decades during the cold war and led to an enormous waste of development resources throughout the ECE region. Even as the general economic and political conditions and the arguments that were used to justify this policy changed, the essential mechanisms in Slovakia seemed to be the same. Maintaining a defence industry was one means and a justification for maintaining the power of old-style bureaucratic direction. The lack of substantial changes in the economic structures that could have offered sources of revenue and employment other than those offered by the defence industry meant that the majority of citizens, high-level politicians and economic decision makers supported this policy.

It is a sad historic paradox that the unresolved problems of the defence industry which were a catalyst for the disintegration of the Czechoslovak Federation were later resolved by the two independent countries in the same manner—by the partial revival and modernization of military-related production. In addition, soon after separation a strong urge to compete with each other emerged in the two successor states. This rather irrational competition gave additional impetus to defence industry development on both sides of the border.

Conversion, which was envisaged as the main track of defence industry restructuring in the late 1980s in the former Czechoslovakia, was gradually eliminated from the government agenda and became entirely an enterprise problem in the Czech Republic. In Slovakia the concept of conversion gained a negative connotation. The difficulties in handling the negative impact of decreasing military production and the lack of convincing positive results contributed to the fact that the bulk of the Slovak population became increasingly hostile towards the whole idea. This disenchantment was skilfully manipulated during the election campaign leading up to the separation of the two republics. Relatively little attention was paid to the fact that defence industry output and arms sales began to fall much earlier than when the conversion policy was launched. In fact, the latter was an attempt to respond to emerging problems. The proposed solution (i.e., conversion) was presented as the cause of the crisis and became the scapegoat for the other economic problems from which Slovakia suffered. The remedies that were followed—that is, a largely unchanged pattern of military production—could, in the long run, only aggravate the structural problems that caused the crisis of defence-related production.

At the beginning of the transformation process, the Hungarian case held the promise of becoming a lesson in conversion for the whole region. Instead, it turned out to be a lesson in the damage caused by the absence of conversion. The entire defence-related sector collapsed, causing enormous economic and human losses, while only partial restructuring and even less conversion took place on its ruins. The development of the Hungarian military sector between 1990 and 1994 represents a curious mixture of market and state influence. As a consequence of market changes, the defence industry suffered a devastating crisis. The fact that it did not disappear completely was due to the efforts of the state agencies that tried to rescue and revamp it. At the same time, since these agencies did not have the financial resources to maintain and finance defence enterprises, the reorganization of the remnants of the sector took place under the aegis of a private holding, Videoton.

One interesting feature of the Hungarian case was that processes of concentration and decentralization took place simultaneously. There was an intense concentration within the Videoton subcontracting system. At the same time decentralization and disintegration went on as a result of the continuous spontaneous erosion of the sector and the enterprise transformation process. Enterprises went through an obligatory transformation that resulted in the establishment of several smaller, independent firms. State agencies occasionally contracted with purely civilian companies for some military projects, which meant further decentralization of defence-related activity.

Promotion and open support of the Hungarian defence sector did not become an organic part of official restructuring policy. The decline of the defence-related sector was too dramatic and its political representation was not sufficiently effective to change basic policy guidelines. The remaining informal contacts and lobbies, however, ensured that military-related enterprises received official help on an individual basis. The surviving enterprises began to reorganize in different interest and pressure groups, partly under the aegis of Videoton.

Despite its difficulties, a diminished defence sector will survive as a loose, informal network of firms able to count on some state and mutual help (even if this takes the form of absorption, as happened with Mechlabor, which became part of Videoton-Rendszertechnika). Their activities will be loosely coordinated by the private Videoton Holding and a state agency, like the Military Industrial Office.

Developments in Polish defence industry restructuring were also the combined result of the impact of recently introduced elements of a market economy together with remaining and new forms of state intervention. Because of the permanent political struggles at the highest level of government, in which questions related to the defence industry often played an important role, both the development and erosion of the sector were frozen. In 1992, when the government at last decided to support military production, the defence industry—

although seriously damaged—could still be rescued. In Hungary the erosion was more intense, decentralization was more advanced and old-style industrial mammoths disappeared more quickly than in Poland—although it should be pointed out that the scale and macroeconomic importance of defence production was always higher in Poland.

After an initial period of hesitation and chaos, the Polish Government decided to introduce a special industrial policy supporting defence-related enterprises. The targets of the official Polish restructuring programme were set rather high. The objective was to concentrate military activity in a restricted circle of state-owned and state-protected enterprises—to maintain and if possible increase output and employment levels and to meet the requirements of the armed forces through local production to the maximum possible extent. This would mean that, instead of further down-sizing, military activity within these core enterprises would be increased. This would require continuous financial and administrative interventions on behalf of the state.

Since the Polish Government decision to back the defence industry took place in the context of a radical macroeconomic and social transformation, several external barriers limited government action. The main obstacle was strictly economic: under the severe austerity programme introduced in January 1990, the state budget and the scope for direct economic intervention were radically trimmed. In addition, the emergence of several new power centres close to or within the government meant that military-related decisions were often questioned and challenged by new actors.

Another serious limitation was the emerging private sector that appeared to be an increasingly powerful economic agent, competing with state-owned enterprises and further limiting state economic resources, not always legally (for example, by tax evasion). Polish defence enterprises had to face multiple challenges: restrictive regulations that affected all the state-owned enterprises, the threat that they would lose their remaining state-guaranteed privileges as well as increasing competition and scrutiny from the emerging private sector. The latter had a strong impact through an intense 'brain drain' and it crowded defence-related factories out of the civilian goods and capital markets.

Since the government faced political, economic and legal limitations, it resorted to multiple and varied forms of direct and indirect support of the defence industry. Special allowances and incentives were created to facilitate the survival efforts of the enterprises. Arms exports and cooperation with foreign firms were actively promoted. Projects to help to resolve the economic and social problems caused by the defence industry's collapse were launched, particularly at a regional level, partially financed by the central government. This latter approach was rather progressive and unique in East–Central Europe.

III. Defence industry transformation as a mirror of socio-economic change

The ECE defence industry and the volume of its arms exports might seem modest or even negligible in international comparative terms. However, the fate of this sector and the way it was transformed after the end of the cold war were crucial as regards overall development in these countries.

During the cold war the military sector remained almost untouched. Even in reform-minded economies like those of Hungary and Poland it was a sheltered residuum of the classic command economy. What happened in the military sector after the change in political system was like a litmus test, demonstrating the depth of changes taking place in the region. Despite loud free-market rhetoric, all the ECE countries revived a certain amount of state protection and special treatment for defence enterprises.

Even in the Czech Republic and Poland, two countries that were declared success stories of market economic transition, the state actively intervened to protect and promote defence-related production. The way the defence industry was treated in the Czech Republic cast doubts on the purity of the liberalism professed by the state administration. While advocating a radical free-market ideology, the state effectively helped some defence enterprises and supported their export activity.

The nature and degree of state involvement in rescuing defence-related enterprises cast a revealing light on the whole macroeconomic transformation process in Poland. The volatility of the Polish political situation initially had a paralysing impact on the defence industry. The prospect of revenues stemming from arms exports, however, reinforced the influence of forces advocating the retention of state control over the sector. Gains realized in the free market contributed to the re-establishment of a modified bureaucratic control. The market economy developed in spite of the lack of genuine restructuring of large defence-related enterprises—the basic pillars of the previous economic system. Despite important reforms and down-sizing, the core of the industry remained largely unreformed and state-protected. Even more important, the position of the sector in the economy remained unchallenged within the overall restructuring strategy.

Developments unfolding within the military sector could only be interpreted thoroughly in the light of other, more widespread changes. Official arguments to justify arms sales in Slovakia claimed that hard-currency earnings from arms exports were indispensable for a genuine restructuring of the entire economy, but hardly any other measures were taken to promote restructuring. In the light of the overall changes taking (or rather not taking) place in the country, the official explanations definitely sounded hollow.

After the initial period of adjustment to the end of the cold war, the new national armies and the modernized defence industries appeared to have survived as important pillars of the socio-economic systems that are in the making in the region. They enjoy and probably will continue to enjoy different forms of state protection and promotion. The amounts of money required for renewed state support of defence-related production might not seem large, but when the resources available for creating the necessary impetus to macroeconomic changes are limited even apparently moderate resources can be crucial.

In addition, there is a danger that the resources dedicated to military-related projects will grow. Defence-related firms have learned how to mobilize additional resources through informal links or by using non-military channels of financing, such as those targeted for technological innovation. Additional resources for military-related activity were also sometimes acquired from the companies' civilian profile. Many defence enterprises at the high-technology end of the sector became involved in infrastructure development—for example, building telephone networks—and benefit from government and foreign financial support for these projects.

IV. The revamped defence industry

The end of cold war and the collapse of the Warsaw Treaty Organization (WTO) military system radically diminished the size of the defence sector throughout East–Central Europe. Defence production fell to 10–30 per cent of its highest cold war level, recorded in the late 1980s. However, this significant drop was not accompanied by a thoroughly thought through macroeconomic policy for dealing with the negative side-effects of this collapse or by a global conversion strategy that could offer attractive and viable alternatives to military production. There is no doubt that most of the defence-related enterprises in the region cut their military production radically after 1990. However, a drop in military output did not represent conversion. In most companies production capacities and workforces became idle rather than engaged in alternative production. This contributed to further economic losses at the enterprise level and to the general fall in output and increasing social tensions of the economies in transformation. This was a high price to pay for the end of the cold war, for both the military-related enterprises and societies of East–Central Europe.

From the perspective of long-term, global development even this unnecessarily high price would have been worth paying if it had been accompanied by guarantees that the social resources allocated to military production would be contained at a relatively low level. This would mean setting the level of military-related production at the minimum and introducing mechanisms which guarantee that scarce resources would not be wasted on excessive and inefficient production. This would require further economic and political changes that current trends do not seem to suggest will occur.

By 1994 defence industry managers and state officials in all four countries had made the assessment that, realistically, only about 30 per cent of the 1988 peak levels of production and employment would be reached once the sector overcame its crisis. The high level of 1988 was reached when the countries were still within the framework of the WTO. In the 1990s the WTO–CMEA (Council for Mutual Economic Assistance) system had disappeared and national armed forces had been cut back significantly. However, in the prevailing security environment in Europe, it is questionable whether even these lower levels of production can be justified, particularly in the context of the state of the economies of East–Central Europe. Reaching and maintaining this level would require a diversion of a significant amount of resources from other important socio-economic uses.

The end of the cold war offered a genuine historic opportunity to change the basic patterns of the defence sector. However, the way the defence sector functions casts doubt on whether the reforms undertaken so far can ensure future control and subordination to broader national policy. While quantitative changes have taken place throughout the region, the key question is whether fundamental qualitative changes in the way the sector is run have been implemented. Is the smaller defence industry also a more efficient, more transparent, less wasteful one?

The sector is definitely under more control and less hidden from society than before. It is subject to official mechanisms as well as some non-governmental, media and social control. Macroeconomic changes have also provided a wider and more varied range of means to tackle enterprise problems. Nevertheless, at the macro-level only minor administrative efforts have been made to reorganize the defence-related sector. The only genuine, large-scale structural change that occurred came as a result of the dissolution of the Czechoslovak Federation. Elsewhere, by and large the same production structures exist on a smaller scale and with minor modifications.

Enterprises have learned to manoeuvre more skilfully but most of them have not changed structurally in ways that could enhance a more efficient and useful way of functioning. By the end of 1994 only a small portion of the defence-related companies had accomplished successful internal restructuring or ensured long-term survival by involving themselves with Western production and markets. The majority of defence-related enterprises have carried out minor reforms and were rescued by their respective governments as the political and economic importance of defence-related production was revised in the region.

In theory, the crisis could have acted as a selection process whereby only the strongest enterprises and managers would survive, and this was to some extent the case. Enterprises that showed the most promising potential and those fortunate enough to have the most committed (or stubborn) managers were able to survive. Relatively rapid government intervention along with lax bankruptcy regulations saved the 'lower end' of the sector as well—the most sluggish and least entrepreneurial enterprises, many of which were producing obsolete heavy weaponry and ammunition. The policy of draining public resources to sustain inefficient enterprises that have no credible demand for their output—which continues—highlights the lack of fundamental changes at both the macro- and enterprise level. In the case of these enterprises, the problems of restructuring have been postponed rather than solved. However, it is likely that they will continue to require subsidies to survive.

Positive linkages between defence industry development and global socio-economic development are as difficult to discern today as they were in the past. Most of the incomes and technological advances achieved by the sector appear to remain locked within it. It is impossible to trace what happened to the export earnings that were created by the sector but they were certainly partly used to offset the costs of arms imports, as before. It is also certain that investments for revamping the sector could be used efficiently and possibly with a wider social usefulness in other spheres. The enormous efforts to modernize WTO-origin military hardware have evident technological and market limitations. However, economic and political decision makers were reluctant to renounce them. It seems that the sector keeps absorbing crucial development resources while creating only limited positive backward linkages in the economy.

During the crisis of the traditional defence industry there was a more or less rapid erosion of the sector accompanied by a silent resistance to change on the part of managers and government officials responsible for the sector. It was fairly revealing that in the Czech Republic and Poland—the countries that seemed to overcome their crisis first—at the first signs of economic recovery the reconstructed military–industrial lobby began to push for an increase in the military budget and for new, expensive military development projects financed from central government funds. Resources recently created by the recovering economy were claimed for reconstruction of the defence industry instead of further conversion and/or for tackling the problems created by the down-sizing of military production. This reflex, to try to divert scarce resources for a narrow sectoral interest, demonstrated that the basic nature of the sector—stemming from the technological features of military-related production and the social position of the military—has not changed in a fundamental way.

V. Renewed defence industry as a vehicle of international economic integration

The national defence industries of East–Central Europe were created and were formerly maintained to serve the Warsaw Treaty Organization. This external need and force shaped their size and structure and the dynamics of their growth through direct political diktat and, in some cases, even direct control over the production process itself. The basic means through which this control was exercised were the fixed and obligatory orders and production quotas, special requirements, prices and barter-like exchange mechanisms that were functioning in the internal trade system of the CMEA. Once the WTO requirements were met, the defence industry management and political leadership of the non-Soviet countries could use available production capacities for exports to non-WTO countries. However, the extent and importance of this activity were minor compared to the volume of intra-WTO exchange.

Internally, the major element that maintained and nurtured defence industries was the national armed forces and their strength, ambition and position in society. The strong and important national army in Poland created an additional pillar for the local defence industry through its relatively high demand for locally manufactured products. In Hungary, in contrast, the relatively low social profile of the army left the defence industry primarily export-oriented.

Since the dissolution of the WTO, no outside force has exerted a similar impact. On the contrary, external conditions became rather hostile as, in the shrinking world market for arms, competition became more fierce. In order to survive, defence industries needed exports. The logic changed and, instead of the 'sucking force' from outside, now there was a push from inside towards those export markets that were still available. This internal push was articulated at both a macro- and micro-level.

All the transforming ECE countries intended to imitate the export-led success of the South-East Asian countries. Export, of anything, became a major slogan for the early 1990s, leading in some sectors to a complete erosion of productive assets. Exports were the main (sometimes the only) means to acquire the hard currency needed for investment, imports of new technology, major infrastructure projects, and so on. Even though the market for traditional military products did diminish, those that were possible to enter were still rather lucrative. Arms could be sold for hard currency at a time when civilian trade was suffering major restrictions owing to the global economic recession and protective trade barriers erected by potential trade partners in Western Europe to defend their own markets and national production from cheap products coming from East–Central Europe.

Another factor in the search for export markets emerged because restricted resources made it necessary for countries of the region to modernize their national armed forces principally with imported equipment. Once the decision was made to retain military production to meet domestic requirements, it became rational to seek economies of scale. Since output systematically surpassed local needs, it seemed logical to export the surplus.

At the enterprise level, exports appeared to be the main road to survival. Even if some state subsidies were received (depending on the enterprise and the country) it was evident that central budgets were not generous enough to finance the entire business. Enterprises needed to create their own revenue—mostly through exports. Even if export activity was of minor importance and even if in some cases its impact was not entirely positive, it was desperately pursued by enterprises since it could bring hard-currency earnings, access to markets that absorbed production and even eventual capital infusions. In addition, if they had promising export potentials, ailing defence enterprises could apply for renewed state support from their respective state authorities.

ECE defence enterprises that were not in deep crisis and which had relatively developed capital assets, significant know-how and a cheap workforce and which were eager to work with Western partners were a good match for those Western enterprises that intended to lower their costs by relocating production and finding new markets. ECE defence-related companies that cooperated with Western firms on civilian or military projects gained additional revenue, access to markets and a new form of legitimacy. Their chances of survival definitely increased. In the explicitly military field, projects to upgrade WTO equipment with Western sub-systems promised long-term advantages to both sides.

Defence-related business became a successful form of economic cooperation with Western companies. Simultaneously, the desired NATO membership became seen as a means of providing political legitimacy and integration into the Western institutional system. During the cold war the ECE defence industry was promoted in order to isolate and reinforce the socialist bloc against the West. Today, governments and business circles in the region promote the defence industry as a means to intensify integration with Western economies.

VI. The challenge of genuine conversion

Conversion was announced as a solution to the crisis of the traditional defence industry in East–Central Europe, but governments took very few measures to promote it. In their struggle for survival, defence-related enterprises tried to keep military-related assets and simultaneously introduce new civilian profiles.

After governments reasserted their control over and support for the defence industry, these survival efforts began to pay off. Some of the enterprises, productive assets and employees were rescued through the strong commitment of workers, managers and ministry officials. The fact that collapse rather than conversion had taken place made it possible to reorganize the remnants of the sector relatively quickly. In the period of economic transformation in the civilian sphere newly established enterprises and green-field investments far outweighed takeovers and privatization. In the defence sector, however, there were almost no green-field investments and new companies were created from the vestiges of former defence-related firms.

Its technical characteristics and its special utility value-centred rationality (as opposed to one driven by exchange values) make arms production expensive. In the European state socialist systems of the cold war period, social conditions were geared towards accommodating military-related production. The state ensured that inputs were cheap, sometimes even free for the defence industry, while the costs of research, development and production were charged to society, not to individual enterprises. At the same time enterprises and the armed forces benefited directly from the profits created through arms production and export, without a significant positive impact on the development of society. The respective societies had to be 'convinced' of the need for this endeavour—hence the special ideological role played by military production and the armed forces in state socialist systems. Military producers and the armed forces in turn contributed to cementing the existing power structures.

Arms production becomes lucrative because arms are sold on political markets, where price relations are largely unrelated to production costs and efficiency. Supply and demand are highly distorted in markets controlled by the state and the national armed forces and on the black market. The first is a typical captive market, where the conditions of sale are personally negotiated between the representatives of sellers and buyers and prices tend to express the actual economic and political power relations of the two. The second is driven by an insatiable need for arms where prices are inflated by the clandestine nature of transactions.

Genuine conversion would imply a change in the social conditions that make arms production a lucrative business and a radical alteration of the present political and economic status quo, far beyond the changes implemented at enterprises. The case of East–Central Europe underlines the fact that conversion is not a technical matter but one that requires changes in thought patterns and behaviour, ranging from new security concepts to truly democratic policy making. It requires flexible and efficient state management that can motivate and collaborate with regional authorities and the private sector. It is only viable if it includes a wide range of active participants at different social levels: central government agencies, local authorities, civil movements, enterprise management and organized labour. This type of multi-level, interdisciplinary, flexible and democratic approach is absent in the transforming societies of the region. Promoting conversion is therefore one way of learning to build a genuinely democratic society as well.

Another lesson of the failure of conversion in East–Central Europe is that market forces are not sufficient for carrying it out, in particular those that naturally gravitate towards short-term gains. Conversion requires a comprehensive state policy that takes into account the predictable negative side-effects of restructuring. Substantial and much more targeted financial incentives and assistance, abundant (possibly preferential) credit and markets for the newly created civilian goods are required. Wide-ranging regional development projects and long-term government strategies in such areas as labour, industrial and housing policy are also needed. Since the ECE national government resources are generally fairly limited, international agencies should be actively involved in creating and promoting conversion projects.

A third lesson is that conversion should be pursued as a global project since partial conversion leaves open the possibility of reversal. As long as arms production and arms trade remain lucrative, individual conversion efforts appear idealistic and even somewhat futile. Genuine conversion is inconceivable without the introduction of strict international control of the arms trade and the strengthening of international conflict-solution efforts. As of today, this would hurt major political and economic interests.

Although conversion should be an international project, for the time being it can be an efficient crisis solution for the enterprises and regions that are affected by the collapse of the defence industry and committed to a medium- and long-term development strategy that involves genuine restructuring. The countries of East–Central Europe should address those areas in which there have been the least changes. Each country has a relatively small segment of its former defence-related sector that has been either successfully restructured (in the military or civilian field) or selected by state agencies to become the core of a revamped national defence industry. The latter companies will be protected and promoted officially, whether or not they have successfully accomplished restructuring. Other companies still have to cope with the negative effects of the collapse of the traditional defence-related sector on their own. They followed the passive or semi-active survival strategies described in chapter 9 and managed to survive the immediate crisis without implementing fundamental changes. This group comprises the majority and without significant changes they will represent a serious burden for the future economic development of the ECE countries. Conversion projects should target these companies.

Proposals could be elaborated together by affected companies, communities, their governments, outside experts, civil society movements and international agencies. Western governments and business circles could offer cooperation through opening markets, providing technical assistance and promoting specific conversion projects at enterprises. They could also assist central or regional government agencies to address regional and sectoral imbalances resulting from the collapse of the traditional defence industry. Future conversion projects could present new types of product and a different enterprise structure and management culture and could be integrated with development projects in the respective regions. They could serve as a positive demonstration, showing that a new form of participative management following a long-term strategy can be as attractive as a strategy based on short-term profit and political interests.

VII. Future prospects

One lesson of the post-cold war history of the ECE region was that major political changes at the national level did not bring fundamental changes in policy concerning the defence industrial sector. There were differences in emphasis, ideology and methods, but politically and ideologically different governments—for example, those of Halina Suchocka and Waldemar Pawlak in Poland, Jozsef Antal and Gyula Horn in Hungary or Vladimir Meciar and Josef Moravcik in Slovakia—followed by and large the same guidelines concerning defence-related production and exports. The only case where a major political change led to a specific turn in government policy was Czechoslovakia in 1992, when the split within the Civic Forum led to the emergence of Vaclav Klaus's Civic Democratic Party (Obchanska Demokraticka Strana, ODS) and the gradual marginalization of opposition figures who advocated radical demilitarization and conversion policy.

This relative independence from the political roller-coaster might mean that trends set in the first period of macro-level transformation will not change fundamentally. It also confirms that enterprise-level changes are likely to have increasing importance in shaping the future.

In the foreseeable future it is unlikely that dramatic changes will upset the present post-cold war trends in East–Central Europe. It would be surprising to see either a sudden, huge increase or a significant cutback in military expenditure or support to industry. Developments in the military industry will be shaped by three main factors: enterprise decisions, the general development of the respective economies and specific government actions.

One major factor shaping the military-related industry will be decisions at enterprises. Although deliberate efforts to intensify inter-enterprise cooperation might reinforce cohesion and make it a stronger socio-political force, it is more likely that enterprises will pursue their future strategies according to decisions taken individually, according to the logic described in chapter 9.

The sector will certainly also be affected by the general development of the economy, including macroeconomic factors such as inflation, unemployment and currency stability as well as the changing structure of industry. The pace or even the continuation of a spontaneous erosion of military-related production will be determined in part by the alternatives offered in the economy as a whole.

The most important government decisions from the perspective of the defence industry may follow from whether or not the aspirations of all four Visegrad countries to become members of NATO are met. Membership will help to drive reform and modernization of the armed forces through which democratic, civilian controls, economic rationality and military efficiency could become entrenched principles. In the framework of alliance, industrial cooperation with Western partners may become easier, at least in some spheres of production. Certainly ECE government and industry representatives assume— rightly or wrongly—that alliance membership will increase external interest in the products of local defence manufacturers.

At the same time, local defence industries might benefit from a government decision to interfere more in sectoral policies in the region. With the return to power of reformed communist parties in Hungary, Poland and Slovakia and the emergence of strong parliamentary opposition in the Czech Republic, these policies may become more acceptable. For all these political actors, a degree of macroeconomic regulation is seen as indispensable if economic growth and modernization are to be accomplished. Decisions to promote certain sectoral industrial policies affecting production of, for example, vehicles, electronics or machine tools might include the military-related industry. At the same time, government decisions (and certainly their implementation) will depend on the availability of financial resources.

The end of the cold war did not lead to radical conversion in East–Central Europe. The military sector did, however, change as a result of both deliberate political decisions and the collapse of traditional forms of defence production. These changes were more costly and painful than was expected. It can only be hoped that in future increased economic efficiency and strict democratic control will ensure that military-related production does not become a source of major economic and social losses.

Index

Adamec, Ladislav 18
Adamov 15, 50
Adamovski 31
Adast 15, 23–24, 25, 26, 50, 53, 139, 160, 170, 171, 176, 177, 178, 179
Aero 13, 14, 37
Aero Holding 43, 47–48, 54, 196
Aérospatiale 127, 128
Aero Vodochody 40, 45, 46–47, 48–49, 52, 53, 54, 153, 164, 165, 170, 176, 195, 199
Afghanistan 50, 119
Africa 15, 40
Alcatel 74
Alena 127
Algeria 16
Allami Fejlesztesi Intezet (AFI) 100
Allami Vagyonkezelo Rt (AVRt) 91, 92, 95, 98
Allami Vagyonugynokseg (AVU) 92
Andrejcak, Imrich 44, 62fn, 63
Antal, Jozsef 221
Arab countries 8, 63
ARMEX 68
arms exports:
    civilian sales and 145, 154, 155
    data on 5
    decline in 196–97
    definition 39–40
    hard currency and 197, 214, 218
    markets lost 143, 145, 153–58
    prices 5, 219
    promotion of 213
    revenue from 218
    tax and 197
    see also under names of countries
Army-Coop 102, 195
Asia 40, 73, 201
AT&T 54, 165
Austria 49, 99
Austro-Hungarian Empire 187
Autoipari Kutato 101

Avia 13, 43, 50, 168

Bakony Fem 87
Bakony Muvek 95, 176
Baksay, Jozsef 28
Balaton, Lake 141
Balaz, Ivan 51
Barak, General Oldrich 30, 52, 55, 193
Baudys, Antonin 33, 39, 40, 42, 45, 55
Bendix/King avionics 118
black market 63, 202–203, 219
Blanicke Strojirny 24
Blatna 21
Boeing 47, 127, 165
Bofors 120, 121, 124
Bojkovice 13, 15, 17, 22, 31
Bosch 177
Bosnia 51
Bratislava 15
Bremer Vulkan 42
Brezno 15
Brno 13, 31, 177
Brno, International Defence Technology Fair (1994) 44–45, 52, 71, 73
Brody, Andras 187, 188
Brown and Root 42
Budapest 94, 101, 102, 188
Budapesti Hiradastechnikai Gyar (BHG) 95, 103
Budapesti Vegyimuvek 102
Bulgaria 75
Bumar-Labedy 109, 111, 115, 119, 121, 123, 168–69
Burma *see* Myanmar

Canada 164
Carnogursky, Jan 31
Caterpillar 100
Cech, Pavel 44
Cenzin 110, 119, 120
Cernak, Ludovit 33, 60
Cerny, Oldrich 27

Ceska Zbrojovka (CZ) 24, 26, 39, 43, 45,
   49, 52, 55, 163, 192
Ceskoslovenska Kolben Danek (CKD)
   Praha 13, 38
Ceskoslovenska Zbrojovka 13
CFE Treaty (Treaty on Conventional
   Armed Forces in Europe, 1990) 28
Chaloupnik, Zdenek 48
Chile 94
China: arms imports 50, 75, 76, 201
Chromec, General Stanislav 55
CKD Praha see Ceskoslovenska Kolben
   Danek
Coca-Cola 129
cold war, end of:
   defence industries and 216
   effects of 6–8, 215
Comasec 102, 192
Comasec-Respirator 37, 153, 164, 170,
   172
conversion:
   advocated initially 8
   capital provision for 162
   commitment lacking 3, 180, 207, 219
   company attitudes to 179
   consumption and 184
   credits for 180
   democracy and 220
   diversification and 175, 178
   economic change and 182–83, 189, 207
   environmental damage and 181
   experience of 174–90
   failures of 178–79, 180–90
   financing 3, 153, 180, 183, 184–85
   forces for, weakness of 181–82
   future prospects 221–22
   half-heartedness of attempts 3, 180, 219
   international dimension 186, 220–21
   investment in 185, 219
   labour content and 140
   macroeconomic level 181–83
   managers 179
   market economy and 183, 189
   market forces and 207, 220
   marketing and 180
   markets and 184
   one town–one enterprise cases and 179
   opponents of 182

political conditions and 208
post-cold war opportunity 174–75
requirements for 220–21
resource shortage 153, 185
scapegoat, as 183
social change and 220
social forces and 181, 182
survival and 171
suspicions of 175
unemployment and 179, 183
Western assistance for 162, 173, 186
worker participation lacking 182
Coordinating Committee on Multilateral
   Export Controls (COCOM) 136
Council for Mutual Economic Assistance
   (CMEA) 5, 7, 52, 85, 86, 144, 188, 217
Credit Lyonnaise 43
Croatia: arms imports 39, 51, 94
Csepel Autogyar 101
Csobay, Jozsef 88
Cuba 16
Currus 100, 162, 179
CZ see Ceska Zbrojovka
Czechoslovakia:
   Academy of Sciences 19, 22
   arms exports 15–16, 18–19, 25:
      policy on 16, 18–19, 27, 28–29, 40–41
   arms imports 30
   bankruptcy law 26
   banks 21, 23, 49
   breakup of:
      effects of 33, 35, 202, 216
      heritage of 34–41, 57–60
      road to 30–33, 211
   Chamber of Industry 160
   Charter 77 20
   Civic Democratic Party 221
   Civic Forum 221
   Communist collapse in 7
   conversion committee 20–21
   credits 21
   defence enterprises:
      bankruptcy 26
      debts 23, 160
      lobbying 26
      survival strategies 27
      Western firms, cooperation with 27
      see also following entry

defence industry:
  arguments justifying 29–30
  characteristics of 13–17
  civilian production 17, 22, 23, 26
  conversion 18, 20–30, 31, 49, 60,
    148, 180, 181–82, 185, 198, 211
  crisis 18–20, 26
  development of 187
  division of labour 16
  economy and 13, 25, 32
  employment 14
  Federation breakup and 31–32
  finances 19
  foreign firms, cooperation with 27
  foreign investment and 30
  history of 13
  impact of 187
  licences 28–29
  markets 24
  policy on 40
  privatization 74, 146, 168, 194–95
  production 8, 13–14, 17, 19, 20, 22,
    23, 24, 25
  production, licensed 16
  profits 29–20
  range produced 15
  regional concentration 17
  reorientation 26–30
  restructuring of 22
  state control over 26
  state support for 21–22, 26, 27, 144
  subcontractors 15
  survival strategies 26
  voucher privatization 25–26, 35
  WTO and 15, 18, 50
  see also preceding entry
economic crisis 26
economic policy 60, 210
Federation, quarrels in 29, 30–33
foreign policy 24
Fund for Structural Changes 22
German occupation 13
Hannomag project 21, 23, 66
Hungary and 33
KOVOM 28
Lombardini project 21, 65, 66, 178
military expenditure 15, 19, 24
Ministry of Control 23

Ministry of Defence 14, 19, 134, 182
Ministry of the Economy 21, 27, 193
Ministry of Finance 21, 134
Ministry of Foreign Trade 21, 27, 28,
  134
Ministry of Industry 21, 22, 29, 134,
  182
Ministry of Labour 182
National Property Fund 26, 160
NATO membership and 24, 30, 49
Peace Society 20
political change in 221
Prague Spring 7
Special Technology Fund 21
unemployment 20
Velvet Revolution 18, 24, 38, 50, 209
World War II and 13
WTO and 13, 15, 50
see also following entry and Slovakia
Czech Republic:
  armed forces:
    arms purchases 48, 55
    inheritance of 63
    modernization 50, 54, 55
    nationalism and 208
    rearming 55
  arms exports:
    competition and 73, 142
    control of 38
    expansion 51
    policy on 37–41, 46
    prices 50
    state and 197, 210
    value of 46
  arms imports 46
  Association of Armament and
    Ammunition Producers and
    Businessmen 159
  banks 43
  corruption 34
  defence enterprises:
    bankruptcy and 41
    debts 160, 161
    managers 149
    privileges lost 38
    success of 52–53
    see also following entry

defence industry:
  civilian products 43
  collapse 44
  conversion 31, 33, 38, 45, 50, 167,
    176, 177–78
  debts 50
  decentralization 35
  diversification 47
  employment 31, 41
  foreign investment 54, 73
  inheritance of 35, 41
  markets 50
  overcapacity 50
  over-employment 50
  policy on 37–41
  price system 50
  privatization 37–38, 42, 43, 47, 52,
    54, 195
  production 20, 38, 43
  R&D 51–52
  reorganization 37, 41–55, 172,
    209–10
  Slovakia and 30, 210–11
  Slovak subcontractors 35
  state support for 38, 41, 44, 46, 214
  Western firms, cooperation with
    42–43, 44, 46–47, 54, 55, 167
  see also preceding entry
economy 34, 38, 46, 54
Federal Union of State Enterprises and
  Joint Stock Companies 159
First Investment Fund 43
foreign investment 34
Gypsies in 34
image abroad 34
industrial base 34
inheritance of 34–41, 63
Israel and 55
liberal–conservative party 9
lustrace procedure 41
macroeconomic environment 34, 172
military expenditure 54, 55, 217
Ministry of Defence 41, 44, 45, 48, 53,
  55, 158–59
Ministry of Foreign Affairs 41
Ministry of Industry and Trade 33, 39,
  41, 47–48, 51
Ministry of the Interior 41

nationalism 208
National Property Fund 48, 54
NATO and 32, 50, 54, 210
parliamentary opposition 222
Prototypa Research Institute 49, 179
public opinion 41
Slovakia and 30, 33, 35, 37, 44
State Defence Council 50
State Glass Research Institute 51
subcontractors and 35
unemployment 34
West European structures and 33
WTO and 37
Czerwinski, Roman 115

Daimler Benz 121
Dana artillery system 71, 72
Dancak, General Karel 51
Danuvia 87, 95, 168
Danuvia Engineering Works 165
data, researching 4–6
defence enterprises, East–Central Europe:
  advantageous position 137
  bankruptcies 9, 134, 144, 145, 150
  banks 160, 162
  barter and 183
  capacity underutilized 134, 138
  capital, search for 161–62
  changes at 191–96, 200–203, 215–17
  civilian companies and 141
  controls over 134–35, 189
  costs, reducing 167
  debts 151, 152–53, 160–61, 183, 195
  features of 133–42
  financial crisis 143, 150–53, 159–62
  'golden share' 139
  government policy and 149
  holding companies 194
  import liberalization and 147, 155
  insolvency 151–52
  investment 135, 153
  management 133, 136, 140, 148, 150,
    157, 166, 171, 172, 173, 192–93, 194,
    208, 216
  marketing 163–64, 167, 191
  material reserves 134
  ministerial supervision 134–35, 137
  organizational features 138–40

overheads, cutting 159–60
political nature 134
politics and 194
privileges 135–36, 137, 138, 144
R&D 135, 136, 142
recovery 10
redundancies 166
reorganization 165, 191
reserves 135, 143
resource shortages 151, 153
retooling 165–66
security 140–41
single-purpose machinery 139
size of 138, 192
social functions 191
society and 133–34
society, military imprint on 186–90
specialization 192
stocks unsold 134, 156
subcontractors 135, 136–37, 138, 139,
   144, 147–48
survival prospects 192
survival strategies 166–74
tax and 147, 183
trade liberalization and 146–47
types of 138–39
wastefulness 151
workforce 135–36, 137, 191
see also following entry and under
names of countries
defence industry, East–Central Europe:
   arguments justifying 29–30
   armed conflicts and 139
   armed forces and 153, 163, 199,
      214–15, 216, 217–18
   arms exports 143, 145, 153–58
   attachment to 137, 190
   banking system and 147
   civilian production 144, 151, 155, 192
   cold capacities 139
   collapse of 8–9, 134
   consolidation 9–10
   cooperation 55
   crisis in 133, 138, 143–90
   data on 5–6
   definitions 5
   demand and 8, 139
   ecological damage 181, 188

economic changes 143, 145
economic status, new 194–96
economy and 9, 134, 199–200, 222
employment and 5
financing 135, 139, 147
foreign investment 195, 200, 202
guild mentality 190
identity crisis 143, 148–50, 157–59
international dimension 141–42, 217–19
investment 151, 153
labour market and 147
macroeconomic environment 145, 146,
   172, 222
markets 143, 145, 163–65
markets lost 8, 145, 153–58
monetary policy and 146
need of declared 10
political changes 145
price system 139
privatization 139, 146, 149, 194–96,
   197
production 9, 136, 137, 139, 166,
   215–16
profits 29–30
quality control 137–38
quantifying 187
R&D 198
restructuring 133, 150, 171, 172, 196,
   207, 208–13, 216
secrecy and 5, 140–41
smuggled equipment, copying of 136
social status and 194–96
socio-economic changes and 143, 145,
   214–15
state, new role of 196–99
state control 134–35, 147, 194, 196,
   197–99
state socialism's collapse and 8
state support 134–38, 145, 150, 174,
   214, 216
state support withdrawn 8, 9, 133, 134,
   143, 144–45
statistics on 5–6
structural crisis 155–56
subsidies 135
technology standard 136, 139
unemployment and 133, 147
USSR and 140, 142

Western firms, cooperation with
149–50, 154, 167, 192, 200–203,
218–19, 222
workers, attachment to 137, 190
WTO and 141–42, 143, 153–58, 217,
219
see also preceding entry, conversion,
and under names of countries
Detva 17, 21
developing countries 15–16, 18, 59, 70,
145, 154, 201
Dienstbier, Jiri 20, 30
Diosgyori Gepgyar (DIGEP) 91, 98–99,
195, 197
Dlouhy, Vladimir 25, 29, 31, 39, 40, 49
Dorries Scharmann 42
Dosek, Jan 179
Droppa, Karol 59
Dubnica 13, 17, 31
Dubnica nad Vahom 66
Duda, Miroslav 49
Dunai Repulogepgyar 37, 97, 98, 102,
160, 170, 194
DV-2 engine 72, 74

East–Central Europe:
armed forces 55
black market 202–3
competition in 202
conflict in 10
cooperation in 55, 201–202
currency conversion 5
currency devaluation 5
definition ix, 3–4
demilitarization and 8
economic changes in 3, 9
economic deformation 188
EU, desire to enter 7
industrial organization 6
industrial units' names 6
market economies and 145
military expenditure, cuts in 9, 199
military–industrial lobby, re-emergence
of 182
nationalist ideologies 208
NATO and 7, 163, 199, 200, 201, 208,
219, 222
OECD and 7

political changes in 1989–90 3, 9
popular dissent in 7
production associations 6
Russia and 202
society, military impact on 186–90
state socialism's collapse 7–8
structural deformation 188
Western technology and 199
see also conversion; defence
enterprises; defence industry *and under*
names of countries
Eastern Europe, definition 4fn
Egypt 48, 63
Elbit Corporation 48, 49
Eldorado Foundation 96–97
El Salvador 119
Erdei, Istvan 169–70
Ericsson 121
Ethiopia 15
EU (European Union) 117, 164, 173 *see*
also PHARE
European Bank for Reconstruction and
Development (EBRD) 173
Exel, Ivo 177

Fabryka Samochodow 121
Far East 84
Fegyver es Gazkeszulekgyar (FEG) 95,
102
Fejleszto Vallalat (AKFV) 101
Fiat–Iveco 98
Fillo, Jan 65
Finland 110
Finommechanikai Muvek 80, 87, 100,
103, 161
France 49, 99
Friedman–Meier 126
Fucik, Josef 18, 26, 31, 51, 72, 193
Fur, Lajos 88, 93, 103
Fuzfo 101

Gabor, Szeles 100, 104, 159, 164
Gamma 87, 92, 95
Gamrat 109
Ganz Hunslet 101
Gdansk 121
Gdynia 94
GEC Marconi 73

General Electric 43, 46
Gerinec, Bohumil 72
German Democratic Republic 18, 47, 94, 162
Germany:
    arms imports 49, 51
    Czechoslovakia and 21, 23
    Hungary and 99
    Iraq and 120
    Nazi 187
    Poland and 120, 124
Glezgo, Stefan 28, 29
Gliwice 109, 115
Glowno factory 121
Godolloi Gepgyar see MN Godolloi Gepgyar
Gorilla tank 118, 121, 122
Goryszewski, Henryk 118
Gregr, Bretislav 46
Grochowski, Ryszard 124, 193
Gumarny 21, 37, 51
Gyor 101

Hannomag 21, 23, 66
Hanzel, Jozef 65, 150
Harvester 124
Havel, Vaclav 18, 20, 27, 34, 38, 40, 61
Hegyhati, Jozsef 90
High Technology Transfer (HTT) 52
HM Radar Rt 100, 103, 161
Hnusta 51
Holan, Vilem 55
Hollandse Signaalapparaten 120
Horn, Gyula 221
Hradec Kralove 51
Hradska, Viktoria 45
Hungary:
    armed forces 77, 84, 93, 94, 104, 218
    arms exports:
        army's low profile and 218
        hard currency and 83–84, 93
        illegal 93
        importance of 218
        increasing 102
        licences 93–94
        MIO and 89–90
        policy on 88–94
        state support 197
    subsidies 81
    arms imports 16, 47, 83, 88, 94, 95
    bankruptcy law absent 86
    budget imbalance 79
    Coal Assistance Fund 162
    communications networks 103
    Communist Party 77, 79–80
    Communist Party resumes power 9, 222
    Council of Ministers 93
    Czechoslovakia and 33
    debts 79
    defence enterprises:
        bankruptcy 87, 92
        debts 88, 160, 161
        disintegration 94–102
        expectations of 86
        managers 149
        see also following entry
    defence industry:
        arguments for 92–94
        cold capacities 82, 88, 91, 101, 104, 139
        collapse 86, 212
        communications equipment 80
        consolidation 102–4
        conversion 77, 79, 88, 165, 175, 176, 212
        Coordinating Bureau 86
        credits 103
        crisis 84–88, 102
        decentralization 88, 102, 212
        development of 187
        economic importance 91
        economy and 77, 93
        employment 80
        foreign investment 73
        Gyor, Programme of 79, 187
        impact of 187
        investment 81
        legislation and 88
        macroeconomic environment 79, 172
        market forces and 89, 105
        markets 82, 84–85
        modernization 79
        need for acknowledged 88
        policy changes 77, 88–94, 149
        precision instruments 80
        prices 84

privatization 88, 91, 97, 146, 195, 209
production 8, 80–81, 82, 83, 85–86, 86–88, 96, 97, 104
production, licensed 83
R&D 81, 82–83, 103, 104
reorganization 88, 192, 212
restructuring 79, 172, 209
state support 81, 82, 85, 88–89, 90, 102, 103, 144, 212
structural features 79–84
subcontractors 80
telecommunications 80, 88
wages 82
Western firms, cooperation with 90
workers' conditions 82
WTO and 83, 84, 85, 99
see also preceding entry
Defence Industry and Defence Technology Development Committee 103
Democratic Forum (MDF) 77, 89, 100
economic changes 7, 77, 93, 105
electronics sector 80, 81
foreign investment 77
Free Democrats 77
Fund for Technical Innovation 89
GDP 79, 105
industrial production 79
Law on Defence 88
macroeconomic environment 79, 85
military doctrine absent 82
military expenditure 81, 85
Military Industrial Office (MIO) 87, 89, 91, 92, 98, 99, 101, 102, 193
Military Price Setting Committee 82, 86
Ministry of Defence 81, 82, 85, 90, 91, 92, 93, 97, 99, 100, 104
Ministry of Finance 82, 88, 90
Ministry of Foreign Affairs 93
Ministry of Foreign Economic Relations 90, 98, 134
Ministry of Foreign Trade 93
Ministry of Industry 81, 83, 88, 89, 90, 92
Ministry of Interior 90, 93
National Committee for Technological Development 103–104

NATO and 92
Parliamentary Defence Committee 97
Poland and 124
political changes 7, 9, 77
politics 77–78
Prime Minister's Office 89
privatization 79, 91–92
reforms, 1968 82
refugees and 162
Russia's debts to 189
Slovakia and 33, 62, 92
social changes 77
Socialist Party 77
State Audit Office 85, 92
state budget 79
State Property Agency 92
unemployment 93
Union of Entrepreneurs 100
University of Technology 102
uprising, 1956, 7, 104
USSR's debts to 84
WTO and 104
Huta Stalowa Wola 109, 110, 121, 123–24, 160, 170
Huzar helicopter 118, 128
Hydral 109

IBM 165
Ikarus 102
India 19, 61, 71, 73, 102, 201
International Standards Organization certificates 127, 153
Investicni Banka 42, 47
Iran:
    arms imports 19, 27, 28, 39, 40, 50
    nuclear industry 40
    Poland and 124
    USA and 28, 40, 154
Iraq:
    arms imports 8, 16, 119, 120, 125
    Kuwait invaded by 145, 154
    UN embargo on 119, 122, 125, 145, 154
Iryda aircraft 118, 120, 127, 129
Isaszegi, Janos 90
Islamic fundamentalist groups 63
Israel:
    Czech Republic and 55
    Poland and 121

Italy 21, 23, 51, 187
Ivanek, Dr Ladislav 20

Jablonec 43, 50
Japan 99
Jaruzelski, General Wojciech 107
Jinonice 21

Kade, Jerzy 120, 122, 175
Kalashnikov rifles 94
Kaliningrad 105
Kampuchea 110
Kaniak, Stanislaw 148–49
Kashin destroyer 120
Kaszub frigate 118
Katowice 181
Kazakhstan 124
Klaus, Vaclav 25, 33, 34, 40, 221
Koblem, Colonel Ivan 63
Kodaj, Samuel 72
Kolin 15
Komarno 15, 22
Komercni Banka 42
Konstrukta Trencin 16, 72, 176
Koprivnice 15, 50
Korea, South 201
Korean War 139
Kovacik, Ivan 71
Kovak, Roman 23
Kozeny, Stanislav 29
Kraus, Milos 74, 75
Krizik 51
Krupp Works 168
Kunovice 15
Kuwait 145, 154, 176
Kvattro 100

L-39 aircraft Albatros 46, 47, 48, 51
L-59 aircraft 48, 55
L-159 aircraft 48
Labor MIM 80, 87, 95
Lada kit 49–50
Lada light weapons 51, 52, 161
Lajzner, Petr 53
Langos, Jan 30
Laszlo, Jeno 89, 193
Latin America 40, 53, 201
Latvia 40

Lebanon 75
Let 15
Letov 15, 48
Leyland 126
Liaz 43, 50
Liaz Jablonec 14
Liberia 119
Libya:
    arms imports 8, 16, 19, 28, 119
    arms production 28
    UN embargo on 119, 145, 154
Line Up 96
Liptovsky Hradok 15, 139
Lithuania 40, 105, 119
Lombardini project 21, 65, 66, 178
Lublin 129
Lucznik 109, 115, 118

Magvasi, Peter 33, 60, 159
Magyar Hitelbank 99, 195
Magyar Honvedseg Haditechnikai Intezet
    (MH HTI) 83, 103
Magyar Optikai Muvek (MOM) 101
Malaysia 201
market economies, statistics and 5–6
Martin 3, 15, 17, 21, 31, 64
Martin Diesel 74, 75–76, 138, 150, 153,
    169, 170, 194
Matav 102
Matrafem 95, 195
Mazowiecki, Tadeusz 105
Mechanikai Labor 80, 83, 87, 101, 139,
    176, 212
Mechanikai Muvek 154
Mechanikai Muvek Gyar Automatika
    Muvek Rt (MMG Automatika) 101, 102
Meciar, Vladimir 32, 33, 56, 60, 61, 62fn,
    68, 210, 221
Meopta 15, 25, 35, 43, 163, 176, 179
Meopta Optical Works 23, 155
Merestechnikai, Informatikai, Kutato es
    Innovacios Reszvenytarsasag (MIKI) 83,
    101, 102, 136, 164, 176
Merkuria 51
Mesit 43
Mesko 109, 115, 121
MHB (Hungarian Credit Bank) 99, 195
Middle East 15, 84, 112, 145

Mielec 109, 117, 120, 153, 162, 163, 165, 170
MiG-21 aircraft 55
MiG-29 aircraft 63, 94
MIKI *see* Merestechnikai, Informatikai, Kutato es Innovacios Reszvenytarsasag
Mikolesek, Jaroslav 172
Misinsky, Jiri 49
MN Godolloi Gepgyar 80, 81, 87, 100
Moravan 15
Moravcik, Josef 59, 61, 68, 69, 71, 73, 221
Moravia 13, 17
Moricz, Gabor 85
Mostaren 15
Motorlet 21
Mozambique 119
Muller, Aleksander 187
Muszertechnika 100
Myanmar 119

NATO (North Atlantic Treaty Organization):
  conversion pilot project 173
  Partnership for Peace 63
  see also under names of countries considering membership
Nemec, Ladislav 29, 72
Nepovim, Jiri 179
Nero 42
Netherlands 120
Nicaragua 110
Nigeria 15, 28, 47, 94
Nike-Fiocchi 135, 168, 178
Nitro-Chem 109
Nitrokemia 101, 141, 168
Nitrokemiai Ipartelepek 101
Nitron-Erg 109
Noriega, General Manuel 39

Odolena Voda 46
oil 15, 67
Olesky, Piotr 169
Omnipol 28, 29, 40, 51, 62
Onyszkiewicz, Janusz 122
Orion 95, 155, 176
Orlik aircraft 118

Orszagos Muszaki Fejlesztesi Bizottsag (OMFB) 103
Ostrava 15
Otkrovice 15

Pakistan 63
Palestine Liberation Organization (PLO) 110
Panama 39
Pardubice 15, 22
Pastula, Wieslaw 126
Pawlak, Waldemar 116, 118, 221
PCO (Przemyslowe Centrum Optyki) 109, 115
Pellegrin, Pierre 73
Penzintezeti Kozpont 100
Persian Gulf War 125, 154, 176
Peru 28
Pestvideki Gepgyar (PVG) 80
PHARE (Pologne–Hongrie: action pour la reconversion économique) programme 117, 164, 173–74
Philippines 47
Pinochet, General Augusto 40
Pionki 120
PLO 110
Plzak, Jan 42
Plzen 43
Pol, Marek 116
Poland:
  armed forces 107, 111, 118, 127, 208, 213, 218
  arms exports:
    barter and 119
    competition 73, 142
    control of 110, 119
    end-user certificates 119
    hard currency and 111
    licences 119
    policy on 113–23
    profitability 111
    promotion 118, 213
    support for 111, 118–20, 197
    value 110–11, 119
  arms imports 16, 75
  Aviation Research Institute 111
  banks 127, 128

black market 105
Central Committee for Scientific
   Research 121
Communist Party resumes power 9, 222
Communist collapse in 7
corruption 105
Council of Ministers 114
defence enterprises:
   bankruptcy 112, 114
   debts 112, 115, 117, 122, 128, 160,
      161
   definition 115
   layoffs 113
   list of major 108
   managers 149
   number of 109, 115, 119
   privileges removed 112
   profits 112
   size 109, 113
   see also following entry
defence industry:
   arguments for 113–14
   civilian production 114, 126, 128
   cold capacity 139
   concentration of 115
   conversion 114, 175, 178
   credits 112, 127, 128
   crisis 111–13, 122–23, 125
   development 187
   development, examples of 123–29
   economy and 121
   employment 108–9, 110, 112, 113,
      116, 117, 128, 213
   foreign firms, cooperation with
      120–22, 125
   foreign investment 120
   geographical distribution 110, 117
   importance of 108
   major producers 108
   markets 112, 126
   one town–one factory situation 114,
      124
   organization of 109
   policy on 113–23
   privatization 107, 117, 129, 146
   production 8, 109, 112, 113, 115,
      116, 117, 124, 128, 212, 213
   production, licensed 124

R&D 111, 123, 124, 127
reorganization 192
restructuring 114–15, 116, 118,
   122–23, 125, 209, 212–13
size of 109, 113, 115, 119
state control 147
state support 112, 117–20, 121, 144,
   213, 214
strikes 115
structural features 105–11
subcontractors 122, 129
unemployment and 117
USSR and 119, 120
Western firms, cooperation with
   120–22, 125, 128
WTO and 119
see also preceding entry
economic change in 7
economic reform 105, 112
economy 9, 111, 121, 122
foreign policy 7
GDP 105
Germany and 120, 124
Hungary and 124
importance of 105
Industrial Development Agency 127,
   162
International Standards Organization
   certificates 127
investment 105
Iran and 124
Israel and 121
Kazakhstan and 124
Lithuania and 105
macroeconomic environment 105, 112,
   213, 214
market economy and 7, 105, 112
military expenditure 112, 122, 217
Ministry of Defence 114, 115, 117, 118,
   121, 122, 127
Ministry of Finance 114
Ministry of Foreign Economic
   Cooperation 110
Ministry of Industry and Trade 110,
   112, 114, 120, 122
Ministry of Privatization 114
National Bank 162
nationalism in 208

NATO and 113
neighbours 105
Parliament 121
Parliamentary Defence Committee 122
Parliamentary Science Committee 118
PHARE and 173
political change in 7, 9
politics 105
popiwek tax 147
privatization 105
Russia and 105, 124
Solidarity 7
speculation 105
Ukraine and 105
USSR and 119
USSR's weapons, dependence on 113
Warsaw School of Technology 128
Western Europe, integration in 7
WTO and 107, 126
Policka 15
Policske Strojirny 15, 43, 53
Pospisil, Bohumir 53
Povazska Bystrica 13, 26
PPS Detva 152, 158
Prague 15, 16, 43, 50, 51
Pratt and Whitney 74, 118
Prelouc 15
Prerov 15, 43
production associations 6
Proxy 114
Przemyslowe Centrum Optyki (PCO) 109, 115
PS 93 Parabellum gun 75
PS Detva 15, 21, 65
PS Policka 22, 25, 26, 53, 179, 180, 196
PS Povazska Bystrica 15, 22, 26, 72, 74–75, 152, 160, 170, 174, 176
PT-91 Twardy tank 120, 121
PVG 87, 90, 96–98, 101
PVG-Dunai Repulogepgyar 91
PZL-130 Orlik aircraft 118
PZL-230 Skorpion aircraft 120
PZL-Mielec 109, 126–28, 129
PZL-Rzeszow 109
PZL-Swidnik 109, 120, 128–29
PZL-Warszawa II 125–26, 154, 159, 163, 176
PZL-Wola 109, 148, 168, 174

Raba 101
Radmor 109
Radom 109, 115
Radwar 109, 121
RDP (Research, Development and Production) Group 38–39, 42, 43–44, 45, 50, 52, 53, 55, 158, 161, 194
recession, worldwide 154, 186, 218
Reda Corporation 67
refugees 186
Rendszertechnika 99
Reorg 92, 96
research 4–6
Research and Development Institute 48
Rexrott 165
Rockwell 48
Romania 50
Russia:
  arms exports 73
  arms imports 67
  debts 94, 188–89
  oil and 67
  Poland and 105, 124
  protectionism 67
Rzeszow 109

Sabata, Jaroslav 20
SABCA 73, 201
SAGEM 44, 118
science associations 6
Sellier & Bellot 25, 52, 53, 161–62, 163, 170, 192
Semtex 63
Siemens 43, 95, 100
Skarzysko-Kamienna 109, 115
Skoda 13, 195
Skoda Holding 42
Skoda-Plzen 13, 14, 37, 39, 42, 43, 50, 55, 192
Skoda Volkswagen 14
Skoda Works 38, 42–43, 161
Skorpion aircraft 120
Slavicin 13, 15, 17, 43, 54
Slovakia:
  armed forces:
    inheritance of 63
    modernization of 63–64
    nationalism and 208

arms exports:
  black market 63
  competition and 73, 142
  decline in 59
  demand 65
  licensing 62
  policy on 31, 60–64
  state support 197
  value of 63
arms imports 49
authoritarianism in 9
banks 59, 67
budget deficit 57, 72
Central Research Institute 72
Communist Party 222
Czech Republic and 30, 33, 35, 37, 44,
  73, 210–11
defence enterprises:
  bankruptcy 64
  debts 69, 160, 161
  management 66, 67, 70, 76, 149
  size of 57
  subcontractors 59, 147
  survival strategies 70
  see also following entry
defence industry:
  arguments for 61–62, 63
  black market 63
  civilian products 65, 70, 75, 211
  collapse of 64
  concentration 57
  conversion 31–32, 33, 61, 64, 67, 69,
    70, 73, 176–77, 180, 211–12
  crisis in 57, 59, 64–76
  Czech Republic and 69
  decentralization 67, 69
  economy and 32, 56–57, 59, 61, 62,
    64, 65, 69, 70, 72
  employment 31, 57, 59, 64, 66, 74
  foreign investment 34, 73–74
  heavy weapons 57, 71
  independence 68–70
  inheritance of 30–31, 35
  international quality certificates 76,
    153
  investment 57
  lay-offs 31

  macroeconomic environment 70, 172,
    211
  markets 66
  modernization 61
  national sovereignty and 62
  overemployment 57
  privatization 68, 76, 146, 209
  production 20, 32, 57, 59, 60–64,
    66–67, 68, 72, 74
  R&D 67, 72, 75
  redundancies 64
  reorganization 65, 67
  restructuring 69, 172, 209, 210–11
  state control 68–70, 147, 199
  state support 61, 68, 70, 72, 210–11
  stocks 71
  wages 66
  Western countries, cooperation with
    42–43, 63, 71, 74
  WTO and 72
  see also preceding entry
economic changes 56
economic policy 32
economy 32, 61, 62, 70, 71–72, 210–11
  see also under defence industry
elections 62
Export Licence Committee 62
foreign investment 34, 73–74
GDP 56–57, 71
Hungary and 33, 62, 92
inflation 57, 72
inheritance of 34, 56–60, 63
international image 56
KOVO union 61
Labour Foundation 66
living standards 56
macroeconomic environment 56
market reforms 56
military triangle 64–65, 181
Ministry of Defence 62, 69, 72
Ministry of the Economy 59, 62, 69, 71,
  72, 134
Ministry of Finance 69
Ministry of Foreign Affairs 62
Ministry of the Interior 69
Ministry of Transport and Public Works
  69

National Bank 67
National Property Fund 69, 75, 177
NATO and 63, 72
Party of the Democratic Left 61
PHARE and 173
R&D 72, 75
Russia's debts to 189
social changes 56
technology 62
unemployment 34, 57, 60, 64
Union of Engineering Industry 61, 159
Slovak Shipyards 22
Slovenia: arms imports 39, 51
Slovenske Lodenice 15
Slovenske Lucobne Zavody 51
Snina 15, 174
SOFMA 43
Sokol helicopters 118, 119, 120, 128
Somalia 119
Soroczynski, Waldemar 125, 159, 163
Soudek, Lubomir 42, 55
South Africa 119
South America 73
South West African People's Organization
  110
Spain: arms imports 51, 53, 119
Spronz, Imre 172
SSUB 15
Stalowa Wola 109, 124, 153, 164, 193,
  196
Stealth aircraft 52
Stema 127
Stocznia Marynarky Wojennej 109
Stocznia Polnocna 109
Stranak, Adam 48
Strauss, Jan 119
Su-22 aircraft 118
Suchocka Government 114, 221
Sudan 119
Sweden 50, 51, 120, 121, 124
Swidnik 109, 129, 164, 176, 192, 199
Syria: arms imports 16, 19, 27, 28, 63,
  154
Szarka, Istvan 86–87
Szekesfehervar 99

T-72 tank:
  exports of 27, 63, 71, 120

modernization 44, 55, 65, 71, 72, 210
  versions of 73, 120
T-80 tank 73
T-84 tank 73
Taiwan 119
Takacs, Bela 90
TAKI see Tavkozlesi Kutato Intezet
Tamara air surveillance systems 28, 40,
  51, 52, 53, 163, 176
Tanzania 15
Tatra 50
Tatra Koprivnice 14, 15
Tavkozlesi Kutato Intezet (TAKI) 83, 92,
  95, 101, 102, 103, 153, 169, 177, 192
Technika 93, 101
Technika Trade Company 102
Technometra Radotin 48
Telefongyar 95, 103
Tesla 15, 21, 22, 35
Tesla Liptovsky Hradok 74, 176
Tesla Pardubice 17, 22, 52, 59, 163, 193
Tesla Praha 54, 74, 163, 165, 172
Thailand 40, 47, 48, 201
Thomson-CFS 121
TOPFIN 43, 44
Torokszentmiklos 100
transnational corporations 201
Trencin 16, 73
Tripoli 28
Turcianske Strojarni 21
Turkey: arms imports 46
Twardy tank 120, 121

Uherske Hradiste 43
Uhersky Brod 13, 15, 17, 22, 24, 39, 43
Ukraine 73, 105, 119, 202
Unimor 121
Unimpex 28
Union of Soviet Socialist Republics:
  arms imports 16, 18, 83
  civilian market collapse 50
  conflict in 186, 207
  debts 188
  demilitarization and 8
  meteorological extremes 140
  military expenditure 84
  new countries 119, 124
  Poland and 113, 119

WTO and 111, 141, 142
United Kingdom 50
United Nations, embargoes 27, 51, 119, 122, 125, 145, 154
United States of America:
  Arms Control and Disarmament Agency 15
  arms imports 49, 51, 98, 171
  Czechoslovakia and 27
  Iran and 28, 40, 154
  Syria and 154
United Technologies 74

Videoton 81–82, 87, 99–100, 101, 102, 103, 104, 160, 194, 195
Videoton Holding 104, 159, 194, 212
Videoton-Rendszertechnika 162, 170, 192, 199, 212
Viet Nam 71
Viet Nam War 139
Vihorlat 15, 158, 174, 176
Visegrad Group see following entry and East–Central Europe; Czech Republic; Hungary; Poland; Slovakia
Visegrad Process 33, 201
Vitkovicke Strojimy a Zelezarny 15
Vlarske Strojirny 15, 43, 54, 153, 176, 178, 195
Vlasim 24
Vlazske factory 22
Vlcek, Jan 42, 45
Vojenska Stavby 38
Volvo 98
Volvo-Michigan 168
Vrablik, Jan 22
Vsetin 13, 22
VSS Kosice 158, 174

Walesa, Lech 107
Warel 109, 152
Warsaw 109, 115
Warszawa-Okecie 109, 120, 122, 162, 179
Weiss, Peter 61
Wojskowe Zaklady Motorizacijne (WZM) 121
World War II 79, 123, 126, 187
Wroclaw 109
WTO (Warsaw Treaty Organization):
  barter exchange 83
  collapse 24, 52, 142, 143, 188
  defence industry production system 141–42, 217
  defence production and USSR 111, 141, 142
  dissolution of 7, 9
  military–industrial cooperation system 8, 32, 141–42
  R&D 142
  USSR's predominance 111, 141
Wytwornia Sprzetu Komunikacyjnego (WSK) 109

X-Trade 42

Yeltsin, President Boris 94, 189
Yemen, South 110
Yuganskorion 95
Yugoslav Federation 28
Yugoslavia:
  arms imports 28, 119 see also Croatia
  conflict 94, 186, 207
  economic changes 7
  UN embargo 27, 51, 119, 122

Zbrojovka Brno 43
Zbrojovka Vsetin 22, 43, 50–51
Zetor 177
Zeveta Bojkovice 15, 22, 25, 26, 136, 167–68
Zimbabwe 15
ZTS 35
ZTS Dubnica 15, 21, 33, 66–67, 72, 73, 152, 158, 176, 178
ZTS Martin 14, 15, 18, 23, 33, 42, 57–58, 60, 64, 65–66, 73, 76, 152, 158, 160, 168, 169, 179
ZTS Prakovice 158
ZTS Topolcany 158
Zubri 21, 51
Zuzana artillery system 67, 71, 72–73, 210
Zvolen 67
ZVS 35
ZVS Dubnica 15, 66, 152
ZVS Meopta 152
Zylna 63